GLOBALISATION AND EMERGING INDIA

GLOBALISATION AND EMERGING INDIA

Edited by

Talluru Sreenivas

MBA, M Com, M Phil, Ph D.

Reader, Department of Management Sciences

RVR & JC College of Engineering

Guntur 522 019 (Andhra Pradesh)

Foreword by

Prof. P. Murali

Vice-Chancellor

Sri Venkateswara University

Tirupathi–517 502 (A.P.)

DISCOVERY PUBLISHING HOUSE

NEW DELHI-110002

First Published-2006

ISBN 81-8356-055-5

Published by

DISCOVERY PUBLISHING HOUSE
4831/24, Ansari Road, Prahlad Street,
Darya Ganj, New Delhi-110002 (India)
Phone: 23279245 • Fax: 91-11-23253475
E-mail:dphtemp@indiatimes.com

Printed at
Arora Offset Press
Laxmi Nagar, Delhi–92

Dedicated to

Dr. Kasaraneni Sadasiva Rao
Former President
Nagarjuna Education Society, and
RVR & JC College of Engineering
Guntur (Andhra Pradesh)

Where the mind is without fear and the head is held high,
Where knowledge is free,
Where the world has not been broken up into fragments
by narrow domestic walls,
Where words come out from the depth of truth,
Where tireless strying stretches its arms towards perfection,
Where the clear stream of reason has not lost its way
into the dreary desert sand of dead habit,
Where the mind is led forward by thee
into ever-widening thought and action
into that heaven of freedom, my father, *let my country awake.*

–Rabindranath Tagore

FOREWORD

Globalisation is not just an economic phenomenon but is driven by powerful political interests, and has tremendous social and cultural consequences. Globalisation, however, provides opportunities through the process of integration with the world economy, which can only be fully harnessed if appropriate strategies are adopted safeguarding the national interests, and those of labour and the vulnerable sections, in particular. The form in which globalisation is occurring while benefiting largely a few sections of the community, seems to have bypassed the majority. A critical look at the Indian experience from early 1990s reveals that significant macroeconomic reorientation is warranted in order to make globalisation work for various sections of people at large.

Globalisation means many things to many people. In a broad sense, globalisation refers to expansion of economic transactions and organisation of economic activities across the national boundaries. This is, however, not a totally new phenomenon. However, what is new is the marked acceleration. It is important to put in place strategies to ensure that economic integration does not result in social disintegration.

It is difficult to isolate the specific impact of globalisation from that of other processes occurring at the same time. Macroeconomic performance of the Indian economy from early 1990s has been fairly impressive. There is also indication that high economic growth has had an impact in lowering levels of poverty. However, these positive macroeconomic trends seem to have also been accompanied by stagnation of employment growth, and deterioration in employment situation as indicated by increased instability and casualisation of employment. The liberalisation processes have accentuated regional, sectoral and social inequalities.

India has tremendous opportunities to overcome the challenges posed by globalisation processes. The overall competitiveness of the economy and productivity levels – not just of labour but also of all factors of production (total factor productivity) – needs to be substantially raised to reap the benefits of globalisation. Its performance on economic and social front is not commensurate with its potential. There is an urgent need to review and reorient macroeconomic policies to undertake institutional reform, and contemplate significant improvements in qovernance. In order to harness the benefits of globalisation, what is critical is striking a balance between high economic growth and increased employment, and between enterprise efficiency and employee empowerment.

The Global Competitiveness Report 2003-04 is the latest publication in the series released by the World Economic Forum, Geneva. This brings out comparative rankings of various countries out of 102 countries covered in the survey. The indices for which rankings of countries are released are: (i) Growth Competitiveness Index (GCI) consisting of three sub-indices, *viz.*, macroeconomic environment index, public institutions index, and technology index. These are the three pillars on which the process of economic growth rests. The three components are combined to calculate the overall GCI. The three factors are interwoven, and are not independent. (ii) Business Competitiveness Index (BCI) consisting of two sub-indices measuring the sophistication of company operations and strategy, and quality of the national business environment. The weighted average of the two sub-indices is defined as the BCI. This procedure results in a weight of 0.66 for national business environment, and 0.34 for company operations and strategy. This means that the benefits of a better business environment for prosperity increase with the sophistication of company operations and strategy, and vice versa. Countries that improve both the business environment and company sophistication in tandem reap disproportionate benefits, while countries where there is an imbalance bear disproportionate costs.

India's ranking indicates that in Business Competitiveness Index, the country is better placed with rank 37 out of 101 countries. In both the sub-indices also, the position is reasonably good. However, in the overall Growth Competitiveness Index in all the sub-themes as well as in the overall index, the performance is much lower compared with business competitiveness index (in overall index rank 56 out of 102 countries). Improvements needed for technology, public institutions and macroeconomic environment should be vigorously pursued.

The companies in the country are integrating technology strategies with business strategies, and are well poised to strengthen their position in the domestic as well as international markets. According to high tech indicators, compiled by Georgia Tech (USA) for 33 countries, India's present high tech production capability is 31, and is likely to be 44 after fifteen years. This is on a scale of 10 implying no capability, and 50 implying capable of producing technically advanced state of the art products. Thus, there lies ahead a great opportunity to make a dent in the global technology trade market, provided healthy government–Industry partnership is established where industry plays a pro-active role, ably supported by conducive government policies.

The importance given to competitive environment in the fields of globalisation, gender disparities and Information Technology in the themes included for the National Seminar on Emerging India : Challenges and Opportunities organised by RVR & JC College of Engineering, Guntur, during March 2004 is indeed laudable. This publication covers the papers received in the three areas mentioned above. In all the themes, the contributors have highlighted the changing scenario and perspectives. Enthusiastic response to the Seminar from the academic and professional circles is noteworthy. The management of the College, and in particular, Dr. Talluru Sreenivas, Reader in the Department of Management Sciences are to be congratulated for having shouldered the responsibility for organising the National Seminar, and bringing out the proceedings of the Seminar into a publication covering the above three themes, focusing attention on key issues influencing the Indian Economy.

I have great pleasure in commending the publication to policy makers, administrators, and implementers associated with the themes covered here. Academics and researchers would benefit from it substantially utilising the analysis and manner of presentation, conclusions drawn, and suggestions emerging from various contributors. I am sure the ideas and suggestions contained in the publication can stimulate further research, and more effective implementation of action-oriented policies.

Tirupathi
Nov. 1, 2004

Professor P Murali
Vice-Chancellor
Sri Venkateswara University
Tirupathi–517 502, AP

PREFACE

At a conceptual level, distinction can be made between technology-enabled (or induced) globalisation and public policy–induced restrictions or easing of restrictions. Globalisation has several dimensions arising out of what may be called enhanced connectivity among people across national borders. Such enhanced connectivity is determined by three fundamental factors, *viz.*, technology, individual taste, and public policy. Cross–border integration can have implications on several aspects affecting the society; cultural, social, political and economic, though we generally discuss the implications or effects of economic integration. Economic integration, in turn, occurs through three channels, *viz.*, movement of people, of goods and, of finance or capital. The pace and nature of globalisation will naturally depend on the combined effect of technology and public policy, both at the national and international level.

Technology, capital markets and management are the three principal drivers of the current globalisation. Whilst each one of them is powerful in its own right, what has given them invincibility in recent years is the fact that they all fit together so neatly. The computer, the telephone and the television stand out in leading globalisation. The Internet is promoting globalisation at an incredible pace. But instead of happening over hundred years like the Industrial Revolution, it will happen over a decade or so. Globalisation signifies five things: movement of capital, goods, technology and people, and incidence of foreign debt. Implementation of macroeconomic policies should be based on human development, not just economic growth alone. All developmental efforts must recognise the importance of people over markets and profits. Human well-being is the end, economic growth is the means. Globalisation should be considered the direction if strategies are devised to implement the policies with a human face. Global integration and interdependence are desirable, if they have something positive for every section of the society. Distributional aspect of growth should form an integral part of developmental strategy.

Global Competitiveness

Global Competitiveness Report 2003-04 is the latest publication in the series released by the World Economic Forum (WEF), Geneva. This brings out the comparative rankings of various countries out of 102 countries covered in the survey. Growth competitiveness Index's (GCI's) main goal is to analyse the potential for the world's economies to attain sustained economic growth over the medium and long term. The index is based on economists' current understanding of the determinants of the complex process of economic growth and development. It summarises the set of institutions, policies and structures during the growth process of heterogeneous countries. The business competitiveness index (BCI) refers to (a) wealth creation at microeconomic level and through sophistication of company operations and strategy, and (b) quality of the national business environment. More productive company strategies require more highly skilled people, better information, more efficient government processes, improved infrastructure, better suppliers, more advanced research institutions, and more intense competitive pressure, among other things. This is what the BCI tries to capture.

Table 1: Growth Competitiveness and Business Competitiveness Indices (2003-04)

(Rank of the Country)

S.No.	Feature	India	China	Taiwan	Korea	Malaysia
Rank out of 102 countries						
1.	Growth competitiveness index	56	44	5	18	29
	(a) Macroeconomic environment index	52	44	5	18	29
	(b) Public institutions index	55	52	21	36	34
	(c) Technology index	64	65	3	6	20

(Contd...)

Rank out of 101 countries						
2.	Business competitiveness index	37	46	18	23	26
	(a) Sophistication of company operations and strategy index	40	42	18	19	26
	(b) Quality of national business environment index	36	44	16	25	24

Source: *World Economic Forum* (2004), Global Competitiveness Report 2003-04, Geneva.

India's ranking as shown in Table 1 indicates that in Business Competitiveness Index, the country is better placed with rank 37 out of 101 countries. In both the sub-indices also, the position is reasonably good. However, in the overall Growth Competitiveness Index in all the sub-themes as well as in the overall index, the performance is much lower compared with business competitiveness index (In overall index, rank 56 out of 102 countries). Improvements needed for technology, public institutions and macroeconomic environment need to be substantially improved. Comparative figures are given for China, Taiwan, Korea and Malaysia. Among the five countries listed here, Taiwan is undoubtedly the leader in competitiveness with 5 as the rank for growth competitiveness index, particularly in technology, macroeconomic environment, and overall index. Korea stands next. Malaysia is the third, and China is slightly better compared to India in the growth competitiveness index, but lower in business competitiveness index. Significant improvement is, thus, to be made both by India as well as China in relation to the attainments recorded in smaller Asian countries.

Technology Intensive Exports

According to World Development Indicators 2004 of the World Bank, India's high technology exports were 5 per cent of its manufactured exports in 2002 compared to 23 per cent in case of China, 19 per cent in case of Brazil, 20 per cent in case of Israel, 32 per cent in case of the Republic of Korea, 58 per cent in case of Malaysia, 60 per cent in case of Singapore, and 65 per cent in case of Philippines. World Bank indicators take into consideration only manufactured exports, and exclude services exports. Recategorisation made by the Indian Institute of Foreign Trade (IIFT), New Delhi in consultation with the Union Department of Science and Technology, reveals that technology intensive exports as per cent of gross merchandise exports and miscellaneous services receipts, has increased from 8.4 in 1994-95 to 18.7 in 2002-03. Technology intensive exports, in absolute terms, have grown from Rs. 7,432 crore in 1994-95 to Rs. 64,335 crore, registering an eight-fold increase. Technology intensive exports are exports of such products/equipment/ plants wherein value of technology input, R&D, knowledge, design, drawings, and expert technical services is much higher than value of raw materials and capital inputs. In an endeavour to analyse technology intensive exports from the country, the following items have been taken into consideration: exports of capital goods, computer software services, turnkey and construction projects, management and technical services, know-how, design and drawings, royalty payment receipts, and receipts from technology-based joint ventures/ wholly owned subsidiaries abroad. Thus, although India's share of technology intensive exports in gross exports has been rising, the country needs to sustain and accelerate the growth of technology intensive exports to enhance their share to 40-50 per cent of gross exports in the next five years or so to catch up with other countries.

Empowerment of Women

A recent survey on Gender status carried out by the Geneva – based World Economic Forum (WEF) in 58 countries finds that full economic and political empowerment remains a dream for millions of women in much of the western world, let alone developing countries. Gender equality is still a distant dream in most countries – developed and developing. Of the 58 countries covered by the Survey for the first time by WEF, India is placed at the 53rd position – embarrassingly behind economically less developed countries such as Bangladesh, and a host of Latin American and African nations, which have done much better in narrowing the gender gap. Despite scoring high in economic opportunity, India is at the bottom of the heap by most criteria – above only Pakistan, Korea, Jordan, Turkey and Egypt. The Survey conducted by WEF is recognition by the international business community that women's status is an area of critical importance for development. The countries have been ranked on the basis of five main criteria laid down by the United Nations

ACKNOWLEDGEMENT

Inspired by the article which I co-authored recently with my Research Director, Professor G Prasad, Department of Commerce and Business Administration, Acharya Nagarjuna University, entitled, Health Care in India – Strategies for Globalisation, I embarked on the humble venture of organising a National Seminar on the very fascinating topic, dearest to our young minded, dynamic first citizen of our country, his Excellency Bharat Ratna Dr. A.P.J. Abdul Kalam, Emerging India – Challenges and Opportunities. The present publication is the outcome of the proceedings of the seminar held under the editor's secretaryship during March 2004 at RVR & JC College of Engineering, Guntur (Andhra Pradesh).

Sizeable number of papers on different functional areas and in different sectors were received from academics, research scholars, and practitioners. These papers deal with various topics which were taken up for discussion in different technical sessions. The sessions were captioned as: (i) Is India Emerging?, (ii) Industry, Infrastructure and Agriculture, (iii) Service Sector and Developed India, and (iv) Human Resources as a strategic strength. In addition to select papers received for the seminar, efforts have been made to include a few more special contributions from prominent professionals and researchers on themes relevant for the publication. The Seminar organisers are highly indebted to all the contributors for their painstaking efforts to make the presentation highly thought-provoking and instructive. We would like to convey our gratefulness to all of them, and look forward to their bringing out greater insight on these themes in future. These papers are distributed over four publications: (i) Service Sector in Indian Economy, (ii) Perspectives of Indian Agriculture, Industry and Infrastructure, (iii) Banking Sector and Human Resources – Changing Scenario, and (iv) Globalisation and Emerging India.

I acknowledge with gratitude the help I received from Professor D Dakshina Murthy, Former Dean, Faculty of Commerce and Business Administration, Acharya Nagarjuna University, who currently heads the Department of Management Sciences of our College, and all other colleagues in our Department for their constant guidance, encouragement and support.

It gives me great pleasure to place on record my indebtedness to Professor G Prasad, whose guidance gave me the strength and courage to bring out this publication. His scholarly guidance and encouragement are responsible for my success in this venture. He has been a continuous source of inspiration to me.

I would like to convey my gratefulness to a number of elders and well wishers for the substantial encouragement and support given to me on various occasions. These include Dr KRR Mohan Rao, former Vice-Chancellor, Acharya Nagarjuna University, Guntur; Professor V Balamohan Das, Vice-Chancellor, Acharya Nagarjuna University, Guntur; Professor L Venugopal Reddy, Vice-Chancellor, Andhra University, Visakhapatnam; Professor GN Brahmanandam, Dean, Faculty of Commerce & Management Studies, Acharya Nagarjuna University, Guntur; Professor DAR Subrahmanyam, Principal, Mahatma Gandhi College, Guntur; Dr K Chandrasekhara Rao, Head, Department of Commerce, Pondicherry University, Pondicherry; Professor PS Sankara Rao, Andhra University, Visakhapatnam; Dr R Murali Babu Rao, Professor of Cardiology on special duty, Guntur General Hospital, and Guntur Medical College, Guntur; and Professor NV Narasimham, School of Management Studies, IGNOU, New Delhi.

I am grateful to Professor P Murali, former Vice-Chancellor, Sri Venkateswara University, Tirupati, for writing the foreword to this work in spite of his busy schedule. I am highly obliged to Professor DL Narayana, Chairman, Third Finance Commission of Andhra Pradesh for delivering the keynote address at the Seminar, and enlightening all the delegates with his extensive research highlights.

It is my privilege to express deep sense of gratitude to the Management of RVR & JC College of Engineering, particularly to our beloved President, Dr K Basavapunnaiah, and our dynamic Secretary & Correspondent, Dr M Gopalkrishna, Sri R Gopala Krishna, Treasurer, and Professor K Pameswara Rao, Principal, Professor B

Diversification of the range of services offered as well as geographical markets, further innovations and ensuring customer satisfaction would remain crucial to maintaining India's competitive advantage in major international markets.

The papers presented at the National Seminar on Emerging India: Challenges and Opportunities, organised by RVR & JC College of Engineering, Guntur, during March 2004, included in this publication refer to three areas: (a) Globalisation, (b) Gender Disparities, and (c) Information Technology. In addition to select papers received for the seminar, efforts have been made to include a few more special contributions from prominent professionals and researchers on themes relevant for the publication. A wide variety of topics have been covered in each section. Special efforts have been made in these papers to examine the recent trends, and bring out suggestions for effective implementation of programmes in future. Conclusions and suggestions brought out by the contributors deserve special consideration of the policy making and implementing organisations. Researchers, academics and professional bodies will benefit from the methodologies followed, and conclusions drawn in the papers. The editor acknowledges the valuable contributions of the authors, and commends them for adoption extensively in the concerned sectors.

Guntur
June 1, 2005

Talluru Sreenivas

special efforts to stretch the reach of education, especially to the girl child. With the objective of achieving economic empowerment and welfare of women, a number of schemes are being implemented. Integrated Child Development Services (ICDS) is an important scheme covering the main components of a holistic and sustainable child development strategy, *viz.*, health, nutrition and education. The scheme provides a package of services. A draft National Plan of Action has been prepared taking into consideration the goals for children set in the UN General Assembly special session on Children held in May 2002, and the monitorable targets set in the Tenth Plan, and goals for Children in related ministries/departments. Political empowerment of women is another important direction, pursued so far at Panchayat Raj Institutions level. At state and national level, it is yet to be operationalised.

Information Technology

India has been consolidating its position as a world leader in software and Information Technology (IT) services. According to the National Association of Software and Services Companies (NASSCOM), the Indian software industry is expected to raise its export revenues by 35 per cent during 2004-05 to US $17.3 billion, reflecting the increasing returns to knowledge advantage. Indian IT industry's market size (exports and domestic) is expected to grow from $ 25 billion in 2004 to $ 65 billion in 2009. The financial services sector including banks, insurance companies and securities firms account for the largest share of India's software and IT services exports at 37 per cent during 2003-04, followed by telecommunication and manufacturing sectors. The Information Technology Enabled Services – Business Process Outsourcing (ITES – BPO) segment generated a revenue of $3.9 billion in 2003-04, and is expected to grow by 44.4 per cent during 2004-05 on top of 45.3 per cent in 2003-04. Alongside the rapid expansion of the IT – ITES sector's contribution to GDP from 1.4 per cent at the end of the 1990s to 3.5 per cent in 2003-04, employment in this sector surged from 5.2 lakh in 2001-02 to 8.4 lakh in 2003-04. Besides capitalising on labour cost, arbitraging on time zone and language, Indian IT companies are increasingly positioning themselves to seek larger shares in the global IT services market, currently estimated at $396 billion. The increasing consolidation through mergers and acquisitions, expansion of services that are being offered from India, higher value end-services, cost competitiveness and expansion in capacity underscore the strengthening of the Indian ITES–market. Even in the ITES–BPO segment, cross-selling, strong balance sheets, end-to-end service offerings are setting the tone of competitive expansion. Indian IT companies have been moving up in the value chain into IT consulting and system integration, hardware support and installation and processing services besides emerging areas such as healthcare, telecommunication, retail and government services.

According to International Data Corporation (IDC), the global ITES-BPO market is expected to grow at a compound annual growth rate of 9.0 per cent during 2002-06. This augurs well for India where the software and services export segment contributed around 73% to India's overall invisible receipts in 2003-04 as against 59%in 2002-03. North America continues to remain India's largest software and services export destination, followed by European and Asia Pacific regions. With the IT services exports rising, India continues to attract a large global share of the offshore business from various countries like the US, the UK and Europe. This has generated a backlash against BPOs particularly in the US.

The BPO activities encompass not only ITES but also a wide range of areas comprising services relating to manufacturing, banking, insurance, sales, marketing, utilities and human resources. India is expected to maintain its lead as the best offshore outsourcing destination, particularly for the US and European countries. Indian entities should strive to diversify their markets to other countries rather than depending only on the US market. India would also have to continuously innovate and maintain its low-cost niche in order to compete with competitors like China, the Philippines, Malaysia, Australia, South Africa and Singapore. India needs to set up more foreign affiliates in the IT segment to provide services offshore, besides attracting more FDI to undertake BPO activities in the country, which would pacify the protectionist reactions by developed countries. The Indian BPO market should also strive to attain maturity through consolidation to withstand the competitive threat, particularly from the emerging East Asian Countries.

Development Fund for Women (UNIFEM) – economic partici-pation, economic opportunity, political empowerment, educational attainment, and health and well-being. *(Source:The Hindu , May 20, 2005, page 11)*.

Among Asian countries, China ranks highest (33), followed by Japan (38). India, at 53 out of 58 countries, is virtually at the bottom of the ladder, scoring, however, way above its league in political empowerment (24). In health and well-being, the country is ranked 34; in economic opportunity 35; in economic participation 54; and in educational attainment a shocking 57. Evidently, the high school dropout rates among girl children and wage inequality are key factors in India's abysmal ranking. Clearly, in the era of globalisation, the lesson for India and the other poorly ranked countries is that they should strengthen and enhance the governmental support systems – not dismantle them in the name of market efficiency. One thing is clear, as economic inequality increases within a country, so does the gap between male and female.

Measuring the magnitude of the problem is a first step. The governments and NGOs (non-governmental organisations) alike are urged to use the rankings of the study to identify issue-areas, and learn from the experiences of nations that have been more successful in narrowing the gender gap. The WEF stressed that improving educational prospects for women should be the main priority for countries around the world, especially in developing countries. It described opening up education for girls as the 'most important catalyst for change in society', and said that progress in other areas such as falling adolescent pregnancy rates and better income opportunities would automatically follow educational empowerment of women. The survey also reveals that there is a link between how a country treats its women and that country's ability to compete globally. The report underlines the 'clear economic incentive' behind empowering women. It is said that countries that do not fully take advantage of one half of the talent in their population, are misallocating their human resources, and undermining their competitive potential.

The report says that 'no country has yet managed to eliminate the gender gap' but the five NORDIC states – Sweden, Norway, Iceland, Denmark and Finland – have succeeded best in narrowing it. They are seen to provide a 'workable model' for the rest of the world to follow. Other female-friendly countries include Britain, Germany, New Zealand, Australia, and significantly several East European countries where women still benefit from the support system built during the Communist era.

Even Britain, which makes it to the top 10, fares badly in a range of areas, lagging behind even India in terms of economic opportunity. USA, ranked 17, with its restrictive maternity rights regime and poor state child welfare system, does not even figure in the top 10 women-friendly countries.

As per the 2001 Census in India, women constitute about 48 per cent of the total population of the country. Women suffer many disadvantages as compared to men in the areas of education, labour participation rate and earnings. The National Policy for Empowerment of Women was adopted in 2001 with the objective of ensuring women their rightful place in the society by empowering them as agents of socio-economic change and development. With a view to translating the National Policy for Empowerment of women into action, a National Plan of Action for Empowerment of Women has been contemplated. To eliminate all types of discrimination against women and girl child, and their empowerment, major strategies being pursued include social empowerment, economic empowerment, and gender justice.

Employment of women in the organised sector (both public and private) at end-March 2003 at 4.97 million constituted 18.4 per cent of the total organised sector employment, compared to 18.1 per cent in 2002. As regards sectoral distribution, community, social and personal service sector employed 56.6 per cent of women workers followed by manufacturing (20.3%), agriculture and allied occupations (9.4%), and finance, insurance, real estate and business (5.5%). States with higher female literacy rates have higher proportion of women in organised sector employment.

Elimination of child labour is one of the concerns for which National Child Labour Projects have been established, and grant-in-aid voluntary organisations are being supported for action–oriented programmes. Two important schemes in the area of education are 'Sarva Shiksha Abhiyan' and 'Mahila Samakhya' being implemented by the Union Department of Elementary Education and Literacy as

Sri Sree Krishna T
Sr Lecturer, Dept. of Management Sciences
RVR & JC College of Engineering
Guntur - 522 019

Dr. Sreenivas Talluru
Reader
Dept. of Management Sciences
RVR & JC College of Engineering
Guntur - 522 019

Sri Subba Reddy C
Lecturer, Dept. of Economics
SGHR-MCMR Degree College
Guntur

Professor Subrahmanyam DAR
Principal
Mahatma Gandhi College
Guntur - 522 006

Dr. Sudhakar A
Associate Professor & Head
Dept. of Commerce
Dr. BR Ambedkar Open University
Hyderabad

Sri Sudhakara Babu Ch
Principal
Jagarlamudi Chandramouli College of Law
Guntur - 522 006

Ms. Sujatha M
Research Scholar
School of Business Management
SV University
Tirupathi, AP

Sri Suryanarayana K
Lecturer, Dept. of Management Sciences
RVR & JC College of Engineering
Guntur - 522 019

Sri Suresh R
Associate Professor
Indian Institute of Financial Management & Research
Chennai

Sri Suresh Babu V V
Lecturer, Dept.of Computer Science
Mahatma Gandhi College (PG)
Guntur - 522 019

Dr. Surya Prakasha Rao BK
Reader, Dept. of Management Sciences
RVR & JC College of Engineering
Guntur - 522 019

Ms. Symala B
Lecturer, Dept. of Economics
Hindu College
Guntur - 522 003

Sri Vasudeva Rao P
Reader, Dept. of Economics
Hindu College
Guntur - 522 003

Sri Venkateswara Rao M
Legal Section
Cotton Corporation of India
Guntur - 522 002

Dr. Venkateswara Rao Malapati
Professor and Head
Dept. of Chemical Engineering
RVR & JC College of Engineering
Guntur - 522 019

Ms. Ziana Shireen Md.
MBA (Final)
Sri Padmavati Mahila Viswa Vidyalayam
Tirupati, AP

Professor Krishnamacharyulu CSG
School of Business Management
SV University
Tirupathi, AP

Ms. Krishna Priya Y
MBA (Final)
Sri Padmavathi Mahila University
Tirupathi

Sri Kumar Ch HKS
Assistant Professor in Management
Alhabeeb College of Engineering
Hyderabad

Ms. Lalitha K
Principal
BHH Degree College for Women
Guntur - 522 002

Ms. Lavanya Latha K
Faculty Member
Sri Padmavathi Mahila Viswa Vidyalayam
Tirupathi, AP

Sri Maruthi Vara Prasad A
Lecturer, PG Dept. of Management Studies
TJPS College, Guntur - 522 006

Sri Murali Manohar B
Asst. Professor, MIS, Debub University
Awassa, Ethiopia

Dr. Nagayya D
Former Director
National Institute of Small Industry
Extension Training (NISIET)
Hyderabad

Sri Nagapavan C
Faculty Member
ICFAI National College
Vijayawada - 520 010

Dr. Nageswara Rao D
Reader, Dept. of Commerce
Hindu College
Guntur - 522 003

Ms. Padmaja Ch K
Faculty
Sri Padmavathi Mahila University
Tirupathi

Professor Prasad G
Dept. of Commerce & Business Admn.
Acharya Nagarjuna University
Nagarjuna Nagar - 522 510
Guntur, Andhra Pradesh

Dr. Prasad LSN
Associate Professor-Economics
Debub University
Awassa, Ethiopia

Dr. Rajasekhar AKVSSR
Reader & Head, Dept. of Economics
Hindu College
Guntur - 522 003

Dr. Rajesh C Jampala
Reader, PG Dept. of Business Administration
PB Siddhardha College of Arts & Science
Vijayawada - 520 010

Sri Ramana Rao SV
Lecturer, Dept. of Management Sciences
RVR & JC College of Engineering
Guntur - 522 019

Sri Siva Prasad AVV
Lecturer, PG Dept. of Business Administration
Akkineni Nageswara Rao College
Gudivada, Krishna Dist., AP

Ms. Soujanya Vamsi
MBA (Final)
Sri Padmavati Mahila Viswa Vidyalayam
Tirupati, AP

LIST OF CONTRIBUTORS

Dr. Adilakshmi P
Reader & Head
Dept. of Business Administration
Montessori Mahila Kalasala
Vijayawada - 520 010

Dr. Aney Thomas
Asst. Prof., Dept. of RDFS
Debub University
Awassa, Ethiopia

Sri Ashok AVS
Faculty Member
ICFAI National College
Vijayawada, Andhra Pradesh

Dr. Balaji Prasad P
Reader, School of Business Management
Sri Venkateswara University
Tirupathi, Andhra Pradesh

Professor Bhavani V
Dept. of Political Science and Public Administration
Acharya Nagarjuna University
Nagarjuna Nagar - 522 510

Professor Bidwai SV
Director cum Professor
Anjuman-I-Islam's Allana Institute of
Management Studies (AIAIMS)
Mumbai

Ms. Bindu Madhavi K
MBA (Final)
Sri Padmavathi Mahila University
Tirupathi

Professor Bose BPC
Dept. of Political Science and Public Administration
Acharya Nagarjuna University
Nagarjuna Nagar - 522 510

Professor Brahmanandam GN
Dean, Faculty of Commerce
Dept. of Commerce & Business Administration
Acharya Nagarjuna University
Nagarjuna Nagar - 522 510

Dr. Chandrasekhara Rao K
Head, Department of Commerce
Pondicherry University
Pondicherry - 605 014

Dr. Durga Nagaveni A
Lecturer, Dept. of Hindi
BHHDegree College for Women
Guntur - 522 002

Smt. Geetha Chew Aycle
Head, Department of Economics
Deebub University
Awassa, Ethiopia

Sri Kishore Babu M
Head, Dept. of Business Studies
Mahatrna Gandhi College (PG)
Guntur - 522 019

Dr. Koteswara Rao MVS
Associate Professor
Dept. of Political Science and Public Administration
Acharya Nagarjuna University
Nagarjuna Nagar - 522 510

Ravindra Babu, Vice-Principal, PS Somayajulu, Registrar, NV Srinivasa Rao, Administrative Officer, G Anantha Narayana, Office Manager, and other senior faculty in the College for providing me conducive work environment to organise this mega event. I specially acknowledge the support of Sri DSR Anjaneyulu, and Sri SV Rattaiah who helped me in the completion of this gigantic task.

I am greatly indebted to Dr C Ramachandra Prabhu, faculty of Department of Physics, RVR & JC College of Engineering, Dr D Nagayya, former Director, National Institute of Small Industry Extension Training (NISIET), Hyderabad, and Professor S Krishna Sharma, formerly of the Dept. of English, Acharya Nagarjuna University, Guntur for the encouragement, help and support extended to me while working on this publication.

My special thanks are due to the Management of Discovery Publishing House, New Delhi for bringing out this publication in an elegant manner in record time.

I also want to thank a number of personal friends for their solid support and involvement in a variety of ways in my academic ventures. These include: Smt & Sri GS Ram Prasad, Smt & Sri K Shyam Babu, Smt & Sri G Subrahmanyam, Smt & Sri M Subba Rao, Smt & Sri Y Durga Prasada Rao, Smt & Sri PN Uday Kumar, Smt & Sri R Vasu, Smt & Sri V Srinivasa Rao and Smt & Sri M Venkateswara Rao.

All my family members have patiently borne the inconvenience due to my involvement in a number of academic activities including the release of this publication, and encouraged me a great deal. I acknowledge their silent and valued contributions.

Talluru Sreenivas

CONTENTS

Section-II: Gender Disparities

Section-III: Information Technology

SECTION–I
GLOBALISATION

1

LIBERALIZATION AND ROLE OF THE BUREAUCRACY

Prof. B.P.C. Bose*

Liberalisation had become a reality. Though a number of academicians feel that the results of liberalisation would be negative, India reached a stage of compulsion to open its commercial and industrial boundaries to advanced countries. Though this process started in early eighties, it reached its logical end in 1990s. Partly, the mismanagement of economy and fiscal anarchy is responsible for it. Once, the liberalisation had become inevitable, the question now is how far the policy making and implementing agencies of this country are tuned to new development. Can the entire bureaucratic structure is ready to adjust itself to the new role and responsibilities. Can it adjust to the new role of facilitator from that of regulator? Uncompromising political will, sychronising the market mechanism and social responsibilities, and the role of the bureaucracy as a catalyst of change are the prerequisites. The need for mobilising the public opinion in favour of new change is also essential. To be precise, In the era of economic liberalization, there is an in evitable and urgent need for redefining the roles and reordering of priorities of bureaucracy, political representatives and public in general and the Government in particular.

* Professor, Department of Political Science and Public Administration, Acharya Nagarjuna University, Nagarjuna Nagar-522 510, A.P.

Introduction

This paper is an attempt to explore the themes of political support, political executive, bureaucracy and its accountability with reference to liberalization policies. The paper also examines certain emerging perspectives concerning the changing role of bureaucracy in India. It also briefly touches upon the policy initiatives needed to reform the bureaucracy in the post liberalization period.

There is no unanimity in the opinions, doubts and criticisms expressed by proponents, opponents and critics on the liberalization policy. Developments in liberal economies in 1980s and 1990s[1] have propelled the competitiveness all over the world. The need for liberalization in India arise partly due to the compelling necessity in the light of serious problem of balance of payments in the 1990s, political expediency, compulsions of development, environmental influences, technological developments, and malfunctioning administrative system, and socio-economic policies etc[2].

Since Independence, various policies and strategies have been initiated for Socio-Economic development by both the union and State Governments in India, the earliest being the Community Development Programme (CDP) in 1952. Various schemes such as National Extension Service (NES), Intensive Agriculture Development Programme (IADP), Integrated Rural Development Programme (IRDP), Minimum Needs Programme (MNP), Drought Prone Areas Programme (DPAP), Desert Development Programme (DDP), National Rural Employment Programme (NREP), Food for Work Programme (FFWP), TRYSEM, Jawahar Rajgar Yojana (JRY), Prime Minister Rojgar Yojana (PMRY), etc. were part of the planning edifice. Because of the centralized planned economic development strategy, most development programmes initiated in the past proved to be inadequate and failed to give the desired results. As a result most of the programmes were either diluted or discontinued. However, bureaucratic apathy and inefficiency coupled with corruption vitiated the efforts of centralized planning. As most of these schemes were centrally sponsored, some of them found to be irrelevant and in some cases inconsistent with the realities and needs at the grass root level mainly due to inter-regional and intra-regional diversities. The implementation of these schemes in an effective way was thwarted by limitedornon-participationofpeopleintheirformulation and implementation. Further, the bureaucracy got strengthened at the expense of the local institutions.

The poor performance of the public sector created some more problems. It is natural that the failure of the public sector in achieving its assigned goals was often projected as the main reason for the failure of Indian policy of mixed economy with emphasis on public sector. The economic and financial health of several Public Sector Units[3] is in very bad shape due to multiple factors. In this context, it is relevant to look at the performance and status of Public Sector Units and several State Governments in India in the recent past.

The CAG in his recent Report[4] identified the following reasons for the failure of public sector units in living up to the expectations.

- Abnormal high inventory.
- Inadequate financial control.
- Inefficient internal audit system
- Deficient cost control system.
- Default in repayment of loans and guarantee fee.
- Over statement/under statement of profit and loss and assets and liabilities.
- Full erosion of paid up capital in 80 Public Sector Units.
- Abnormal increase in staff cost.
- Time overruns/cost overruns[5].

Making the problem more complex, the financial performance of various state governments is alarming. The finances of most governments are in deficit, thus making the maintenance of healthy fiscal policy impossible.[6] Perhaps the failure of public sector in mobilising the extra resources necessary for investment in core sectors, and the fiscal indiscipline of the governments forced the government to go for liberalisation on the dictates of the lending institutions.

Whether is it public sector or Government, it is the bureaucracy which plays a crucial role. The role of the bureaucracy had been decisive in implementation of various policies and programmes. As such, the bureaucracy has to shoulder major responsibility along with the political executives for the present state of affairs in our country. The Indian administrative system is known for its rule bound, rigid, conservative, slow and unresponsive behaviour. Can we afford to have the same traits in the era of liberalisation, where the competition form the private sector challenges the hitherto captive areas of operation? Isn't the proactive and committed bureaucracy is the need of the hour? The experience from the private sector and the countries, which assigned a limited role to the state, demonstrate that the liberalization policies involve far reaching implications and fundamental changes in public administrative systems – structures, functions, attitudes, and behaviour patterns. The million-dollor question is what is the role of the bureaucracy in the changed context? Does it leave the space to voluntary and philanthropic organisations by withdrawing itself to its traditional role as argued by the Public Choice theoreticians[7]? Or does it takes more burden and responsibility even in the changed context?

Different academicians perceive the process of liberalisation differently. According to some, liberalization means rolling back of the Government or limited governance resulting in reduction in size and role of the bureaucracy. Others viewed it as privatisation, deregulation, disinvest-ments, debureaucratisation, decentralization, re-inventing government etc. Viewed from a different perspective, discounting the misgivings and doubts expressed by critics, several academicians have opined that state and the bureaucracy continue to play an important and major role in the era of liberalization by redefining its role and redesigning its structures and functions. One of the much visualised role being a change from 'regulator' to 'promoter' and from 'rule orientation' to 'goal orientation' or 'result orientation' (Jain, 1996; Singh,S.S. 1996 and Ramesh K.Arora and Rajani troll, 1996). This view believes that it can play an effective role as a facilitator and enabler.

Irrespective of the different perceptions and expected contribution of the liberalisation, it is a fact that the process of liberalisation had become a reality. For any reform political support is an essential and basic ingredient. The role of bureaucracy, where the master is competent, to a large extent depends upon the nature of the political will and support it derives from the political system. However, the reform process indicates that there is political vacillation dictated by electoral compulsions and it appears that bureaucracy is taking advantage of this (See, Corbridge and Harris, 2000 and Currie,1996). Bureaucrats often complain that there is frequent interference or over critical or fault finding postures on the part of politicians. On the other hand, the politicians have their score of complaints against the attitude of the bureaucracy. The situation indicates a wide gap between the perceptions of politicians and bureaucrats about each other's roles.

Another relevant aspect is the accountability of the bureaucracy for performance. The traditional or existing devices of ensuring accountability proved to be either ineffective or inadequate. Politicians face electorate every five years. Private sector executives are accountable to their shareholders. The moot question in this context is why should bureaucrats continue to be unaccountable? So, there is need for espousing the bureaucrats for their non-performance.

As a part of the British legacy, we have inherited a bureaucracy with generalist orientation. It was observed that the generalist bureaucracy is more resistant to change and conceives every reform of radical nature as a step that disturbs equilibrium. This tendency underscores the need for creation of structures with specialist orientation since the generalist tradition cannot cope up with the demands of liberalization. Liberalization paradigm placed the revamping of bureaucracy on the top of reforms agenda. Consensus in terms of reversal of roles in favour of "a regulator to promoter" is clearly evident. Analysts argue that since India has plural democratic system and multiple actors involve in influencing the liberalization process, the implementation gets slowed down. It is very difficult to bring about consensus. The moot question here is can stern-faced regulators switch roles to play smiling professional men shown in brochures? Can rationing officers become marketing men?

According to some observers, currently the focus is on the "discretionary controls" of the bureaucracy. One presumption is that deregulation and debureaucratisation may not be whole heartedly appreciated by the bureaucracy desirous of retaining whatever powers and authority it has. Whatever may be the attitude of bureaucracy to liberalization, it is essentially the question of political will that matters much. But one positive side of the Indian bureaucracy is that it has shown adaptive capabilities atleast to some extent.

Presumably, the main thrust of bureaucratic reform is one the reduction of the size of bureaucracy itself. It means, efforts have to be directed to physically move it away from its former area of activity where it did the damage in the days of permit raj.

Public

One of the major concerns relating to the liberalization policy is the implications for the public? From the general public, the response to the liberalization seems to be indifferent, passive, ill-informed, ignorant, misguided and confused. Neither the advocates nor its opponents have any clear idea to offer as an alternative to the general public in such a situation. Critics of liberalization policy argue that there is a neglect of social dimension in government claims that the policy will be pursued with 'human face'. Commenting in his editorial note T.N.Chaturvedi (1996, VIII) has expressed the feeling that "haunted by newer apprehensions on account of burgeoning corruption at different levels with news papers reporting on new scams and scandals threatening to push public accountability and concerns for the poor to oblivion". He further states that no attempt was made in any systematic and sustained manner to take people into confidence about Structural Adjustment Programme and liberalization policy. It is necessary to take public into confidence in attempting such radical departures in public policies through awareness campaigns and public education programmes.

Dr. Sharma (1996: 235) says that in the capital centered approach, public had been reduced to the status of passive spectators concerned largely with receiving whatever benefits this approach bestow up on them. He felt that "people centred approach on the other hand" may be distorted and self defeating unless the people, their education and organization became the prior focus, Dr.Bhaskara Rao (1996: 321) while commenting on the role of the state in the liberalization era called for exercise of caution. According to him, "it is the special responsibility of the state to correct standard market failure and guide the market towards achievement of social policies through people entered approach". Dr. Arora (1996: 664) has expressed the hope that emergent administrative system ought to be client oriented or people oriented with its major focus on empowering people".

In spite of the criticisms and misgivings about the impact of liberalization policies from various quarters, it is hoped that the positive results of reform process will, to some extent, contribute for the socio-economic development of the country. After all one component of the beneficiaries are the public. Liberalization visualizes improvement in administrative systems for better performance aimed at attaining the larger social goals.

Apart from these, one tends to raise questions like :

(a) Can the bureaucracy with its present form and orientation is relevant to the liberalization philosophy?

(b) How do we redefine the role of the state and the government in relation t the social realities?

(c) What are the goals, processes and organizational structures for implementation of liberalization policies?

(d) Whether there is any incompatibility in the existing regulations and statutes governing the public bureaucracy?

(e) If so, what are the changes required to re-orient the bureaucracy and sensitising it towards implementation of liberalization policy?

The following suggestions may be considered for better exploitation of the changed situation for achieving the desired results:

(a) Reforms will not be effective unless there is a strong political will and support and bureaucracy's active participation.

(b) There is need to develop adequate administrative capacity, sufficient infrastructure and technology to support ongoing liberalization programme.

(c) Bureaucracy shall be encouraged to bring in innovations as catalysts of change.

(d) Government have to become competitive.

(e) Emphasis shall be on result and performance orientation.

(f) Administrative systems must be proactive rather than reactive.

(g) Right to information provides an opportunity to the general public to scrutinize administrative organizations.

(h) Need to balance the market mechanism with social and public concerns.

In the era of economic liberalization, there is an in evitable and urgent need for redefining the roles and reordering of priorities of bureaucracy, political representatives and public in general and the Government in particular.

NOTES

1. Though few people remember it, the process of economic reform was initiated in 1980s. The post emergency rule of Indira Gandhi (1980-1984) and her successor Rajiv Gandhi (1984-1989) tried to liberalize the economy by opening doors to foreign goods, liberalizing licence procedure and diluting the existing industrial policy Rajiv Gandhi wanted a judicious combination of deregulation, import liberalization and easier access to foreign technology (Kohli, 1989:312), Bardhan, 1989, Sanjay Baru, 1985, Prabhat Patnaik, 1986 and Aggarwal and Chowdary, 1991).
2. There are conflicting views on the necessity, nature and consequences of liberalization. Some argue that it is unavoidable (Ahluwalia, 1999 and Narasimham, 1993) and some other argues from other extreme (Prabhat Patnaik), 1993 and 2000.
3. For details on the role and performance of public sector units in India see Raghavulu, C.V., "Privatisation and Public Enterprises in India", The Indian Journal of Public Administration, Vol. XLII, No.3, July – Sept, 1996.
4. Out of the 259 Public Sector Units, 144 units made a profit of Rs.30,680 Crores and 113 units suffered losses to the tune of Rs.9499 Crores. In addition to this seven public sector units (FCIL, JFCL, IISCL, HECL, HSL, NTPC and IDPL) sustained cumulative losses to the tune of Rs.14,471.15 Crores. The number of employees working in public sector units stands at 19.28 lakhs. Other problems include, avoidable loss, unproductive expenditure, avoidable payments and loss of revenue to insurance public sector units to the turn of Rs.2152.82 Crores. Comptroller and Auditor General of India, Activity Report 1999-2000, IAA Dept. Singh Graphics, New Delhi, 2000, pp. 32-34.
5. However, there is an alternate view that public sector is not only a burden, but also income generating one for Indian Economy: An alternative Survey, 1998-2003 (Yearly), Delhi Science Forum.
6. The following are the major features of state finances:

   Low growth rate in tax revenue; Abnormal rise in revenue expenditure; Stagnant/decline in plan expenditure (capital); Increasing burden of administrative cost; Financing of Social Sector expenditure through borrowings; Lack of initiative in recovery of loans given by the state Governments; Spiralling rise in borrowings; High cost of debt servicing; and Proceeding towards debt trap.

The following table present the actual economic situation of several states in India.

Name of the State	*Rev. Deficit*	*Debt.*
	1998-1999	*1989-1999*
Andhra Pradesh	2684	21388
Karnataka	1215	18617
Maharashtra	3926	27456
Rajasthan	2996	24170
Madhya Pradesh	2872	21959
Kerala	2030	10073
West Bengal	4856	26444
Uttar Pradesh	8696	62725
Gujarat	2863	17079
Tamilnadu	3437	N.A.

Source: CAG Activity Report 1999-2000.

7. To be very brief, the Public Choice Theory favours down-sizing the government's role and expansion of the activities of market forces. In administrative language it amounts to the handing over of government functions to the private sector, wherever it is possible.

REFERENCES

1. Aggarwal, J.C. and N.K. Chowdary (1991) *Indian Economy: Crisis and Reforms,* Delhi, Shipra.

2. Ahluwalia, Montek, S. (1999) *India's Economic Reforms* in Jeffrey D.Sachs, Ashutosh Varshney and Nirupam Bajpai (eds.), *India in the Era of Economic Reforms,* Delhi: Oxford.

3. Bardhan, Pranab (1984). *The Political Economy of Development in India,* New Delhi, Oxford University Press.

4. Bata K.Dey, (1992) Beyond Bureaucracy, Beyond Hierarchy, *The Indian Journal of Public Administration* (IJPA) Vol.XXXVIII (Oct_Dec).

5. Bhaskara Rao, V. (1996), *Liberalization Policy: Need for People Oriented Approach,* (IJPA), Vol.XLII, No.3, July-Sept.

6. Chaturvedi, T.N. (1996). Editorial, *(IJPA)*. Vol.XLII, No.3, July – Sept.

7. Corbridge, Stuart and Hariss John. (2000) *Reinvesting India: Liberalization, Hindu Nationalism and Popular Democracy*, Cambridge: Policy Press.

8. Currie, Bob (1996) *Governance, democracy and Economic Adjustment in India: Conceptual and Empirical Problems Third World Quarterly*, Vol.17, No.4.

9. Jain R.B, (1996). *Globalization, Market Economy and Human Security: The Indian Experience, (IJPA)*, Vol.XLII, No.3, July-Sept.

10. Kohli, Atul, (1989). *Politics of Economic liberalisation in India, World Development*, Vol.18, NO.4.

11. Narasimham, M, (1993), *Economic Reforms: The Unfinished Agenda*, New Delhi: Rajiv Gandhi Institute of Contemporary Studies.

12. Patnaik, Prabhat (1986). *New Turn in Economic Policy: Context and Prospects, Economic and Plitical Weekly*, Vol. 21, No. 23.

13. ...., (1999). Notes on the Political Economy of Structural Adjustment, *Social Scientist*, Vol. 22, No.23.

14. ...., (2000). *Economic Policy and its Political Management in the Current Conjuncture in Frankel*, Zoya Hassan at.al (eds.) *Transforming India: Social and Political Dynamics of Democracy*, New Delhi.

15. Ramesh K.Arora and Rajini Goyal, *Indian Public Administration: Institutions and Issues*, (2nd ed), wishwa Prakashan, New Delhi, 1996,

16. Sanjay Baru (1985). *The State in Retreat, Economic and Political Weekly*, Vol. 20, No. 16.

17. Sharma, A.K. (1996). *People's Empowerment, (IJPA)*, Vol.XLII, No.3, July-Sept.

18. S.S.Singh, (1996). *Liberalization and Public Service: Agenda for Reforms, (IJPA)*. Vol.XLII,No.3, July-Sept., 1996.

2

THE EMERGING, NON-EMERGING AND ILL-EMERGING TRENDS IN THE LEGAL ARENA

AN OVERVIEW

Ch. Sudhakara Babu*

No institution is ever drawn in such a way that it can alone lead a nation to prosperity. The in-built qualities of an institution excel itself in its elevation whereas emerging, non-emerging and ill-emerging trends shall have a great influence on its relevance. Constitution of India is the best area for testing the trends. When the continued reverence of the people to the Constitution is an emerging trend, the destructive attitude of the politicians is an ill-emerging trend. The continued patronage of the people with the Judiciary is an emerging trend whereas the growing corruption, nepotism etc. are the ill-emerging trends. Let better trends emerging elevating the Nation.

Introduction

The importance of mechanisms of Law and Justice in the nation building cannot inspite of being in two of the three organs of State, be over estimated and over-emphasised. No institution has ever been drawn such that it can solve, with all ingenuity, the infinite variety of problems or challenges that may emerge in the race to prosperity. The political philosophy that lies in the hearts of the people in general and the people in power in particular, the means and methods that

* Principal, Jagarlamudi Chandramouli College of Law Guntur- 522 006, A.P.

they have chosen in achieving the values and goals and the avenues within which they allow the institutions to function and perform, determine the prominence and profoundness of an institution.

When the in-built qualities of an institution are the main factors in its relevance and elevation, the emerging trends will always be a boon, the non-emerging trends will always be a bane and whereas the ill emerging trends would be disastrous. In a developing nation the existence, working and growth of the institutions would be a tri-mixture of these trends. The same is true with the Indian Legal system and the institutions associated with Law and Justice. Among the numerous branches and institutions of law an attempt has been made in this piece, to through some light on the trends on the Constitution, Law-making, Judiciary and emerging International Criminal Law.

Constitution of India

Inspite of being the world's largest written constitution amended hundred times, the in-built potential of the constitution in giving a viable polity to this nation is highly debated. Out of scores of areas under the constitution enabling discussion four areas viz. Fundamental rights, Parliament, Governors and Article 356 are focused.

Regarding the Fundamental Rights it is submitted that the unenumerated rights be made explicit rights in the form of appropriate amendments to Part III of the Constitution. The efforts of the Supreme Court in blossoming the scope of Fundamental Rights, particularly Article 21 of the Constitution be complemented in the form of adopting them into the Constitution. The aspirations of the people be cherished at least to the extent they have been judicially deduced.

As the Nation has been 'glowing' the claim for more reservation under Articles 15(4) and 16(4) of the constitution in favour of more backward communities and minorities may not be satisfied. The reservation scheme be revamped in such a way that the dependants or children of the vulnerable avocations like agriculture, craft be benefited.

Freedom of Press, Freedom of Information, Right against torture and inhuman degrading and cruel treatment and punishment, Right to compensation for being illegally deprived of one's right to life or liberty, Right to Privacy, Right to work – both to urban and rural downtrodden for a minimum of one eighty days in a year, Right to speedy and effective justice and legal aid, Right to education – up to any age and level in case of people below the poverty line and Right to safe and adequate drinking water and clean environment, be added in Part III of the Constitution, at appropriate places vitalizing the existing fundamental rights.

The bicameral Parliament is entrusted with the job of making Law for this Land and the State Legislatures at State level. The composition of the Houses as enshrined in Articles 80 and 81 of the Constitution has nurtured the Houses into a broken reed. The law-making bodies in the course of time have become more the deliberate bodies and the deliberation of late has become shouting and shutting, ultimately pushing the legislative business to its back seat. The composition of the bicameral Parliament should be such that the upper house be a Legislative body composed of Law-people and the lower house be a deliberate body composed of peoples representatives who deliberate on the national interests and approve the law recommended by upper house. The same mutatis mutandis be applied to State legislatures, making bicameral legislatures compulsory to each State. The Hung Houses may be taken care by the "constructive vote of no-confidence" as recommended by the National Commission to Review the Working of the Constitution.

The appointments of Governors made by UPA Government brings forth the Governor's position under the Constitution to limelight once again. Once the 'constitutional dictator' 'an autocrat presiding over provincial despotism' and originally intended by the framers of the Constitution to be a 'non political' 'impartial' and 'person to uphold the dignity of the Head of a State in the Indian Federal system', the Governor has emerged as a 'favourate boy' of the Centre, a 'fallen horse' of the ruling party and so on. The Raj Bhavan has become a refugee camp for the 'burnt-out' politicians and it is made a 'stepping stone for those still burning with political ambitions'. The sage of the pre-independence and pre 1967 period has been reduced to a saboteur of the elected governments. No other institution under the Constitution has been so vehemently, venomously and contemptuously attacked and abused. The office of the Governor has lost most of its earlier prestige and dignity and it enjoys scant respect. Even those that held the post viz. Mrs.Vijaya Lakshmi Pandit suggested the abolition of the office from our polity.

The bizarre state of affairs was not unknown to the constitution framers. But the partition and its ghastly aftermath and the communist upsurge in Telangana forced the founding fathers towards a strong centre and to retain the age old office of the Governor which was 'pregnant with its colonial origin, autocratic ethos and bureaucratic background'. The constitutional arrangement went on well till the fourth general election in 1967. But, the role that the Governors played later has vitiated the 'parliamentary climate' and 'constitutional niceties' of the office so much that some Governors were humiliated, some were recalled and compelled to resign.

The ambiguous language of the constitution, political considerations, previous political affiliations and the future political ambitions of most of the Governors, centripetal tendencies and such other factors have degenerated the person of the Governor.

It is the high time to restore the lost prestige and honour of the office of the Governor. The lacunne lies with the appointment and removal of Governor. The National Commission to Review the working of the Constitution has recommended on the line of the recommendations of Sarkaria Commission, that the following matters should be kept in mind while appointing the Governors:

- He should be eminent in some walk of life.
- He should be a person from outside the State.
- He should be a detached figure and not too intimately connected with the local politics of the State.
- He should be a person who has not taken too great a part in politics generally and particularly in the recent past.

The National Commission further opined that the Governor of a State should be appointed or transferred or removed by the President after consultation with the Chief Minister of the State. The success or failure of an office depends upon the quality and ability of people who work on it. If the men who work the system are honest men of integrity and character, it will be successful. If the men work on it are dishonest it is bound to fail. With this type of politicians available in the country no constitutional arrangement or set of rules shall hold good. Let good sense prevail over the appointing authorities, in appointing Governors.

The office of the Governor has not failed. In the 'Indian type of federalism' the 'link' between the Union and States must be strong. Though the office of the Governor is not the corner stone of our democratic apparatus, it has unique importance in the working of our Union-State relations and in filling-up the political vacuum as and when the constitutional machinery in the state breaks down.

Article 356 of the Constitution which provided for a giant control of one tier of the constitutional structure over the other, has been the one most talked about and the one that has been frequently used, misused and abused. According to a study of Lok Sabha Secretariat the Article has been invoked 111 times. On 13 occasions it was used against Union Territories. In the remaining 98 instances on 10 occasions it was used for technical reasons like delay in completion of the process of election etc., in 54 cases its use was warranted and on 13 occasions it was misused and on 21 occasions it was abused.

Even after 10 amendments, Article 356 which was intended to be a bulwark of the constitution assuring discipline on the part of representative governments in States, continues to be a sword of democles hanging over the elected governments in States, provoking an end less debate on its delection. But the odds are in favour of its continuation. The situations requiring its invocation are numerous. Its misuse can be prevented by creating the necessary constitutional conventions governing its use and by availing the measures provided in the analogous provisions viz. Articles 256, 257, 355 and 365. Article 356 may be invoked as a matter of last resort, as stated by Dr.Ambedkar in the Constituent Assembly and before issuing a proclamation the concerned State shall be given an opportunity, except in urgent cases, to explain its position.

Law-making

"The public good ought to be the object of the legislator, general utility ought to be the foundation of his reasonings. To know the true good of the community is what constitutes the science of legislation, the art consists in finding the means to realize that good." (The theory of Legislation by Jeremy Bentham page 1). The good the Law-makers intend to do is known by the quality of Law they find (Law was found not made – Savigny). The National Commission to Review the Working of the Constitution has observed –" If there is a sense of unease with the way the Parliament and the State legislatures are functioning, it may be due to a decline in recent year in both the quantity and quality of work done by them. Over the years the number of days on which the houses sit to transact legislative and other business has come down very significantly. Even the relatively fewer days on which the houses meet are often marked by unseemly incidents, including use of force to intimidate opponents, shouting and shutting out of debate and discussion resulting in frequent adjournments. There is increasing concern about the decline of Parliament, falling standards of debate, erosion of the moral authority and prestige of the supreme tribune of the people.(Report of the National Commission to Review the Working of the Constitution, Universal Law Publishing Co. Pvt. Ltd. 2003, page 105) The suitability and the quality of legislation made can be doubted on several fronts. Even on a pivotal area like terrorism, which has been effecting the sovereignity and integrity of the nation, the political manoeuvre dominate and the nation could not have a viable legislation even at present. The passing and repeal of TADA and POTA show the dilemma of Parliament on a matter of highest national importance.

The problem of 'quality legislation' is not peculiar to modern parliaments. Even the second parliament, which was composed of great nationalist leaders was not an exception. The Hindu Succession Act, 1956 which was passed by the second parliament as piecemeal of Dr. Ambedkar's Hindu code was enacted in such a way that in certain cases the property cannot be distributed at all. The Act provided for the distribution of a Hindu intestate's estate. Two different sets of rules are made for Hindu male and female intestates. Sections 15 and 16 provided for Hindu female intestate succession. According to Section 15 (1), the property of a female Hindu dying intestate shall devolve upon the sons and daughters (including the children of any predeceased son and daughter) and the husband. But, in the absence of any son or daughter of the deceased (including the children of any predeceased son or daughter) the property inherited by the female Hindu from her father or mother shall devolve not on the husband but on the heirs of the father. Imagine a situation where a Hindu female had inherited property from mother and died leaving behind the same and her father. It devolves on the heirs of the father and not on the father! One cannot have heirs during the life time. There are a few such anomalies in Hindu female intestate succession. (for a detailed study on the subject please refer to Supreme Court Journal, 1993, Journal Section, page 13 for an article of the same author titled " Rules of Succession to a female Hindu – A Jumbled Lot? Or a languished lay in inaptness"). The anomaly has not been rectified even after almost half of a century. This is just the tip of the ice berg. "Corrective steps are urgently needed to strengthen Parliament's role as the authentic voice of the people as they struggle and suffer to realize the inspiring vision of a free and just society enshrined in the Constitution. Also, it is of the utmost importance for survival of democracy that Parliament continues to occupy a position of the highest esteem in the minds and hearts of the people." (Report of the National Commission to Review the Working of the Constitution)

Judiciary

"On the one hand, in popular discussion of forms and changes of Government, the judicial organ often drops out of sight, on the other hand, in determining a nation's rank in political civilization, no test is more decisive than the degree in which justice, as defined by the law is actually realised in its judicial administration ...." (Hearld Laski "a Grammar of Politics, S. Chand & Co. Ltd. 1979 page 541). Judicial reform, particularly, timely delivery of judgments is being debated within the judiciary. Judiciary has become even against several odds, more efficient and the justice delivery mechanism has been speeded up. But, the statistics of pending cases are still astonishing. The 20.6 million cases pending in 1995 before the District courts swelled to 23.4 million in 2004 and the 3 million cases pending in 1995 before the High Courts came to 3.4 million in 2004. But, the 36,000 cases pending in Supreme Court in 1995 came down to 30,000 cases in 2004. These figures one way suggest the relevance of judiciary and confidence the people repose, when there has been a pervasive disenchantment with the working of the other institutions of democracy, on Judiciary by filing millions of cases each year and on the other hand emphasize the need for sophistication in justice delivery system and the cooperation that the judiciary requires from various other quarters in performing its uphill tasks. The legislature should make timely and qualitative laws, amendments and repeals. The executive should provide necessary infrastructure to the courts and be prompt in making appointments at both the higher and subordinate judiciary and be positive in filing cases, preferring appeals and in enforcing judgments. The National Commission to Review the working of the Constitution has advocated that the governments should have a 'litigation policy' directed towards reduction of government litigation and protection of public interest by preventive strategies.

Advocates are blamed to be a stumbling block to any reform to judicial procedure. The failure of judicial dispensation has resulted in Alternate Dispute Resolution (ADR) systems. ADR is in derogation of professionalism of Advocates. The Bar and Bench should strive at quicker and qualitative judicial dispensation and at marginalisation of ADR so that people would get justice as defined by law and not weighted verdicts.

Litigant friendly courts is the need of the hour. Our courts have still retained the colonial colours. Honourable people hesitate appearing before the courts. The large difference between the accused and the witness is made thinner. Certain courts still retaining the witness boxes is thrusting a sense of guiltiness on the part of the witnesses. Lack of minimum facilities like drinking water, toilets and seating arrangements make the vindication of greater rights before the courts a laughing stock. The plight of the people at the doors of the court hall during call work and the subsequent longer wait probably till evening in the corridors and under the trees speak volumes of apathy at the very seat of justice. When every other public office including police stations got some face lift and become more public friendly, courts remained as they were depriving people their guaranteed dignity under the Constitution. It is the high time for providing minimum amenities in the courts.

International Criminal Court

'King can do no wrong' has been the pervading principle of soverign immunity that has saved the perpetrators of grave atrocities that have deeply shocked the conscience of humanity. For centuries together and particularly in the recent past millions of children, women and men have been made the victims of unimaginable atrocities. Of late it is recognized that such grave crimes threaten the peace, security and well being of the world. Affirming that the most serious crimes of concern to the international community as a whole must not go unpunished and that their effective prosecution must be ensured by taking measures at the international level, the International Criminal Court (ICC) was established on 1st July, 2002 at the Hague, the abode of International Court of Justice.

Rome statute of the International Criminal Court 1998 has enabled the establishment of International Criminal Court, which is a permanent institution, having jurisdiction on the most serious crimes of concern to the international community like the crime of genocide, crimes against humanity, war crimes and the crime of aggression. The statute has defined these crimes in all the detail. But, terrorism has not been defined and included in the statute as a crime. This was due to the problem of religion-based terrorism.

ICC's jurisdiction can be invoked at the instance of a State or Security Council of United Nations. The statute has established individual responsibility for international crimes. It further recognized the criminal responsibility of the Commanders and Superiors for the acts of the forces. The court can impose a sentence not exceeding 30 years of imprisonment and fine.

India had actively participated in the preparatory committee meeting of the statute. But, it did not ultimately sign the statute. India expected that ICC would be based on the principles of complementarity, State soverignity and non-intervention in internal affairs of States. Indian objections to ICC are mainly two fold. India objected the Security Council's control over ICC. There is no legal basis for Security Council to either refer matters of peace and security to ICC or veto cases from coming before ICC. Any role to Security Council in triggering ICC jurisdiction is violative of sovereign equality. The other objection was to the definition of crime of aggression. Externally inspired terrorism, according to India is a proxy war and poses a great threat to the human rights of innocent people and it was not included in the definition of aggression. The first use of nuclear weapons and the possession of weapons of mass destruction are not made international crimes.

America had first signed the treaty before the 31-12-2000 deadline but later in May 2002 had repudiated its signature and embarked a worldwide campaign to undermine the ability of ICC by entering into Impunity agreements with over 40 countries.

The creation of ICC is an unprecedented exercise in the development of international law and in innovocating new forms of international co-operation for the protection of Human Rights in post war era and the States shall have a duty of strengthing the hands of ICC in punishing international crimes.

REFERENCES

1. Harold J. Laski – *Grammar of Politics* S.Chand & Company Ltd. New Delhi.
2. Report of the National Commission to Review the working of the Constitution Universal Law Publishing Co. Pvt. Ltd. Delhi.
3. William A. Schabas – *An introduction to the International Criminal Court* Cambridge University Press, UK.
4. Antanio Cassese – *International Criminal Law* Oxford, New York.
5. *Bentham's Theory of Legislation*, Tripathi, Bombay.
6. H.M. Seervai – *Constitutional Law of India* Tripathi, Bombay.
7. *Mayne's Hindu Law and Usage* – Bharat Law House, Delhi.

3

CHALLENGES TO DEMOCRACY IN INDIA

Dr. P. Balaji Prasad*

In Part-A of this paper the Democracy in India is presented in its three phases viz., ancient, after independence and at present or modern in every finer detail. In Part-B, the working of democracy in India before the recent elections of 2004 is explored in a comprehensive political framework. In Part-C the state of A.P. is considered as a specific case reflecting many indicators of change demanded by the people and the dynamics of a working democracy are presented. The intraspection on working of democracy was used as method to conclude on what strategies are to be adopted during the present crucial period of Indian emergence as super power by 2020. It was finally identified that awakening the common people and building the strong civil society in India is the solution for security of individual leaders and society as well to develop collectively as an emerging super power.

PART – A

Indian Democracy – An Introduction

The concept of democracy: A form of government in which the supreme power is vested in the people. The aim of democracy: is good life for every individual which includes certain satisfaction of the essential economic needs which would create in him a chance to

---

* Reader, School of Business Management, S.V. University, Tirupathi

develop his creative faculties. The dignity of the individual or sacredness of the human personality is the fundamental principle of democracy.

Evolution of Democracy: India having been under the domination of Britain for a considerable period, was influenced by the British traditions. This was the main reason for the Indian constitution to be based upon the British Parliamentary System.

How Democratic is Indian Democracy?

The democracy gives a vision, a way of life, asks the people to accept certain ideas norms or standards of behaviour. The objectives and obligations presented in the preamble provide complete guidance. The government is not called democratic simply because the people have voted it to power by the majority. The only test that the government is democratic in true sense of the words when it gives democratic rights to its subjects. Adequate and proper communication between the political leaders and the people are essential for a healthy growth of political processes and rapid economic development. In his speech Gandhi said, "I am pained at the unemployment here". He gave the impression to end the poverty is to end unemployment. Due to indiscipline the state of Indian Democracy had been brought far from reassuring. There are members of Indian legislatures whether at the centre or the state level who have been elected without any academic, social or political background but have succeeded due to various extraneous considerations. The elected members seldom go deep into the internal or external problems facing the country. No code of decency or ethics is observed during the sessions of the legislature. The present democratic working has been misunderstood by some parties and individuals which tried to speak in different voices.

The role of people: In India the political adult franchise is quite a recent achievement it is a long process resulting in the introduction of institutional democracy that what the best has achieved through a long struggle has come to the Indian population through the struggle of independence. The acceptance of the principles of universal sufferage is an expression of the belief in the equal role of all men and women. The ballot is a machinery or a method of the expression of men's manhood. The natural right is that man expresses himself in a valid form touching the interest which affects him. The adult franchise has enabled him to recognize his real self.

Role of Elections : A democratic political system should provide adequate opportunities for the people to discuss political issues and express their will on them. The press, public meetings and the parliament are the institutions to express public opinion. In a democratic government the people are the final arbiter of political authority. The government in power is formed by the political party commanding a majority in the legislature and the people choose the government through elections and get the government as they desire and as they deserve.

The Role of Political Party : In order to make democracy a true representative institutions the modern working cannot operate without well-organized political parties in the assemblies and also in parliament. The day-to-day business cannot be conducted if there are no disciplined political parties. The present system of elections with a single member constituency one man one vote and election by a simple majority has resulted in defective working of the Indian political parties. The problems include (a) Existing system of election gives importance to the individual candidate then the political party (b) Elections and campaign generate primordial and ethnic instincts, work in the mind of the voter at the time of elections. (c) Instead of concentrating on programmes and policies parties try to measure the constituency in terms of religious or caste arithmetic and search for candidates who quality in that arithmetic (d) Not only the existing system of elections dilute parties programmes or ideology it leads to all sorts of nepotism in the body politic (e) The phenomenon of independents a special feature of Indian parliamentary system not aligned to any party is the result of existing electoral system. These independents win elections on the basis of 'personalism' and are immune from any kind of discipline. Their accountability is diffused and alignments are always shifting. They do not defect because they are unattached.

The Role of Civil Services : The civil services and the political system have been considered the two wheels of the administration cart. With the independence of our country the responsibility of the services have become one of ours. They make or mar the efficiency of the machinery of administration – a machinery so vital for the peace and progress of our country. No government particularly the democratic administration can properly function without the help of officers who serve as administrators in every department. The ministers in charge of the portfolios are not permanent as they come and go. They are amateur in the work of the administration. The essence of the good government is the efficient administration.

Doctrine of neutrality in civil services : The ideologies of political parties differ but the motive of the services is to serve according to the policy laid down. Political interference in administration – a great factor which saps the morale of the civil service is interference of the ministers and other politicians in the day to day work of the administration on behalf of party men, friends and relatives. There is an importance of public behaviour and also the art of dealing with the people. The officers should also develop the habit of being courteous and polite, should try to adopt with the changing condition. The role of politician is to take advantage of the matured experience and ability of civil servant. They should be shown due regard and their services should be appreciated.

The Background of Indian Democracy – Part I

Democracy in ancient india : In 1605 at the time of the death of Akbar, the Moghal ruled an empire stretching from Kandhar in the west to Dacca in the east and from Srinagar in the north to Ahmedabad in the South. Akbar had no proper education in his youth and perhaps he was not literate but he was endowed with wonderful memory and a wide catholicity of mind. He had consolidated his conquests and devised an administrative system by choosing his lieutenants irrespective of their race or creed and he was served by able and trusted counselors like Todarmal, Man Singh; Abdur Rahim and the witmaster like Birbal.

He devised a system of perfect equality between the Hindus and Muslims in public life. There after his succesors-Jahangir, Shah Jahan and Aurangzeb – ruled vigorously. Aurangzeb was a king of austere habits with a puritanical turn of mind. The collapse of the Moghal empire followed the passing away of Aurangzeb in 1707.

From 1627 onward, Maratha power became a great force in north and south upto 1680. in 1761 the Marathas and Abmadshah Abdali met at the field of Panipat and by that time the Moghal empire was virtually reduce to a small territory around Delhi. The hold of Afghanistan was lost altogether.

The British East India Company was established in India in 1600 which acquired political power later on. The British influence increased and the East India Company, as for its trading functions, came to an end. At the instance of great patriotic Indians like Raja Rammohan Roy and Ishwar Chandra Vidyasagar, certain social reforms were undertaken by the Company. English was officially adopted as the medium of instruction in schools and colleges set up by the Company. In 1853-54 steam power was introduced, cotton mills were started, railway lines were laid and telegraphic lines were extended and the development of communication was undertaken.

The Indian Mutiny

This was the first war for Indian independence in 1857. This revolt succeeded in brining about the end of East India Company but the administration of the country passed under the British crown. The 1857 Mutiny roused great feelings against the British rule. It shaped itself into a national rebellion. The movement against-the alien rule was mostly confined to the Gangetic Valley and Central India. In Delhi, the Moghal emperor was made the symbol i.e. head of the movement. The revolt was crushed and the old Moghal emperor was tried in a British curt, dethroned and exiled to Burma.

Roots of Democracy in India – Birth of Indian congress : British Impact on Indian Economy – The traders from British continued to increase and the Indian masses were exposed to mounting distress which became acute during the periods of scarcity and famine. The economic discontement : The main causes were the land revenue policy of the government the draining of wealth from India and the failure of the government to help in developing Indian resources and industries. The national movement gained momentum consequently upon the turning events marked by the extension of the means of communication and transport large increase in foreign trade of India and modernization of Indian economy. The spread of western education the impact of modern political thought and modern science and technology created a ground for political revolution.

Birth of Congress : All the educated and politically awakened people in India thought of having a country-wide organization to speak for common cause and formed an all India political party named Indian National Congress. The struggle for independence gained momentum and even the British policy of "Divide and Rule" failed to weaken the movement.

Beginning of Gandhian era : As soon as the first world war August 14-18 ended the movement for Indian independence had gained momentum. Gandhiji emerged as the undisputed leader of the Indian National Movement had great effect. His heroic fight for the Indian community in South Africa won the confidence of the Indian Population as his novel methods of non-violent passive resistance yielded good results. At the end of the struggle India became independent with self-confidence, faith and hope to move forward to meet the challenges of freedom and democracy and social justice for all. All politically conscious persons were at the back of the national call for independence initiated by Mahatma Gandhi.

PART II

Indian Constitution Under Indian Independence

Preamble of the constitution: "We the people of India, having solemnly resolved to constitute India into a sovereign democratic, republic and to secure to all its citizens-justice social, economic and political, liberty of thought, expression, belief-faith and worship. Equality of status and of opportunity and to promote among them all fraternity assuring the dignity of the individual and the unity of the Nation. In our constituent assembly this ......of......day of May 1948 AD do here by adopt; enact and give to ourselves this constitution".

Distinctive Features of Constitution

Right to equality – Right to freedom –

Freedom of religion – cultural and educational rights

The directive principles are based upon economic democracy because a parliamentary form of government should be accompanied by Instructions regulating its exercise. They are like Instrument of instructions issued to the governor general or the governors by the British Government under the Government of India Act 1939.

Democracy in Modern India – Part III

Emergency and After : The 19 months period of the Emergency declared in June, 1975 by the Congress Government is responsible for the downfall of the Congress and the then Prime Minister of India Shrimati Indira Gandhi was responsible for pulling down an edifice built earlier. The Congress Leaders were a party for its destruction.

Excesses of the Emergency : The Emergency was declared on 26th June, 1975. During the 19 months of emergency the Congress became most unpopular. It was considered by a large section of people in the country as enemy of the people and it was hated more than the British had been hated before 1947.

The Emergency period of 19 months created revolutionary feelings in the people in a revengeful spirit as almost all the sections of society suffered in one way or the other. The press was affected the most due to harsh provisions or ordinance and Government proclamations to curb the liberty and people and free and impartial expression in the newspapers. Not only in Congress circles that great discontentment prevailed but also her trusted colleagues and cabinet members felt sore about the swift happening and the changing events. Autocracy within the Congress Party, in a large measure, helped the former Prime Minister in successfully imposing emergency and in silencing the critics within the party.

Misdeeds of the Party in Power : What are the fundamental misdeeds of the previous Government ? It abused the emergency powers to preserve the personal powers of Mrs.Gandhi. It subverted the Constitution by enacting the 38th, 39th and 40th and 42nd Amendments during the Emergency. It arrested thousand of citizens from all walks of life, political opponents, University Professors, Congress party, Members of Parliament, Journalists, Lawyers, Authors and practically anyone it did not like without giving any reason. It muzzled the press and converted All India Radio and Doordarshn and almost the entire press of India was converted into a propaganda department of ruling Congress Party. It systematically interfered with the independence of the Judiciary. It used reprehensible method to enforce a programme of family planning. The family planning programme got momentum for which lakhs of rupees were forcibly collected from the people. It made an attempt to establish a personality cult and Nehru dynasty. A reign of fear prevailed among the people. There are severe instances in almost every field about the atrocities committed at the instance of politicians who were counted in the party in power. Each political party must be subjected to the rules of democracy within itself, i.e. its central committee, its State and District Committees, should be elected by the rank and cadre of the party, and not nominated from the top.

Sanjay Gandhi became a force : There was a time when the son of the Prime Minister of India, Shri Sanjay Gandhi rose to high esteem in the name of personal approach to the people at the Centre and the State level. He was not a member of the Congress nor he had any connection with the administration. He carried voice simply because he happened to be the son of the Prime Minister and he got full backing in press statements and eloquence of Shrimati Indira Gandhi. Whenever and wherever he visited, in any part of the country, he was treated by the people and the administration as a big boss as of commanding control of the Government machinery. His visits attached the poor masses because he posed to be the guiding factor for the Government. The people thronged in thousands and some-time in lakhs to attend meetings addressed by him. The Chief Ministers, other ministers and the Prime Minister. The Government spent lakhs of rupees over his receptions and arrangement of his meetings. The people were approached by the Congress workers for donations in connection with such reception programmes. The people were compelled for face of lifting their houses in order to give good look. At some places the over enthusiastic workers managed to get rose flowers spread on the passage where Shri Sanjay Gandhi was to walk for the meeting.

Declaration of Election by the Prime Minister : To the surprise of all the top rank politicians, all at once the Prime Minister made a public announcement in a broadcast that the political prisoners would be released and election would be held at an early date. The MISA detenus were released one after the other to create atmosphere for fair and free elections.

Divided Opposition Joins Hands : As soon as the repressive policy was relaxed Shri Jai Prakash Narayan, an accredited leader of the people, rose to the occasion, exerted his influence and pressed the political parties and regional groups for joining hands to become a single party. The Congress (O), the Jan Sangh, the Socialist Party, Bharatiya Lok Dal held individual and collective meetings as inspired by Shri Jai Prakash Narayan. Meanwhile a strong group lead by Shri Jagjiwan Ram the then Agriculture Minister openly announced in a press conference that he had resigned from the Congress Party and also as a Cabinet member to support the move to defeat the Congress. He announced that the Congress for Democracy would extend support to Shri Jai Prakash Narayan.

Emergence of Janata Party : It seemed a fact that the divided opposition, as before would have given the control of the country to Congress again. All its leaders, workers and sympathizers were the worst sufferers in the Emergency period and individually everybody felt a necessity for a common All India Party. Shri Jai Prakash Narayan proved a boon to the scattered elements that he succeeded in bringing them together for a common symbol and common manifesto and programme. The symbol adopted was that of Haldhar of Bharatiya Lok Dal Party and thus was declared the formation of the Janata Party. This announcement was welcomed by all the people affected by the Emergency. The Janata Party claimed to defend the people's democractic rights and livelihood as a national party of India. The party drafted an election manifesto defining all the programmes for the advancement of the country if voted to power by the people. The following political character was prepared and circulated liberally, with a view to educate the masses about its high ambition and future prosperity programme for the people of the Republic of India.

PART – B

Working of Democracy – in Inda

Which way will Political India Go? : The importance of the assembly elections in five states – Mizoram, Madhya Pradesh, Rajasthan, Delhi and Chattisgarh – Scheduled for November – December 2003 stretches beyond the immediate. This is the final round of Assembly polls before the 14th general election is due by the end of 2004. the outcome is widely expected to influence the decision of the Bharatiya Janata Party-led Government on the precise timing of the Lok Sabha contest. A convincing win in several of these States could prompt the ruling coalition to bring forward the general election to early next year. An adverse outcome could seed the National Democratic Alliance Government opting to meander to the end of its term. The elections in the four Hindi – speaking States will conclude a series of direct contests between the two leading parties in the political system that began with the BJP retaining Gujarat in December 2002 and saw the Congress wresting Himachal Pradesh in February 2003. Since there is no question of any party winning a majority of seats in the next Lik Sabha election, the real contest is for single largest party status. Whoever scores in the coming Assembly contests will emerge as the automatic favourite for 2004. Since alliances play a crucial role in both electoral success and government formation, the front-runner status could prove decisive.

In four of the five States, the Congress faces a factor that is sometimes dreaded and sometimes made light by politics : anti-incimbency'. The Madhya Pradesh Chief Minister, Digvijay Singh, was able to overcome this factor impressively in the 1998 Assembly election even if the BJP has scored heavily in the State over its adversary in three successive Lok Sabha contests – 1996, 1998 and 1999. Retaining power in Bhopal is expected to be tougher this time. In Chattisgarh, Ajit Jogi, after appearing to be in control has gone on the back foot and rather mystifyingly, faces a Central Bureau of Investigation chargesheet relating to forgery. In Rajasthan, Ashok gehlot, who has been painted by his adversaries as a weak Chief Minister, seems to be responding resourcefully to the challenge from Hindutva forces led by the VHP, apart from hijacking the BJP agenda of providing reservation for the Economically Backwardness Classes. Whether such efforts are enough to overcome the antiincumbency factor remains to be seen. In Delhi Chief Minister Sheila Dixit has concentrated on good, clean governance and not allowed the BJP to run away with the State hood issue as an electoral plank. In Mizoram, where the Congress is not directly threatened by the BJP, the stakes and pressures are considerably less.

It is well known that there can be considerable variance between the outcome of Assembly and parliamentary elections in the same State even when these contests are held in reasonable proximity. Local bread-and butter and governance issues, the image and resourcefulness of the Chief Minister and local leaders, and the opportunity given to the national party leadership to do concentrated campaigns explain some of the differences. Local factors can also play out quite differently in the two categories of elections. Significantly, the BJP has lent of its Union Ministers, Uma Bharti and Vasundhara

Raje, to Madhya Pradesh and Rajasthan, to counter the wiles of Mr.Singh and Mr.Gehlot, who have established themselves as regional chieftains of the Congress. The current round of Assembly polls will also witness a novelty : the filing by candidates of affidavits with information on criminal antecedents (if any), movable and immovable properties, liabilities, and educational qualifications. The Election Commission of India made this mandatory on Mach 27, 2003. The interesting questions are : How effectively will such information be communicated to the electorate ? And will the information make a real difference to the outcome?

PART – C

Working of Democracy – A Case of Andhra Pradesh

Politics of Padayatra : The Padayatra undertaken by CLP leader YSR galavanized the party raise hopes among party cadre. But how does it help congress in the Fourth Coming assembly elections is to be watched. YSR returned to State Capital in the last week of June at the end of his 68 days grueling 1471 km in the mid summer. During the entire campaign it was virtual showers of rights, complaints and demands of the people from wherever he set his foot in the entire state covers 676 villages of 56 Assembly Constituency located in 11 district of state. Eventhough initially the padayatra has been treated as election gimmick by the Chandrababu realizing the response evoked by the CLP leader padayatra announced at once various welfare schemes of the people.

Not only he took the anti establishment he went ahead appealing positively with popular schemes mainly free power to framers, loan waiver in the drought hit areas, etc., realizing the potential of YSR campaign Babu had to shift his focus on five years of efforts from industralise the state to irrigation and agriculture. Despite his personal victory of sorts through Padayatra yet his campaign could not bring the leaders of congress onto single track which remains the main weakness. For eg. It is significant in a rally in Rajhmundry while one of the state incharge Vayalar Ravi participated but the present incumbent incharge of PCC affairs of state Gulam Nabi Azad did not participate in Padayatras. It is predicted that if TDP forgets an alliance with BJP once again like in 1999 the congress calculations of victory might go wrong. YSR realizes this and he feels lack of competent candidates for congress is its one of Chief weaknesses. The Padayatra campaign proves one point that it establishes an unassailable lead to YSR during the run up to assembly poll within the congress.

Case of Politics of Chittoor District : The MLAs rude and violent behaviour is well known in the constituency. However, on Saturday one Ravishankar and his friends are quarreled leading to sensational murder and political conspiracy, paralyzing for two days the common mans life in the Chittoor district. The student who had been murdered is son of Y.V.Rajeswari Deputy Chief of Women's Wing of TDP Chittoor district has taken political overtones and the district being the home district of CM Chandrababu adds the extradimension to the whole episode.

MLA is said to be unlawfully indulging in many criminal activities for the past many years. This fresh incident became a nightmare to the District Congress establishment and unable to take up the issue and respond in the matter. Police are aware of his excesses and does not dare to interfere with his activities. As per the AICC Principal Secretary Gulam Nabi Azad orders PCC has suspended CK Babu. Further PCC leadership has agreed to approve the action taken by AICC establishment.

In general killing, threatening for political purposes is a normal way of living in the Rayalaseema district. However, for the last few years such acts are on the wane but CK Babu incident once again brought out the face of politics of killing and threats into broad day light. Further, the gunman Prakash Reddy's involvement in the criminal act is of great concern to one and all. Especially the police were disturbed as instead of preventing the murder and kidnap their aiding the MLA is shocking. This brings out the issue of giving gunman to the MLA's with bad history for a review according to the police DGP P.Ramulu. At the time when elections are nearing the murder might have strong impact on the minds of people and especially in the coming elections might have a negative fall out. To restore the party's stakes will be an arduous task especially for the PCC leadership quite an uncomfortable position. Especially in the context of issuing tickets and selection of candidates and renomination of existing candidates will be a challenging affair.

On one hand leaders like YSR completed Padayatra to motivate people excite the sagging spirits of party cadre, the MLA of the same party indulging in criminal acts and thereby ending the chances of renomination. Now for the ruling TDP can announce Rajeswari as the candidate for Chittoor. But if congress rejects the renomination CK Babu might contest as independent and still win the election. Such is the issue of criminality versus morality in the minds of people or electorate. While criminal acts might be punishable in the eyes of the law but may not be immoral in the hearts of the electoralate.

Assassination as Politics : The authors of the deadly claymore mine blasts in Tirupati, of all places, narrowly failed in their latest bid to take out the Andhra Pradesh Chief Minister, N.Chandrababu Naidu.

This dastardly terrorist attack brings into focus the fanatical belief of the ultra-left extremist party, the CPL-ML People's War (PW), in assassination and terror as the pith and substance of politics. In this respect, the PW can be likened to the Liberation Tigers of Tamil Eelam and the Sendero Luminoso (Shining Path) guerrillas of Peru, both claiming to represent liberation or revolutionary causes while specializing in killing sprees. Despite some success in unifying scattered naxalite groups and factions and linking up with new extremist pockets, the PW finds its revolutionary armed struggle reduced to isolated actions of killer squards. This is not people's war, but excitative terrorism at its most grotesque. By carrying out a high precision attack on the Chief Ministers' convoy, the PW might have revived its fading image in Andhra Pradesh and dispelled the notion that the State has nearly succeeded in controlling it. The attack also demonstrates that although the movement seems to be at a low ebb in the Telangana district, its underground cadre posses dangerous military strike capability. The PW cadres killing spree has gone under the name of the Tactical Counter Offensive Campaign. The State must avoid the temptation of responding in kind, that is through resort to assassination of naxalites or their sympathizers in the name of counter – terror. In the present situation, whre the political and ideological basis of the armed extremists has declined steadily, some amount of legitimacy is being accorded to 'encounter' killings, for which sections of the State's police have acquired national notoriety. While the PW must be further isolated politically and put down with a stern hand, there must be scrupulous respect for democratic and human rights, the rule of law, and the procedure established by law on the part of the Government.

The basic political reason that made Chief Minister Naidu as prime PW target is his consistent stand against the extremist party and his refrain that development is not possible as long as the most deadly naxalite party in India is allowed to continue its activities. While Cabinet colleagues have chosen reticence in public as the best policy on this risky issue he has chosen to be bold and vocal. It must be recalled that Mr.Naidu's former Cabinet colleague, A.Madhava Reddy, who was extremely vocal in denouncing the PW's atrocities, met a glory end when the organization blasted his vehicle in 2000.

Naidu preparing for Early Poll? : The speculation that the Chief Minister, N.Chandrababu Naidu, will go in for dissolution of the Assembly and order early elections is gaining credence as he has begun the process of consulting his cabinet and party colleagues about the political advantages of such a move.

The basis of this speculation is the perceived sympathy factor in favour of Mr.Naidu, particularly among women, after he survived the assassination attempt by the People's War on October 1 Mr.Naidu has been brushing aside that his immediate priorities are to ensure smooth conduct of the Afro-Asian Games and providing succour to the drought – hit farmers.

But, political observers, believe that Mr.Naidu is preparing for such an eventuality by instructing officials to distribute 13 lakhs white ration cards to the poor before October 31 and expedite the implementation of welfare schemes he announce at the Telugu Desam's Mahanadu at Tirupati in May. On Saturday morning, he held a meeting with senior Ministers and officials to hasten the construction of 70 lakh individual sanitary latrines, a component of the one crore boons, to woo the weaker sections, farmers and women.

A clearer picture about the party's thinking will emerge on October 20 when the TDP chief has covered a meeting of the Politburo and the party's extended executive committee in which all important leaders, including district unit chiefs, are expected to spell out their views on the advantages of advancing the polls. Elections to the Assembly are due in September 2004 but TDP leaders are gradually veering round the view that the opportune time for holding the elections would be beginning of 2004 in the hope that the sympathy factor would sustain till then. Senior party leaders feel that there might be several imponderables like drought and political controversies between now and September 2004 which harm the TDP's interests. A snap election would also given very little time to the Congress to forge a possible tie-up with the Telangana Rashtra Samithi (TRS) before the elections.

This move is also in recognition of the fact that things were not going well for the TDP till October 1. The TDP's image got denoted after some of its leaders were suspected to have been involved in the multicrore fake stamp paper scam in the wake of C.Krishna Yadav's arrest undoing the feel-good factor which Mr.Naidu wanted to project after the Godavari Pushkarams. The resentment among farmers over the Government's wavering attitude on the issue of distribution of Krishna waters among the three regions of the State also posed a major worry to the TDP leadership. Organizationally, the party witnessed dissensions at the grass root level, although it had successfully enrolled nearly 90 lakh members and conducted the elections without any major hitch. At many places, the party had to face embarrassing situation with the TDP functionaries proposing no-confidence motion against their own Mandal presidents.

The Chief Minister who was earlier planning to reshuffle his team and create an election Cabinet by balancing the caste factors and giving more weightage to efficiency, has apparently dropped the move since there is no longer any talk in party circles about the proposed changes.

PART – D

Working of Democracy – An Introspecton

The twin threats posing problems to Indian Democracy are the threat to individuals in the form of deteriorating law and order, loss of confidence of the citizen in the ability of the state upon war of gang lords, increased criminialisation of politics. The other threat looming large is to the integrity of the state due to unhealthy linkage between corrupt politics and corrupt business. To face the seemingly diverse challenges of the country means bracing upto the twin tasks of meeting the demands of the poorest of the poor in the country under liberalization of economy on one hand and facing the challenges from the mightest of might under globalization of economy on the other.

Chomsky on Democracy : According to Chomsky Liberatlization of capital was undermining democracy as it created virtual parliament of business that can veto decisions. On one side there would be the voters and on the other the speculators with unaccounted conclusion of power.

Politics and Democracy : The world of politics conjures upto the common man often on the wrong side of its traditional cousins namely constitution, caste, communalism crime, corruption from the infamous politicians tool kit. However, there appears a change now to see on the right side some of its new cousins in the eyes of citizen as a hope on horizon. A few of them may include culture violence, election, cinema, backwardness and women to capture some of the issues and trends of the service economy from the discipline of business management.

Democracy and election : 1996 parliamentary elections is a unique mandate is given by Indian Electorate in the past independent Indian Political history it signifies the end of the one party dominance and beginning of a new coalition era in parliamentary democracy. The mandate therefore makes the political parties to sit up and introspect rather seriously vis-à-vis electorate whom do the serve, by adopting to reduce the gap between what they promise to what they deliver with the maturity of the democracy the party managers must realize that there is a need to formulate people friendly policies in the context of rising expectations of people. People cannot be taken for granted any more.

Culture and Democracy: Indian in all walks of life had gained more exposure to the world these last 10 years than in the 40 years before that. An imagination for good quality of life as a result of exposure which lead to an action it is prelude to action. This cultural shift also owes its existence to the changing politics in India. There has been a churning in caste politics and the rise of Mayawati and Mulayam are visible symbols of it. Laloo's success sends out the signal that "to reach power you to not have to become like them" and wear a gentleman's dress. It's okay to come riding cow.

An Introspection

The immediate context is assassination attempt on a Chief Minister. The cause may be terrorism and extremism what causes such an eye for eye approach by the people. Moreover it is the poor and ordinary who are worst hit in this anarchy. If we draw lessons from history of the recent past we will be able to appreciate some of the courses of this anarchy. The collapse of east Germany and end of communists dictatorships during 1989-91. the story of China where the economic development is without any ideological overtones of Maoist China's revolution. The struggle of Vitenamese against the hegemony of America in 1970s and their victory. The merciless rule of polpot regime in Cambodia in which one third of country's population is reduced to ashes. The end of dictatorships in Mangolia and Albania and even Cuba the lst vestage of communist rule how it has changed will give us great learning for democracy because it is not the defeat of socialism per se in these countries but it is rather the success of western nations in the quest for individual rights, freedom, quality of life that has a great value and impact in all these developments. It does not even mean success of capitalism because even today in America there are nearly 5 crores or 20 percent of population which has not got the benefit of health insurance cover.

Hence, what we need is to solve the defects of our democracy we have to adopt much more rigorous democracy alone which is known to even ordinary men. The democracy in India survives because the majority of ordinary and poor who cast their votes without any fear or favour in every election and unseat the unpopular governments and remove the arrogant rulers. They alone fight for the rights of fellow ordinary men. The fight of such people include usual methods of logic, rational argument and public debate. There by they attempt to change the hearts of people through facts, win an argument through logic. When we don't do this people become impatient, often violent and resort to eye for eye in the absence of any grievance solving democratic procedures.

What are the causes of such a state of affairs in our democracy, the fate of majority of our citizens is decided by birth rather than on their merit, achievement and hard work. Many of them not even have access to sound health and good education facilities. It is important therefore on our part to wage an unconditional war against a system overhaul. After all it is neither a win or loss for somebody nor denying any one's rights and privileges. It means respecting both individual and collective interest.

Very often we are relying on personal charishma rather than institutional arrangement and trying to protect the individual leaders through the power of gun, protection by police and through bullet proof cars etc. The threat to the security of individual leader is because of our excessive reliance on individual rather on the system. Unless we shift to the multiple leadership rather than one man's influence in our practice of democracy we will be losing people like what happened in the case of Indira & Rajiv.

The name of political stability should not be either Vajpayee or Chandrababu Naidu because they being in the highest position of power would be natural prime targets of antisocial elements with their hatred, frenzy born out of ideological overtones.

The political system of ours has come to such a pass because often the irresponsible, power hungry among them behave like fighting cocks, lack consciousness that all of them are there for the sake of well being of ordinary and poor. Such demeanor of their creates a hate campaign and vicious atmosphere. The result of such behaviour will be lack of credibility on loose reign of terror and kill even those politicians. Because the politicians of today are obsessed with power as single most motive irrespective of their political background. Eventhough there are many a politician who are honest and decent and of integrity due to majority of power mongers for the sake of personal benefit. Politicians in general are disrespectful lot in the eyes of the public.

When criminals become politicians politics itself will be a bane on the hungry stomaches, burning hearts, minds which have been subjected to humiliation at these hands.

No doubt there is an achievement in the last 56 years of post independence but there is a mismatch between expectation of the people and opportunity that could have been created. Due to the gap between what is aspired and what is actually achieved leading to a vacuum. That vacuum to unrest. Hence there is need for political system overhaul.

The political reforms areas include electoral reforms and judicial reforms so that poor and rich have equal access constitutional reforms to make elected answerable and remain the servants of people. Former secretary general of Lok Sabha Subhash C.Kasyap advocated changes in the first-post-the post system being practiced in the country.

Delivering the Prof.Rasheeduddin Ahmed Khan second memorial on "electoral reforms in India" organized by the Southern Regional Centre of ICSSR at Osmania University, Kashyap said a candidate should be declared elected only if he or she secures 51 per cent of the total votes cast. "The present system perpetuates vote bank politics. Candidates securing even 15 per cent votes are getting elected to the Loksabha and state legislatures. The anomaly could be rectified if a runoff is held between the two candidate who secure maximum votes".

Awakening the common people and building the strong civil society will be the need of hour. It's the only real security for individual leaders and society as well.

REFERENCES

1. R.K.Bhardwaj, *Democracy in India*, National Publication House, New Delhi, First edition, 1980.
2. Balaji Prasad, P. *Management Challenges of Service Economy of India – Issue and Trends*, Serial Publications New Delhi first edn. 2003.
   (a) Chomsky on the trend of *liberalization* p. 41-45.
   (b) Should we be governed by iron rule and thumb rule p.60-65.
3. Editorial, *The Hindu, Assassination as Politcs*, Friday October 3, 2003.
4. Jayaprakash Narayan, *End of Terrorism with Political Overhaul-Central Essay, Eenadu*, Sunday October 5, 2003.
5. Amarnath K.Menon, *Politics of Padayatra, India Today*, First July 2003 p.38&39.
6. Amaranat K.Menon, *Murder in Chittor - India Today*, First July, 2003, p.40&41.
7. Editorial, *The Hindu, which way political India go?* Saturday, October 11, 2003.
8. News report, *Naidu preparing for early poll? The Hindu* p.1, October 19,2003.
9. News report Kashyap advocates changes in Poll pattern, *Deccan Herald* June 29, 2003.

4

CAN INDIA EMERGE AS A SUPER POWER?

Dr. A. Sudhakar*, S.V. Ramana Rao and K. Suryanarayana*****

The world economy has changed a lot over the past few decades. Over the next five decades, the change will be more dramatic. The Indian economy is one of the fastest growing economies of the world. There is a definite feel good factor in the Indian Economy. All parts of the economy are firing together, the result is that India is poised to take the great leap forward, from being a mere 'developing' to 'emerging' economy to a developed one. In 2002-2003, Indian companies have churned out the highest earnings growth since 1994-95. The three sectors-agriculture, industry and services are predicted to grow more than 6%. The Goldman sachs report "Dreaming with BRICS: The path to 2050" states that over the next 50 years, Brazil, Russia, India and China – The BRICS economies – could become a much larger force in the world economy. Mark Anson, Chief investment officer, Cal PERS expects that both India and China will be in the top six economies by 2050, and that their economies will exceed that of Japan with in the next 50 years. Professor R. Vaidyanathan, Professor

* Associate Professor, Head, Dept.of Commerce, Dr.B.R.Ambedkar Open Univ., Hyd-36.

** Lecturer, Dept.of Management Sciences, RVR & JC College of Engineering, Guntur-19.

*** Lecturer, Dept.of Management Sciences, RVR & JC College of Engineering, Guntur-19.

of Finance, IIM, Bangalore, said that there is an increasing awareness in the west that the axis of economic development is shifting to Asia. In other words, one can say that the 19th century was the century of Europe and 20th was that of US and 21st is going to be that of Asia particularly that of India and China. By 2020, both India and China will be economic powers to reckon with.

This paper mainly explores the issues and challenges to emerge India as a super power. It touches aspects like feel good factors, GDP, economic reforms etc., and also barriers for the growth and measures to over come it.

Introduction

India's progress and development over the next few decades will be intimately linked to the events that would happen within the region as well as around the world. India's per capita income has doubled over the past 20 years with population growth slowing now to about 1.6 percent per annum, a growth rate of the gross domestic product (GDP) of around 9% percent per annum would make India as a mere 'developing' or 'emerging economy' to a developed one. The Goldman Sachs report "Dreaming with BRICS: The path to 2050" mentioned that India has the potential to show the fastest growth over the next 30 and 50 years. Growth could be higher than 5% over the next 30 years and close to 5% as late as 2050 if development proceeds successfully.

An essential requirement for national development is realizing the potential opportunities that the country has and creating competitive and sustainable advantage over them. The sectoral composition of the GDP changes with economic development. This transition is now occurring globally and is reflected in the explosive growth. The same is true with in the case of India. India's services sector has already become the dominant contributor to GDP, accounting for 4.6 percent of total, but its share is still far below the UMI reference level of 60 percent. Knowledge has replaced capital as the most determinant of development. India has become a knowledge workers hub.

This paper explores the possible opportunities and challenges to India to emerge as a dominant Global Player and also measures to be adapted to make India as a super power.

Economic Growth

The Gross domestic growth is the basic measure of the health of any economy. The growth rate forecasted by various institutions are as follows:

GDP Growth Forecasts

Institution	*Forecast for 2003-04(%)*
CII	7.2
IMF	5.6*
ADB	6.7
NCAER	7.1
RBI	7.0
CRISIL	7.1
ICRA	6.5 – 6.9
CMIE	7.4

* IMF forecast refers to 2002-03; is set for revision.

Source: www.businessworldindia.com

When the Government of India announced its first estimates for economic growth, it said that the GDP had grown by an awesome 8.4% in the second quarter of the financial year. It is highest quarterly growth since 1996-97 and it was far better than the 5.7% growth seen in the first quarter. It also makes India one of the fastest – growing economies in the world. China is still a head of us, at 9.1%; but ours is better than other countries in the region – Hong Kong (4%), Indonesia (3.9%), Malasia (3.5%), Singapore (1.7%) and Thailand (5.8%).

According to Dr.Omkar Goswami, Chief Economist at the CII, the Indian economy could either grow at "an extremely feasible target" rate of 6.5% or a "stretch" growth rate of 8%. He predicts that growth rate would increase at 0.5% points per year to stabilizing at 8%. He projects macro economic indicators by 2010 as follows:

Projects of Select Macroeconomic Indicators by 2010

Indicator	*At 8% growth $ bn*	*At 6.5% growth $ bn*
GDP	869	809
Industrial Output	283	227
Exports	103	83
Market size	550	584
Household savings	210	223

Source: CII data.

As the Goldman sachs report entitled "Dreaming with BRICs: The path to 2050", stated that India has the potential to show the fastest growth over the next 30 and 50 years. Growth could be higher than 5% over the next 30 years and close to 5% as late as 2050 if development proceeds successfully. Overall, growth for the BRICs is likely to show significantly over this time frame. By 2050, only India would be recording growth rates significantly above 3%. The macro economic trends are started showing positive signs. And it is expected to continue years to come.

Macroeconomic Trends

	1980s	*1990s*	*1992/93 to 1996/97*	*1997/98 to 2000/02*	*2002-03*
GDP growth (% per annum)	5.6	5.8	6.7	5.5	4.4
- Agriculture	3.4	3.0	4.7	1.8	-3.1
- Industry	7.0	5.8	7.6	4.5	6.1
- Services	6.9	7.6	7.5	8.1	7.1
Investment rate (% of GDP)	22.0	23.0	23.3	22.5	22.1
- Public	10.0	7.8	8.0	6.6	6.3
- Private	12.1	15.2	15.3	15.9	15.7
Govt. deficit (% of GDP)	8.1	7.8	7.2	9.3	10.4
Current account balance (% of GDP)	-2.1	-1.4	-1.2	-0.7	1.0

Source: The Hindu Survey of Indian Industry, 2004.

Disinvestment

The story of India's disinvestment programme since 1991-92 has been one of ups and downs, reflecting the difficult transition from an era of socialist planning to a market economy. The BALCO'S privatization led to more privatizations such as ITDC hotels, IBP, Paradeep phosphates and VSNL. The only way India can unlock her assets and derive value from them, is to disinvest all non-strategic PSUs. This has to go on at a faster pace which would ensure the economic development of the nation. Disinvestment has a role to play in the fiscal consideration of the government finances.

Infrastructure

The transport infrastructure in India largely consists of roads and railways, the other modes such as air and inland water transport having minimal and only supportive roles. Between roads and railways, road transport has evolved as the preferred mode both for people and goods. The share of freight traffic by road is about 60 percent as compared to 40 percent by rail. The share of passenger traffic by road is about 80 percent as compared to 20 percent by rail.

The road network is vast around 3.3 million km. National highways and state highways covering 1.72 lakh km have a pre-eminent position in road transportation, carrying nearly 60 percent of the freight traffic and 87 percent of the passenger traffic. Road traffic is growing at the rate of 7 to 10 percent a year while vehicle population growth in recent years has been at the rate of 12 percent a year. A well developed infrastructure cuts down a lot of operational expenses of companies in the industrial as well as in the service sector. Infrastructure development is going on at a good pace in the country. The growth of national high ways over the decades is shown in the following table.

Growth of National Highways

Year	*Length of NH (km)*
1	2
1947	19,811
1951	21,440
1961	23,798

(Contd...)

1	2
1971	23,838
1981	31,671
1991	33,650
1995	34,298
1998	38,517
1999	49,585
2001	58,112

Source: The Hindu Survey of Indian Industry 2004, P: 143.

To give a boost to the country's economic development, a massive programmed for 4/6 laning of 13,146 Km of national highways has been taken up since 1999 under the national highways development project (NHDP). The project includes the Golden Quadrilateral on the National Highways connecting the four metropolitan cities Delhi, Mumbai, Chennai and Kolkata. The program includes 4/6 laning of National Highways from Srinagar to Kanyakumari in the North-South corridor and Sinchar to Porbander in the East-West corridor. This is one of the largest programmes of road development ever taken up in any country. In addition, the centre is taking up four laning of 10,000 Km of Non-NHDP high traffic density National Highways corridors including connecting state capitals to the NHDP. Alongwith these, four laning of about 400 Km the country has been taken up by the NHAI under the port connectivity programme.

A forecast of the road transport scenario in 2015 according to a study conducted in 1997 is given as follows:

Road Transport Scenario in 2015

Indicator of Infrastructure	*1997*	*2015*
1	2	3
Population	950 million	1250 million
Urbanization	27 percent	35 percent
Car population	4.0 million	15-20 million
Car ownership	4 per 1000	11-15 per 1000

(Contd...)

1	2	3
Truck population	22 million	75 million
Bus population	0.5 million	1.7 million
Road based passenger movement	2,847 bpk	15,830 bpk
Road based freight movement	815 bpk	4531 bpk
Petrol consumption	6 million T	25 million T
Diesel consumption	30 million T	100 million T
Village connectivity	50 percent	100 percent

Source: The Hindu Survey of Indian Industry – 2004, p: 144.

Security Markets

No other securities market in the world has undergone such dramatic and rapid changes in such a short period as the Indian market. The changes took place in different areas such as products and services, processes and procedures, technology, governance and investor relations. The most important development in recent years which made India in a position comparable to the best systems in the world. From almost a fortnight a few years ago, the settlement period has now been brought down to two days after trading (T+2) and Indian Securities are poised to move towards T+1 settlement in the near future. Higher standards of surveillance, compliance of corporate Governance, greater disclosure and investor education have strengthened the securities markets. This really making India to be on par with Global markets.

In spite of all the feel good facors, there are certain quarters where deficiencies are removed to be India as a super power.

The McKinsey Global Institute (MGI) has studied the country's economy to see what is holding it back. The study found that there are three main barriers to faster growth. These are:

1. The multiplicity of regulations governing product markets;
2. Distortions in the market for land; and
3. Widespread Government ownership of business.

EXHIBIT

What's slowing India's economic growth?

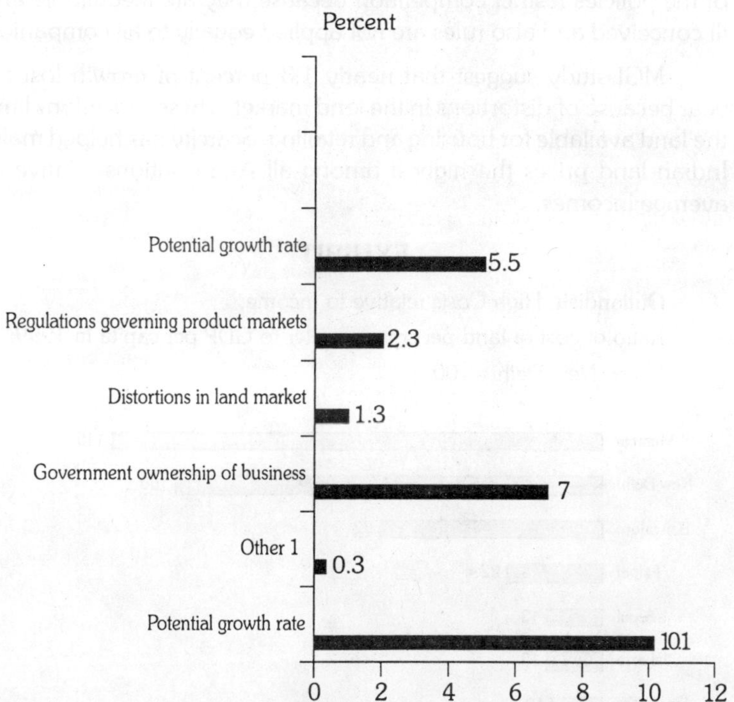

1 Includes transportation insfrastructure and labour laws.

Source: McKinsey Quarterly.com.

The researchers calculated that these three barriers together inhibit GDP growth by more than 4 percent a year. Removing them would free India's economy to grow as fast as China's, at 10 percent a year. And it would create nearly 75 million new jobs outside agriculture which could virtually absorb the fastest growing work force.

Barriers to Growth

The rules and policies governing different sectors of the country's economy, together impede GDP growth by 2.3 percent a year. For Instance in car making Industry, after 1991reforms competition increased dramatically between domestic and foreign companies. The demand for new, cheaper and high quality Indian-made automobiles has increased, as a result the employment in the industry rise by 1 percent from 1992-93 to 1999-2000. The other deterrents are some of the policies restrict competition because they are inequitable and ill conceived and also rules are not applied equally to all companies.

MGI study suggest that nearly 1.3 percent of growth lost for year because of distortions in the land market. These distortions limit the land available for housing and retailing. Scarcity has helped make Indian land prices the highest among all Asian nations relative to average incomes.

EXHIBIT

Outlandish: High Costs relative to Income.

Ratio of cost of land per square meter to GDP per capita in 1999:

Index: New Delhi=100

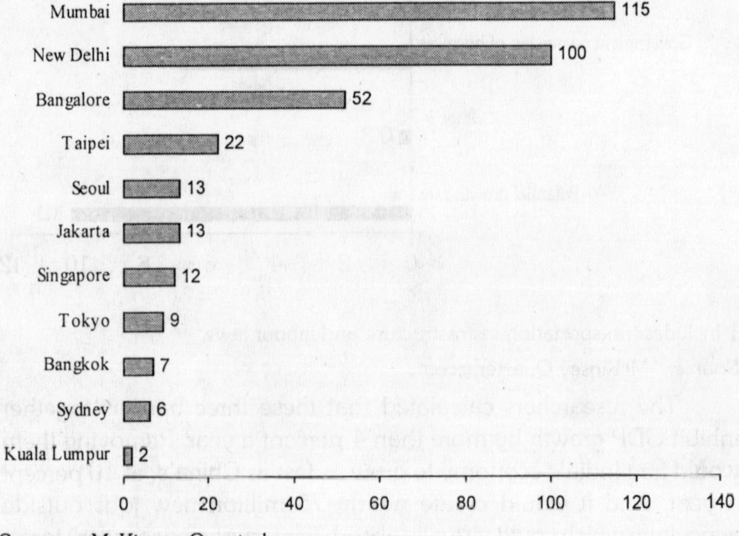

Source: McKinsey Quarterly.com.

Three distortions in the land market are especially significant.

Those are:

1. Unclear ownership
2. Counter productive taxation
3. Inflexible zoning, rent, and tenancy laws

Lack of clarity about who owns makes it immensely difficult to buy land for retail and housing development. Not surprisingly, most new housing developments are constructed on land already owned by the developers or the few insiders who know how to speed up the bureaucratic title-clearing process. Low property taxes, ineffective tax collection and subsidized user charges for power and water leave local governments unable to recover the cost of their investment in infrastructure, particularly in suburban areas. For instance, in Delhi, water is supplied at only 10% of its true cost. Property taxes collected in Mumbai amount to only 0.002 percent of the buildings estimated capital value, the ratio in developed countries is 1 to 2 percent. Stamp duties are extraordinarily high in India: close to 8 to 10 percent of the value of the property changing hands. Not surprisingly, this expense discourages the registration of land and real estate transactions. Land in city centers that would otherwise be available for new retail outlets and apartments is "frozen" by protected tenancies, rent controls and zoning laws. Protected tenants cannot be evicted and will never voluntarily surrender their cheap tenancies, so their ancient buildings can never be sold or rebuilt.

Another barrier for growth is Government ownership of businesses. Government controlled entities still account for around 43 percent of India's capital stock and 15 percent of employment outside agriculture. Their labour and capital productivity levels are well below those of their private competitors.

Fiscal Deficit

The average fiscal deficit (as a % of GDP) of the centre from 1990-91 to 2002-03 is 5.3%. This is one of basic structural deficiencies of the economy. The combined revenue deficit of centre and states in 1998-99 was 2.9 percent of GDP at current market prices. This rose to 3.6 percent in 1994-95, the base year for the Tenth Finance Commission and to 6.3 percent in 1999-2000, the bas year for the Eleventh Finance Commission. It has exceeded 7 percent of GDP in 2001-02. Going by this trend, one may wonder what the magnitude of imbalance would be in 2004-05, the year immediately proceeding the reference period of 2005-06 to 2009-2010 for the Twelth Finance Commission. The following table indicates the combined deficit of centre and states.

Combined Deficit of Centre and States (Rs. Crore)

Items		*2002-03 revised estimate*	*2002-03 budgeted estimate*	*2001-02*	*1995-96*	*1990-91*
Gross	Centre	1,45,466(5.9)	1,35,524(5.3)	1,40,955(6.1)	60,243(5.1)	44,632(7.8)
Fiscal	States	1,16,730(4.7)	1,02,882(4.0)	95,986(4.2)	31,426(2.6)	18,787(3.3)
Deficit	Combined	2,48,979(10.1)	2,26,864(8.9)	2,26,418(9.9)	77,671(6.5)	53,580(9.4)
Revenue	Centre	1,04,712(4.2)	95,377(3.7)	1,00,162(4.4)	29,731(2.5)	18,562(3.2)
Deficit	States	61,302(2.5)	48,314(1.9)	59,233(2.6)	8,201(0.7)	5,309(0.9)
	Combined	1,66,014	1,43,691	1,59,395	37,932	23,871
Primary	Centre	29,803(1.2)	18,134(0.7)	33,495(1.5)	10,198(0.9)	23,134(4.1)
Deficit	States	42,584(1.7)	30,629(1.2)	33,497(1.5)	9,494(0.8)	10,132(1.8)
	Combined	88,492(3.6)	64,442(2.5)	84,048(3.7)	18,598(1.6)	28,585(5.0)

Source: The Hindu Survey of Indian Industry, 2004.

The overall fiscal deficit target set at 6.5 percent. Clearly, the fiscal situation is far from achieving these targets. The data indicate that the combined fiscal deficit of the centre and states for 2001-02 was in excess of 10 percent of GDP with the center's deficit at 6.1. The eleventh finance commission had also recommended that the combined debt of the centre and the states should be brought down from a level of 65 percent of GDP to 55 percent in 2004-05. This ratio instead of declining had gone up to about 75 percent in 2001-02.

Measures to Accelerate Growth

India has the potential to show the fastest growth over the next 30 and 50 years. Growth could be higher than 5% over the next 30 years and close to 5% as late as 2050 if development proceeds successfully. India's economy has three types of sectors.

1. Modern sectors
2. Transitional sectors
3. Agricultural sectors

Modern ones, with production process resembling those in modern economies, provide 24 percent of employment and 47 percent of output. Transitional sectors provides 16 percent of employment and 27 percent of output. Agricultural sectors provide 60 percent of employment and 28 percent of output. The MGI report states that if India could able to dismantle all the existing barriers, that the resulting increase in labour and capital productivity will boost growth in the overall GDP to 10 percent a year, release investment capital worth 5.7 percent of GDP, and generate 75 million new jobs outside agriculture, in both the modern and the transitional sectors.

Govt.of India fiscal policies should be framed to accelerate growth with low inflation and sustainable balance of payments. Fiscal policies will have to be restructured not only to facilitate but play a pivotal role in bringing about this acceleration in growth with macro economic stability. Public spending in areas such as roads, water supply, power, primary education and primary health will need to be stepped up to provide the appropriate physical and social infrastructure necessary for accelerating growth.

The reservation of products for small – scale industry should be eliminated completely. The process should be started with 68 sectors accounting for 80 percent of output of reserved sectors and also equalize sales taxes and excise duties for all categories of palyers in each sector. Establish an effective regulatory frame work and strong regulatory bodies similarly the GOI, remove all licensing and quasi licensing restrictions that limit the number of players in industries.

Conclusion

The Indian economy is on a path of a greater success in time to come. India will be very different country, if the economic reforms carried on successfully and fruitfully and also by dismantling the bottlenecks/barriers which are impediment for accelerate the economy growth. Goldman sachs report mentioned that growth in the G6, Brazil, Russia and China is expected to slow significantly over the next 50 years, India's growth rate remains above 5% through out the period, India's GDP out strips that of Japan by 2032. Demographics play an important role in the way the world will change. The Goldman sachs report says that by 2010, India will start growing faster than China. This is driven by demographic advantage the India has. Today India has a working population is about 525 million, by 2020, this will be 762 million. But the non-working population will not increase at the same rate. This would help to enhance the growth and productivity which the other countries are lacking. The stage has been set for India to really shine in the coming future above all it has all the potential to transform from 'developing' status to "Developed one" and can become a "super power" if the Government and people of the country act quickly by a "mental revolution".

REFERENCES

1. www.gs.com
2. *Dreaming with BRICs* : The Path 2050.
3. G. Kumaraswamy Naidu & Ali Mohammad Anwer, *The Gaint Rises-Again*, Portfolio Organizer, Vol.V. issue 1, pp.21-28, Jan.2004.
4. Portfolio Organizer – Various issues.
5. Analyst – various issues
6. McKinsey Quarterly.com
7. *India Vision 2020*.
8. www.Businessworld.com
9. The Hindu Survey of Indian Industry 2004.

5

INDIA AS A SUPER POWER IN THE NEW MILLENNIUM

Prof. S.V. Bidwai*

Is it possible for India to become the most developed country by 2050. Most expected answer is yes, India can become developed country, and a super power this is the main theme of the paper. When we dream of India becoming a superpower by 2020, we have to look at four different dimensions (1) people, (2) economy, (3) strategic strengths and (4) ability to sustain and improve on these over very long periods of time in the future. It is in this context, the paper pursues from four different perspectives viz.:

- India past, present and future
- India as a knowledge superpower
- Will India ride the Demographic Wave
- India as an industrial and financial super power in the globalised environment.

The paper looks at these different dimensions and tries to arrive at the conclusion that India can emerge as a super power vindicating the dream of our president who has a vision of India in the new millennium.

* Director cum Professor Anjuman-I-Islam's Allana Institute of Management Studies (AIAIMS), Mumbai.

"The nation can use its core competence in IT, natural resources and human resources to become a knowledge superpower by 2020. The 21st century belongs to the knowledge age, where acquisition, possession and application of knowledge are the most important resources."

-A.P.J. ABDUL KALAM

Hon. President of India

Introduction

When the whole world is in turmoil, with people fighting over borders & religion, the Indian shall rise above all this & lead this world into the future, full of ethics, morals & values. This is the real definition of a super-power, a country which leads the world with its power to unite it to one world vision.

Is it possible for India to become a Super-Power by 2020? Most expected answer is yes, India can become a Super-Power this is amply substantiated by This amply substantiate by the vision put forth by our Hon. President A.P.J. Abdul Kalam and Goldman Sach Report. The paper pursues the question from four different perspectives these are

- India past, present and future
- India as a knowledge superpower
- Will India ride the Demographic Wave?
- India as an industrial and financial super power in the globalised environment.

India Past, Present and Future

In the 3rd millennium BC, the Indus-Saraswati civilization was the world leader in science and technology as well as in trade and philosophy. We are witnessing a return to India's roots, considering the bright prospects of India in the new millennium. In current discussions about this development, the Pokharan nuclear tests were the inevitable main points of reference, because they have acted as an eye-opener to Indians and foreigners alike. The tests have made the point that India now plays in the top league: technologically, because Indian scientists have demonstrated their mastery of that very technology which, after 1945, decides a country's status in geopolitics; and politically, because India has demonstrated the will and capacity to assert its vision of a multipolar world, as opposed to the unipolar "new world order" inaugurated by the Soviet implosion.

The following quote of former UN Secretary General Boutros Boutros Ghali is relevant "In the next 25 years, we will have new important states, among them new super powers India, China, Russia, USA and European Union. This will help in democratisation of the UN," he said in New Delhi. Favouring the expansion of the UN Security Council, Ghali said without the political will of the member states it would not be possible to achieve. "The extension of the Security Council is something positive and again it depends on what will be the direction of countries like India or will they accept to have a permanent seat without the veto, Observing that unilateral decisions have created crisis for the UN, he said the new world order might help making the body a more democratic one."

Infact the latest Central Intelligence Agency report mentions that India will be a super power by 2020 is a mind opener even without debate as to how much of it is true and it should prompt introspection. The CIA's aim is to prepare the US for future economic challenges from China and India. In this paper, I would like to look into some of the implications of the emerging power equation. Not from the military point of view but from other more broader and long lasting perspectives within the vision laid down by the president.

India as a Knowledge Super Power

The nation can use its core competence in IT, natural resources and human resources to become a knowledge superpower by 2020

According to an article by A. P. J. ABDUL KALAM President of India. India can indeed be a super power not in terms of military might but in terms of knowledge the following is a brief extract by an article written by our Hon president

"In the 21st century, knowledge is the primary production resource and it will be used as a tool to drive societal transformation and create wealth.

The knowledge industries where India can shine are:

- IT Software and IT enabled services, including BPOs

- Entertainment and media
- Bio-technology
- Pharmaceutical
- Health Services

Besides, above India will do very well in the following sector, which also have substantial involvement of knowledge.

- Auto components
- Energy

Knowledge has always been the prime mover of prosperity and power. The acquisition of knowledge has therefore been the thrust area throughout the world, and knowledge society can be the foundation for building a developed India.

During the last few centuries, the world has undergone several social transformations. First there was an agricultural society where manual labour was the key factor and economic growth was dependent largely on agricultural products. With the advent of the industrial revolution, economic progress was propelled largely by technological development leading to machines replacing human resources.

India could not fully reap the results of the industrial revolution as the nation was ruled by foreign powers. However, licensed industrial institutions did emerge. This society added value to its products through explicit knowledge, which is technology, to produce industrial products that led to the economic growth of nations. Thus management of technology, capital, and labour provided the competitive advantage to bring about this transformation in economic growth.

The world today has already moved into an information society. This society derives its economic growth by further value addition to the explicit knowledge through networking. Connectivity and software products are now driving the economies of the nations. While tomorrow's world would be one that would recognise knowledge in its most comprehensive form and add further value to products through innovative knowledge-intensive products/services in a networked ambience. It is these knowledge products that will contribute to the economic growth of nations.

While a knowledge society has a two-dimensional objective of societal transformation and wealth generation, a third dimension emerges when India has to change into a knowledge superpower-knowledge protection. The knowledge superpower status brings in its wake a tremendous responsibility to strengthen intellectual property rights and protect our vast biological and microbial resources. Our ancient knowledge and culture should be protected against multiple attacks launched from many directions.

Thus a knowledge superpower has to focus on two important issues-economic prosperity and national security. Our communication network and information generators have to be protected from electronic attacks through surveillance and monitoring and building technologies to handle such attacks. Thus the core requirement for knowledge protection is two-fold. There should be a focused approach on intellectual property rights and related issues and major private sector initiatives in the area of technology generation for information security.

Is India an IT Super-Power?

Information technology. It is a $16 billion industry. It has changed the perception of the world about India, and India's own perception about itself and has helped productivity of other industries

In recent years, there has been a small chorus of voices promoting the notion that India is an IT Super-Power. Not only has this been touted by a section of the Indian Press, but it has also found an echo in the writings and statements of Indian NRIs. Undoubtedly, India's progress in the field of Computer Science has been quite remarkable. The reputation of India's best IT professionals is entirely well-deserved, and Indian researchers have been publishing some of the best papers in the field.

Moreover, according to a recent article in Forbes magazine, India's intellectual acumen has now drawn 150 global business giants to set up research and development facilities in India. Not only does the list include important technology companies such as IBM, HP, Texas Instruments, Motorola, Samsung, STMicro and Infineon, but also large manufacturing companies such as GE, Daimler Chrysler, Tyco Corp, and Electrolux.

Although not all of these R&D facilities are working at the cutting edge of technology, several of these centers are critical to the success of the parent company. For instance Intel's India Research Center filed 63 patents in the past year, and has now emerged as Intel's most significant international center, edging out counterparts in Malaysia and Israel. Guillermo Wille, head of GE's India Research center has noted that GE's Indian scientists and engineers are working in leading edge fields such as nanotechnology, hydrogen energy, photonics, and advanced propulsion. And in the ultimate compliment to Indian talent, Oracle co-president Charles Phillip said recently: "The kind of intellectual figure you people have is phenomenal..." .

Although there has been remarkable progress in just the last five years, until the benefits of high technology flow to all sections of Indian society - (and raise living standards across the board) - the designation "IT Super-Power" will have a somewhat hollow meaning.

Will India ride the Demographic Wave?

When we dream of India becoming a superpower by 2020, we have to look at four different dimensions

(1) people, (2) economy, (3) strategic strengths and (4) ability to sustain and improve on these over very long periods of time in the future.

In this section, we will focus on the first dimension i.e. people and continue with the remaining three in other parts of this paper.

Population Growth

Naturally, we need to look at population growth. World population is estimated to be 7 billion by the year 2000 and projected to be 9.4 billion by the year 2020. In India the current population growth rate of 1.8 per cent can be envisioned as coming down to 1.5 percent by 2020. Investment in primary education and basic health care facilities is vital if the rate is to be brought down, as it must be if we are to achieve the vision of a developed India. With certain assumptions it is possible to envision a population of about 1.2 billion by 2010 and therefore a per capita GDP of $762 at constant prices (being $3146 with purchasing power parity – PPP_; and a population of about 1.4 billion by 2020 and per capita $1540 at current prices ($6355 with PPP).-

Facing the Challenge of the 21st Century

With the advent of 21st century, the management requirements are undergoing a sea-change. The markets have started changing discontinuously. To be successful in this situation, the managements require creativity and intuition rather than quantitative analysis. They will have to be proactive with speedy response to competitive environment rather than reactive. They will require permanent flexibility with leadership from everybody according to requirements. Consequently, information has to be shared with efforts to reinvent competitive advantage and create new markets. This means a change in the mind-set of the population.

Riding the Demographic Wave

Even while there will be greater urbanization, there would also be greater rural-urban integration economically and socially. Integration with the world economy is also likely to bring a number of different consumption styles and value systems. With increasing prosperity there would also be greater attention to protection of environment. It will be possible to ensure better nutritional and health standards for all our people.

The literacy rate can be expected to improve from 52 percent in 1991 to roughly 80 percent in 2020. The life expectancy at birth in expected to improve substantially.

Demographics play an important role in the way the world will change. Even within the BRICs, Demographic impacts vary greatly. The decline in working-age population is generally projected to take place later than in the developed economies, but will be steeper in Russia and China than India and Brazil.

The following graph shows how India compare with other BRIC's in term of growing:

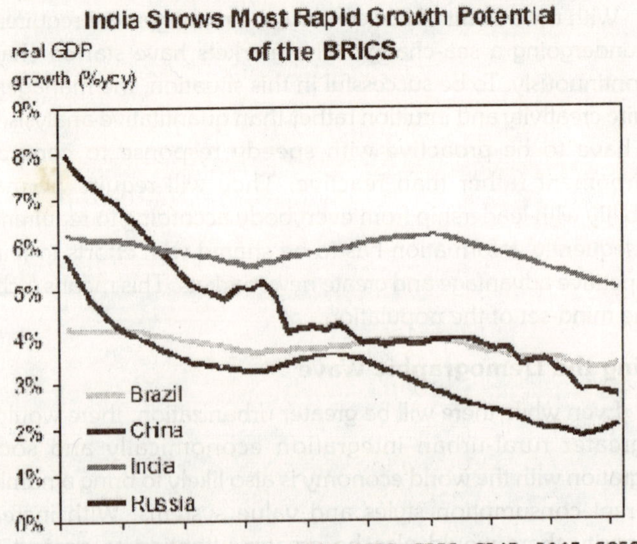

Source: Goldman Sachs Report.

There is likely to be a large population of young people with aspirations of a better lifestyle. There would be a large reservoir of literate and skilled persons. There is also a greater likelihood of more women taking part in direct economic activities including entrepreneurship.

India as an industrial and financial super power in the globalised environment

The Goldman Sachs Report

Indian economy will overtake UK, Japan by 2035: Goldman Sachs The Indian economy is expected to overtake the United Kingdom and Japan by 2035, making it the world's third largest economy after the US and China, according to a new report.

Global investment banking and securities firm Goldman Sachs says in the report that by 2050 China, Brazil, Russia and India will be ahead of the six largest industrial states in overall GDP.

"If everything goes smoothly, these four countries will become the most attractive region in the world for placing direct as well as portfolio investment," Goldman Sachs states in its report *Brazil, Russia, India and China - A Road in 2050*.

Its prediction is based on the assumption that the current six leaders of the world economy, USA, Japan, Great Britain, Germany, France, Italy, will experience only 2 per cent annual growth in the next half a century.

According to Goldman Sachs this will allow India to overtake Japan in GDP by 2032 and China to get ahead of the US by 2041.

Goldman Sachs senior analyst and co-author of the report Dominique Willson explained the calculations were based on existing trends in each of the four countries, including demography, a possible slowdown in growth and expanding production and services sectors.

"To achieve these results, the countries do not have to carry out any special economic policy in order to repeat the wonderful experience of 'Asian tigers'," Willson is quoted as saying. "It is enough to ensure macroeconomic stability, transparency of the economy and to work at improving public and market institutes, infrastructure and education."

The Goldman Sachs analysis comes on the back of reports that Europe's economic problems are worsening. French bank Societe Generale says France, Germany, Italy and the Netherlands are in recession. On the other hand China has replaced the UK as the world's fifth largest exporter and the Chinese economy is growing by 8 per cent a year.

In making its forecasts, Goldman doesn't focus on the four developing nations' current economic-growth rates, even though these certainly haven't been too shabby. Instead, using demographic projections and a model of capital accumulation and productivity trends, it calculates likely gains in gross domestic product and income per capita, and currency movements.

Over the next 50 years, the model assumes that GDP will rise at an average annual clip of 3.8 per cent in Brazil, nearly 6 per cent in India, 4.7 per cent in China, and 3.2 per cent in Russia, versus the US' projected 1.7 per cent. It also assumes that the value of the four nations' currencies will rise.

For America, the report says, the news isn't all bad. Although the US would cease to be the most dominant single force in the global economy, it would reap trade benefits from the new megapowers' hefty gains in spending on goods and services.

Although these nations, particularly China, are often viewed mainly as competitors to the US, "probably more important in the long run is that these are economies that are going to be generating a substantial part of the world's demand growth," Wilson says.

The four nations have a projected GDP of $2.75 trillion for this year, versus the G-6's $21.25 trillion, but the report reckons that in another five years, the annual increase in spending from these economies could be greater than that from the G-6 and more than twice as much in dollar terms as it is now.

By 2010, the annual increase in spending from the four economies could reach $521 billion, versus the current $159 billion.

To be sure, the forecast assumes that China, India, Russia and Brazil "maintain policies and develop institutions that are supportive of growth."

According to Geoffrey Dennis, an emerging-market strategist at Smith Barney, China's biggest challenge is to move towards a fully free-market economy, while Russia's is to diversify away from its heavy dependence on oil and gas, while creating a consumer society.

India's biggest need, he maintains, is to raise the per-capita standard of living for its huge population, while reducing the "tremendous government interference" in its economy.

The authors acknowledge that the projections about the new economic powers aren't sure things, particularly because they assume the removal of a good number of political and structural barriers.

And indeed, they point out, it's well to remember that economic predictions frequently go awry. In the 1980s, Japan — which later began floundering in a lengthy deflationary spiral that may still not have concluded — was being trumpeted by some forecasters as the nation that would overtake the US by now.

Another point: "If you go back and say which have been the emerging markets people have been the most excited about, you wouldn't necessarily pick the same four" as Goldman, says Dennis.

He notes that several years ago, Mexico, Korea, some central European countries, and Argentina, were viewed as the next big things. Still, he believes the Goldman report is "conceptually correct."

Dennis acknowledges that China, India, Russia and Brazil "are growing very rapidly," although to achieve the dominance outlined in the Goldman report, they would have to expand their economies and avoid major crises.

While the Goldman economists concede that there's a good chance their projections won't be met, they say that even if they merely come close, "the implications for the pattern of growth and economic activity could be very large indeed."

A Summary of the Report and its Implications are given below

1. Over the next 50 years, Brazil, Russia, India and China—the BRICs economies—could become a much larger force in the world economy. Using the latest demographic projections and a model of capital accumulation and productivity growth, we map out GDP growth, income per capita and currency movements in the BRICs economies until 2050.

2. The results are startling. If things go right, in less than 40 years, the BRICs economies together could be larger than theG6inUSdollar terms. By2025 they could account for over half the size of the G6. Currently they are worth less than 15%. Of the current G6, only the US and Japan may be among the six largest economies in US dollar terms in 2050.

3. About two-thirds of the increase in US dollar GDP from the BRICs should come from higher real growth, with the balance through currency appreciation. The BRICs' real exchange rates could appreciate by up to 300% over the next 50 years (an average of 2.5% a year).

4. The shift in GDP relative to the G6 takes place steadily over the period, but is most dramatic in the first 30 years. Growth for the BRICs is likely to slow significantly toward the end of the period, with only India seeing growth rates

significantly above 3% by 2050. And individuals in the BRICs are still likely to be poorer on average than individuals in the G6 economies, with the exception of Russia. China's per capita income could be roughly what the developed economies are now (about US$30,000 per capita).

5. As early as 2009, the annual increase in US dollar spending from the BRICs could be greater than that from the G6 and more than twice as much in dollar terms as it is now. By 2025 the annual increase in US dollar spending from the BRICs could be twice that of the G6, and four times higher by 2050.

6. The key assumption underlying our projections is that the BRICs maintain policies and develop institutions that are supportive of growth. Each of the BRICs faces significant challenges in keeping development on track. This means that there is a good chance that our projections are not met, either through bad policy or bad luck. But if the BRICs come anywhere close to meeting the projections set out here, the implications for the pattern of growth and economic activity could be large.

7. The relative importance of the BRICs as an engine of new demand growth and spending power may shift more dramatically and quickly than expected. Higher growth in these economies could offset the impact of greying populations and slower growth in the advanced economies.

8. Higher growth may lead to higher returns and increased demand for capital. The weight of the BRICs in investment portfolios could rise sharply. Capital flows might move further in their favour, prompting major currency realignments.

9. Rising incomes may also see these economies move through the 'sweet spot' of growth for different kinds of products, as local spending patterns change. This could be an important determinant of demand and pricing patterns for a range of commodities.

10. As today's advanced economies become a shrinking part of the world economy, the accompanying shifts in spending could provide significant opportunities for global companies. Being invested in and involved in the right markets—particularly the right emerging markets—may become an increasingly important strategic choice.
11. The list of the world's ten largest economies may look quite different in 2050. The largest economies in the world (by GDP) may no longer be the richest (by income per capita), making strategic choices for firms more complex.

Globalisation and the Industrial and Financial Sectors

The impact of globalisation on the following major sectors and how India has shaped up

- industrial sector
- agricultural sector
- external sector
- financial sector

Impact on the Industrial Sector

Often a question is asked whether India can compete with the big economies of the world in industry and trade. My answer is that we are already competing well. Take the case of the hardcore manufacturing sectors. In automobile components, our exports have gone up from $375 million a year ago to $1.5 billion this year, with 18 of the world's largest auto manufacturers outsourcing components from India. Many of them are getting components designed in India. We have the marriage of design, information technology and manufacturing.

Reforms in the industrial sector were fallout of the realisation that resources to meet the enormous capital requirements cannot be generated from within the economy, and that restrictive licensing policy and over-dependence on public sector would not provide the desired catalytic action. Hence, the policy thrust was directed towards delicensing, allowing infusion of foreign capital, partial privatisation of some public enterprises, and opening of the financial sector to encourage foreign participation.

It is believed that in response to the incentives of the liberalisation programme, particularly improved access to imported capital, and easier possibilities of foreign collaboration, the 'animal spirits' of private entrepreneurs set off a wave of investment that helped in lifting the rate of industrial growth. It was observed that while capital formation in the private corporate sector rose, in the household sector it fell and this decline was much more than the increase in the private sector capital formation. Later in 1994-95, however, the household sector contributed significantly to the rise in overall capital formation.

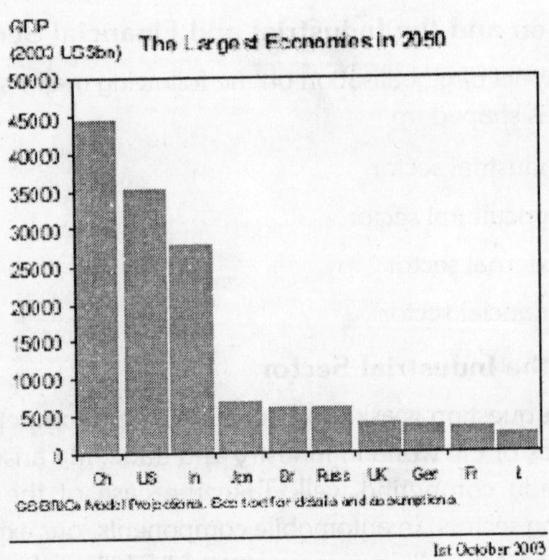

The post 1991 relaxation of rigorous controls succeeded in increasing market competition in India. The threat of market entry is believed to induce efficiency as it has in the reformed regime in India. Such efficiency growth is considered critical for industrial expansion as well as for generating large amounts of national income to support superior standards of living of India.

Prior to liberalisation, the government controls, including reservation of certain industries and restriction on foreign capital, import of technology, components etc. created sources of advantage for different groups of companies. While liberalisation has created opportunities for improving competitive position, it has also eroded many traditional sources of advantage thus posing a threat.

It appears that there is a general lack of clear thinking in terms of private equity participation and regulatory and monitory mechanisms. The infrastructure development with respect to power, telecommunications, oil and gas, and human resource development along with the financial sector all lack in co-ordinated thinking and proper implementation of the regulations. The intellectual property rights issue is an example of neglect, which is allowing the foreign companies to patent the long established products of our country. India also lacks behind China in industrial development

Impact on the Agricultural Sector

So far, economic reforms in India have been confined mainly to the non-agricultural sector. However, agriculture being an integral part of the economy and given the strong linkages between the different sectors of the economy, reforms are having a strong impact on the agricultural sector.

With the increased pace of economic liberalization, the anti-agriculture bias of the policy makers has been reducing. While the focus of the policy makers has been on the industrial sector, agriculture gained primarily due to reduced protection to the manufacturing sector and an appropriate increase in the relative prices of the major farm products.

The time series data on GDP reveal an overall increase in real terms during the post-liberalization period. It is the growth in the agricultural sector that is believed to have contributed to a great extent to the observed acceleration in the growth of the Indian economy in the post-liberalization period. In this respect, it is interesting to note that the increase in the money income in the agricultural sector is to a level that has offset the rising inflation rate. For the first time, this increase is comparable to that in the non-agricultural sector.

When we look at the sources of this accelerated growth of net agricultural output, we can very clearly distinguish a departure from the labor-induced growth in the pre-liberalization era. It is the increase in the total factor productivity – itself a product of improved capacity utilization, technical progress, weather conditions, etc. – that is stated to have emerged as the most important factor during the post-liberalization period.

The constant upward revision in the minimum support prices of major agricultural products has brought about a significant increase in the relative price of agricultural products and moved the terms of trade in favor of agriculture. In today's changed context, when the global prices of primary products have started to turn in favor of the developing countries, there is hope for agricultural exports from India. The success would, however, depend much on the policy initiatives, rather than on the global economic environment as in the past.

Traditionally, both internal and international terms of trade have been against the primary goods and in particular, agricultural goods. It is believed that structural transformation of the economy reduces the relative share of agriculture in GDP. However, as manufactured goods become relatively abundant in comparison with agricultural goods in the course of industrialization-based development, terms of trade move in favour of agricultural goods. It is argued that in the early phases of planned development, possibly due to low level of agricultural development and per capita income, the terms of trade of agriculture vis-a-vis industry were adversely affected. The rise in the dependence of industry on agriculture for intermediate inputs led to a steady improvement in the 1st phase of liberalization(1986-87 to 1990-91). The trend was, however, reversed during the 2nd phase of liberalization (1991-92 to 1997-98) when the terms of trade for manufactured goods improved at the cost of agriculture, thus reflecting a pro-rich slant of the New Economic Policy.

Impact on External Sector

The main impact of globalization has been the effect on the competitive strength of the Indian exports in the world market. Specifically, there is an increased focus on the competitiveness of Indian exports in the EU market.

The basic reforms that have taken place in this sector since 1991 generally relate to the following areas :

- Industrial reforms - affecting the Foreign Capital and Technological Policies
- Exchange Rate reforms
- Trade Policy reforms

The sweeping reforms have certainly affected the external sector favorably. For instance, consider the growth in exports as a percentage of GDP.

Table-1: Export, Import and Trade as a Percentage of GDP

Year	*Export*	*Import*	*Trade*
1990-91	6.2	9.40	15.6
1991-92	7.3	8.30	15.6
1992-93	7.8	9.80	17.6
1993-94	8.8	9.70	18.5
1994-95	8.8	10.5	19.3
1995-96	9.9	12.6	22.5
1996-97	9.5	13.0	22.5

The table shows that exports have grown faster than GDP in the post reform period. The annual export growth rates reveal a remarkable recovery from a negative export growth of –1.5% in 1991-92 to an impressive growth rate of 18-21% during 1993-96. Since April 1996 exports have however suffered some setbacks. This is mainly due to the fact that, the entire business world has been facing a slump for the past couple of years.

There has also been a definite increase in India's share in world trade in the post-liberalization era. The following table shows India's share in world trade in percentages.

Table-2

Year	*Export*	*Import*	*Trade*
1950	1.85	1.71	1.78
1960	1.03	1.69	1.36
1970	0.64	0.65	0.65
1980	0.42	0.72	0.57
1990	0.52	0.66	0.59
1991	0.50	0.56	0.53
1992	0.53	0.61	0.57
1993	0.58	0.60	0.59
1994	0.60	0.63	0.61

The growing outward orientation of the economy has also led to an increase, though nominal, in the country's share in the world trade from 0.53% in 1991 to 0.61% in 1994 as can be seen from the table above. But when we compare this to the performance of India during the earlier decades of this century, we find that India is lagging far behind.

Liberalization has also helped the external sector to bring a greater balance in trade account. The reforms have helped to cover as much as 85-92% of the import bill as against only 60% in the later half of the eighties. The growing globalization is also reflected in the rising number of foreign collaboration approvals, from 703 in 1990 to 1797 on an average between 1992-95. The technical collaborations have also increased from 502 in 1990 to 823 p.a. during 1992-95. The improved external sector performance is also reflected by the fact that the external debt burden has decreased from a peak of $99 billion in March 1995 to $90.9 billion in March 1997.

The above evaluation clearly reveals that the liberalization reforms of 1991 have considerably improved the external sector performance. Still, with all the latest technology and emerging challenges coming up, it would not be easy to sustain this improvement for long unless appropriate back up action is taken. With the present Government promoting Swadeshi, it is very difficult to understand the implications. After all, one thing that counts is consistency, and if a policy is not given ample times to show its worth, it is useless to implement it in the first place.

Impact on the Financial Sector

As a result of globalisation there has been an unprecedented growth of the financial sector, particularly the banking sector. But there were infirmities and serious problems in the system that was essentially owned and controlled by the Government. This called for reform measures to manage this transition to globalisation, in an efficient manner. Thus the essential impact of globalisation in the financial sector has been the introduction of reforms to firm up certain practices of the financial system. These reforms are guided by the free market philosophy, which forms a corner stone of the globalisation policy.

The pre-reform growth in the financial system is attributed to the supply-led strategy and government ownership of the large part of the system. The weaknesses in the system are considered to be inevitable fallout of the growth process. However, weaknesses needed to be corrected and for this, policies and practices were changed to revitalize the financial system. The uncritical acceptance of the free-market philosophy is a hindrance to the genuine reform of the financial system. The goal of globalization can be considered as premature and infeasible, given the current state of the socio-economic development and the sensitivity of the financial markets. Regarding monetary control, usage of direct instruments - like the variations in reserve requirements, regulation of size and distribution bank credit, etc. - is considered more suitable than the present single-measure monetary targeting approach.

The distortions caused by some of these measures broadly reflect the growing insensitivity of the banking system to the development needs apart from encouraging unhealthy practices to counter competition. While the government authorities retrace some of their steps, some experts propose a socially desirable reform package that is aligned with the national priorities of improving employment opportunities and living standards in the informal sector. Within the recommendations of the Narasimham Committee, to ensure operational flexibility and autonomy, the reform agenda stressed on a shift of focus from money to credit, cross-subsidization of interest rates in favor of deserving and bankable customers. It advocated a restoration of the promotional role of IDBI to retain the functional distinction between banks and financial institutions.

The Path Ahead

The evolution of India as a superpower in 2020 presupposes rapid economic growth in the intervening period. If the nation has to reach that status, then the rate of growth would necessarily have to be 8-10 per cent per annum. The record of the developed countries shows that the growth of consumption of energy has been higher than the rate of economic growth itself. Do we have to follow the same path?

Perhaps this trajectory is not essential for India, mainly because energy supply is a capital intensive activity. For a capital-scarce economy like India, a very different path would have to be explored and pursued, a path that does not demand the same levels of capital for the energy sector that were required by the developed nations at the same stage of development.

When the developed countries were at the same stage, there was limited choice of technologies and fuels, which constrained them to follow an energy-intensive path of growth. Fortunately, for a variety of global as well as local reasons, the developed countries have had to create technological solutions that are far less energy intensive. We could employ them effectively.

The dream of India becoming a superpower by 2020, a goal set by the President and the Prime Minister, can be realised if we are clear on the focus, scale and execution. In all these areas we have to do much more. Focus has to be a national effort; so far our efforts at nation building are scattered in many directions. Even when children prepare for an exam, they have to give up other things and focus on the exam. In the same way, we have to focus on a developed India. It is not something we can do on a part-time basis.

To Conclude

We have a long way to go before we become the best, but we can achieve this target provided we stay focussed, think big and execute our projects on time.

REFERENCE

1. *India 2020 – A vision for the New Millennium* by A. P. J. Abdul Kalam with Y. S. Rajan, Viking – Pengium Books India (P) Ltd.
2. *Wings of Fire – An Autobiography* by A.P.J. Abdul Kalam with Arun Tiwari, Universities Press (India) Private Ltd.
3. *Goldman Sachs - Report.*
4. Various Newspapers.
5. CIA Website.

6

EMERGING INDIA

CHALLENGES IN EXTERNAL DEBT

Dr. L.S.N. Prasad*,: Geetha Chew Ayele** and **P. Vasudeva Rao*****

The article presents the logic that foreign debt used for productive purposes which results in income for the nation, would not be burdensome from the national angle, as it facilitates repaying capacity. Alongwith a few other developing countries, history of Indian foreign debt is traced, and its implications analyzed. Debt distress periods of recent years are presented for a number of countries. For India, the period recorded in the table is 1981 to 1984; a relatively short period, compared to a few countries where it ranged from 10 to 15 years. Debt distress is considered as periods in which countries resort to exceptional financing in any of the three ways: (1) incur substantial arrears on their external debt, (ii) receive debt relief from the Paris club of creditors, or (iii) receive non-concessional balance of payments support from the International Monetary Fund. In addition, three factors that affect the gravity of debt distress are debt burden, quality of institutions and policies, and shocks that affect: the real GDP growth. The decreasing per capita consumption/availability of necessities in the country causes concern, and warrants immediate corrective steps. In India, per capita consumption during 1990s increased at 1.2 per

* Dept. of Economics, Hindu College, Guntur, Presently: Associate Professor, Dept. of Economics, Debub University,Ethiopia.

** Head, Dept. of Economics, Debub University, Ethiopia.

*** Reader, Dept. of Economics, Hindu College, Guntur, AP.

cent for low income groups,: 6.2 percent for middle income groups, and 3.8 per cent for high income groups. Efforts should be made to improve the growth rate further.

Introduction

Despite persistent analysis and debates on foreign debt and loans, the debt related issues are still not well understood in our Country. Politicians with non-economic background, people with vested interest who are in the decision making levels make the foreign debt a heavy burden on the Indian Economy. If the foreign debt uses in productive income generating facilities, the repayment – debt service – would not have that many burdens to the economy.

India is one of the countries in the world, which has been approaching for foreign debt for various reasons. In our country there is a notion that lender influence the borrower –in decision making. In 1980 for the first time, the then government headed by Late Prime Minister Indira Gandhi, approached the International Monetary fund (IMF) to go for a loan worth of 5 Billion US $. At that time it was equal to Rs.5000 crores. There was a lot of hue and Cry against this borrowing. Since then the Indian governments irrespective of the party or policy are approaching the world Bank, IMF, Paris Club, Aid India Consortium for foreign loans. It is now in rumor that even the state governments are also approaching the various international organizations for foreign debt.

International borrowing is for various reasons becoming obligatory. The main reason in Indian contest is the structural adjustments. It is nothing but getting loan for repaying the old loans. In the year 1990 the Indian government did not have sufficient foreign reserves to repay its interest obligations. No international organization came forward to rescue us. The then government, in spite of its efforts to mobilize the foreign loan, put 27 tones of gold for mortgage in the international market and pay debt obligation. It seems that profit motive lenders lend as long as credit worthness of the economy appears solid the will come forword to lend the loan. In the long run if the credit worthiness of the economy will decrease it will be a big problem to debt service.

The Golden rule: the golden rule relate to the growth rates and foreign debt. It can be compatible with any set of relative sizes of debt and the economy, yet it is intitutively obvious that a tiny economy growing at the same rate as its huge debt are not in true equilibrium. There must be a equilibrium in between debt and the growth of GNPA relationship is sustainable only if it can resist minor variations and posses endogenous forces capable of returning its equilibrium. A borrowing economy must be able to adjust changes in its own growth rates and other characteristics and in the value and conditions of new flows (borrowing).

Repayment: Repayment of debt is an obligation but it is an obstacle to economic Development, Many countries in the world from Afghanistan to Zimbabwe unsustainable services is an euphimenonomenon of the generalized failure of development rather than its cause. India in one of the example for some time in the case less optimization of foreign debt.

Debt in some countries: The African country cote D ivories is a small country. Its debt is to private lenders. The increase in debt is faster than its growth in GNP. In 1980 the private inflow is turned into out flow. In the 1990 there was relief but the political turmoil and civil strife have joined economic stagnation and to reduce the debt burden quite unsustainable. Take other example, Indonesia. The debt crisis has derailed the development. Out flow contribute 13% in Gross National Investment (GNI). Around 40% of central government budget allocated to debt services. Another country, Uganda is nation of political disturbances. Its economy depends on Aid, which is highly concessional. The export earnings barley finances 20% of its imports.

Going for debt to repay the debt: There were number of occasions that debt repayments can be directly deducted from the new loans. The government of India never questioned its absolute obligation were meant without specific assistance, the remaining free foreign exchange earnings would not sufficient to meet minimal other developmental needs. If we go back in 1964, the US helped to import 10 million tones of wheat under PL 480, when India was in dire need of food grains. The Indian debt relief was not lessened in over the years, and the world bank helped in obtaining the aid from Aid India consortium. The government approached for flexible bilateral non-project aid. It was helped to procure non-aided bonds. It is continues and there were debt distress years in the Indian foreign debt.

Methods of Debt relief: There are three methods of debt relief. They are :

(a) Simple cancellation of payment

(b) Postponement of payment

(c) New loans usable for debt relief

In addition to this The debt distress is considered as periods in which the resort to exceptional financing in any one of three ways:

(i) incur substantial arrears on their external debt,

(ii) receive debt relief from the Paris Club of creditors, and

(iii) receive non-concessional balance of payments support from the International Monetary Fund.

In addition to this they are three factors-the debt burden, depends. They are a, the quality of institutions b. policies, and c. shocks that affect real GDP growth-are highly significant predictors of debt distress. The World Bank in 1990's asked the aid consortium members to provide sufficient debt relief to India so as to reduce the total debt service burden to less than 20% of its export. At that time most of the countries on the principles which were commonly accepted but they were not in agreement on burden sharing.

Impact of excess debt: The data available from the international Financial Statistics and Global Development Forum during 1999-2000, the growth of per capita consumption in low income countries is estimated around 1.6. Only 12 out of 49 highly and moderately indebted countries having decreasing per capita consumption. In the case of India the per capita consumption among high income groups increased 3.8 percent where as in Middle income group it has increased at the rate of 6.2 percent. In the low income group it has increased at 1.2 percent. It is very good to say that India is not the bunch of the 12 countries. But with the 1 billion population we must be cocious to increase the per capita availability of necessaries to the people who are living near above and below the poverty line. The decreasing consumption rate among these groups is not an ordinary one. It should be tackled in macroeconomic concept.

The debt distress is considered as periods in which countries resort to exceptional financing in any one of three ways: (i) incur substantial arrears on their external debt, (ii) receive debt relief from the Paris Club of creditors, and (iii) receive non-concessional balance of payments support from the International Monetary Fund. In addition to this there are three factors-the debt burden, the quality of institutions and policies, and shocks that affect real GDP growth. These are highly significant predictors of debt distress.

The debt distress as periods in which any one or more of the three following conditions hold: (a) the sum of interest and principal arrears is large relative to the stock of debt outstanding, (b) a country receives debt relief in the form of rescheduling and/or debt reduction from the Paris Club of bilateral creditors, or (c) the country receives substantial balance of payments support from the IMF under its non-concessional Standby Arrangements or Extended Fund Facilities (SBA/EFF). First condition is the most basic measure of debt distress: the inability to service external obligations resulting in an accumulation of arrears. But countries that are unable to service their external debt need not necessarily fall into arrears; they can also obtain balance of payments support from the IMF and, in addition, seek debt rescheduling or debt reduction from the Paris Club. The Paris Club assesses the "extraordinary external financing needs" of countries based on balance of payments projections set within a macroeconomic framework agreed as part of an IMF program, and takes into account all other sources of external financing available to the country. (which involves a reduction in the debt of Paris Club members by 67 percent in present value terms).

Conclusion

In this analysis a simple description is given to assess the debt and its repayments. In the present globalised world, lifting of various restrictions on movements of capital, it is the time to the Indian government to make a suitable macro economic policy to adjust with the changes in international trade and to generate and earning of the sufficient foreign capital and by having the favorable balance of trade.

Debt Distress Periods of the Selected Countries

Country	Start Year	End Year
Albania	1992	2002
Argentina	1983	1996
Brazil	1983	1986
Chile	1983	1990
Cameroon	1987	2000
Ecuador	1983	1997
Egypt	1977	1981
Ethiopia	1991	2000
Ghana	1996	1999
Indonesia	1997	2002
India	1981	1984
Jamaica	1977	2000
Jordan	1989	2001
Kenya	1975	1978
Kenya	1992	1997
Mexico	1983	1993
Pakistan	1980	1984
Pakistan	1995	2001
Philippines	1976	1979
Somalia	1981	2000
Thailand	1997	2000
Turkey	1978	1985

REFERENCES

1. Aylward, Lynn and Rupert Thorne (1998). *An Econometric Analysis of Countries' Repayment Performance to the International Monetary Fund. IMF Working Paper* No.98/32.
2. Berg, Andrew and Jeffrey Sachs (1988). *The Debt Crisis: Structural Explanations of Country Performance, Journal of Development Economics.* 29(3):271-306.
3. Birdsall, Nancy, C.Claessens, and I.Diwan.2002. *Policy Selectivity Foregone* Debt and Donor Behavior in Africa. *Centre for Global Development, Working Paper* No.17.
4. Cline, William (1984). *International Debt: Systemic Risk and Policy Response. Institute of International Economics:* Washington,DC.

5. Cohen, Daniel (1996). *The Sustainability of African Debt*. World Bank Policy Research Department Working Paper No.1691.

6. Detragiache, Enrica and Antonio Spilimbergo (2001). *Crises and Liquidity: Evidence and Interpretation. IMF Working Paper* No. 01/2.

7. Dikhanov, Yuri (2003). *Reconstruction of Historical Present Value of Debt for Developing Countries, 1980-2001: Methodology and Calculations*. Manuscript, The World Bank.

8. Lloyd-Ellis, H.,G.W.McKenzie, and S.H.Thomas (1990). *Predicting the Quantity of LDC Debt Rescheduling*. Economics Letters. 32(1):67-73.

9. Manasse,Paolo, Nouriel Roubini, and Axel Schimmelpfenning (2003), *Predicting Soverign Debt Crises*. Manuscript, University of Bologna, IMF and New York University.

10. McFadden, Daniel, Richard Eckaus, Gershon Feder, Vassilis Hajivassiliou and Stephen O'Connell (1985), *Is There Life After Debt? An Econometric Analysis of the Creditworthiness of Developing Countries*, in Gordon Smith and John Cuddington. Ed.,

11. *International Debt and the Developing Countries*. World Bank: Washington, DC.

12. Reinhart, Carmen, Kenneth Rogoff, and Miguel Savastano (2003). *Debt Intolerance*.

13. Brookings Papers on Economic Activity, forthcoming.

14. Reinhart, Carmen (2002). *Default, Currency Crises, and Sovereign Credit Ratings*.

15. World Bank Economic Review. 16(2):151-170.

16. Underwood (1990). *The Sustainability of International Debt*. Manuscript, The World Bank.

17. Wooldridge, Jeffrey (2002). *Simple Solutions to the Initial Conditions Problem in Dynamic, Nonlinear Panel Data Models with unobserved Heterogeneity*. Manuscript, Michigan State University.

18. World Bank (2003), *Annual Report: Special Purpose Financial Statements and Internal Control Reports of the International Development Association*. Washington: The World Bank.

7

HUMAN POVERTY IN INDIA
A CASE STUDY OF GUNTUR DISTRICT (ANDHRA PRADESH)

Dr. A.K.V.S.S.R. Raja Sekhar*

Poverty is a state of deprivation. In absolute terms it reflects the inability of an individual to satisfy certain basic minimum needs for a sustained, healthy and a reasonably productive living. Conceptually, any attempt at quantifying the incidence of poverty in any population requires taking into account the level and pattern of an individual's personal consumption expenditure, as well as their access to social transfers and public provisioning. However, it is not easy to measure the consumption shares of an individual in the publicly provided goods and services or the benefit he or she derives from the overall social contexts, for often it is not possible to price them or they are provided free of charge, even though it all adds up to the well-being of the concerned individual. In general, therefore for identifying the poor one looks at the level of personal expenditure (or income) that enables the individual to satisfy a certain minimum consumption level.

* Reader & Head of the Dept. of Economics, Hindu College, Guntur.

It is in this context an attempt has been made in the study to calculate the Human Poverty, to assess its impact and to suggest appropriate measures to tackle this problem in Guntur District of Andhra Pradesh.

Introduction

Poverty is a state of deprivation. In absolute terms it reflects the inability of an individual to satisfy certain basic minimum needs for a sustained, healthy and a reasonably productive living. Conceptually, any attempt at quantifying the incidence of poverty in any population requires taking into account the level and pattern of an individual's personal consumption expenditure, as well as their access to social transfers and public provisioning. However, it is not easy to measure the consumption shares of an individual in the publicly provided goods and services or the benefit he or she derives from the overall social contexts, for often it is not possible to price them or they are provided free of charge, even though it all adds up to the well-being of the concerned individual. In general, therefore for identifying the poor one looks at the level of personal expenditure (or income) that enables the individual to satisfy a certain minimum consumption level. The proportion of population not able to attain the specified level of expenditure is then segregated as poor. Using such an approach the Planning Commission, Government of India has been estimating the Head Count Ratio of the poor at State level, separately for rural and urban areas for over three decades. It currently uses a minimum consumption expenditure, anchored in an average (food) energy adequancy norm of 2400 and 2100 kilo calories per capita per day to define State specific poverty lines, separately for rural and urban areas. These poverty lines are then applied on the NSSO's household consumer expenditure distributions to estimate the proportion and number of poor at State level.

Human Poverty in India

At the national level, the incidence of poverty on the Head Count Ratio declined from 44.48 per cent in 1983 to 26.10 per cent in 1999-2000.

It was a decline of nearly 8.5 percentage points in the ten years period between 1983 and 1993-94 followed by a further decline of nearly 10 percentage points in the period between 1993-94 and 1999-2000. In absolute terms, the number of poor declined for about 323 million in 1983 to 260 million in 1999-2000.

The decline has not been uniform either across States or across rural and urban areas. While the proportion of poor in the rural areas declined from 45.65 per cent in 1983 to 27.09 per cent in 1999-2000, the decline in urban areas has been from 40.79 per cent to 23.62 per cent during this period.

At state level, among the major states, Orissa, Bihar, West Bengal and Tamil Nadu had more than 50 per cent of their population below the poverty line in 1983. By 1999-2000, while Tamil Nadu and West Bengal had reduced their poverty ratios by nearly half, Orissa and Bihar continued to be the two poorest States with poverty ratio of 47 and 43 per cent respectively. Among others, Jammu & Kashmir, Haryana, Gujarat, Punjab, Andhra Pradesh, Maharastra and Karnataka have also succeeded in significantly reducing the incidence of poverty. Rural Orissa and rural Bihar continued to be the poorest among rural areas both in 1983, as well as in 1999-2000. In urban areas, the poorest three states in 1983 were Madhya Pradesh, Uttar Pradesh and Orissa whereas in 1993 it was Orissa followed by Madhya Pradesh and Bihar.

Status of Human Poverty

Human poverty on the HPI has declined considerably during the eighties. The decline was from nearly 47 per cent in the early eighties to about 39 per cent in the early nineties. The decline has been marginally more in rural areas in comparision to urban areas, resulting in a narrowing down of the rural-urban gap. At the national level, the magnitude of human poverty on HPI and the Planning Commission's head count ration anchored in a food adequacy norm are comparable. However, in terms of the rural and urban incidence, as well as at State level, there are considerable variations. The rural-urban ratio for the proportion of the poor on the HPI is nearly twice as high as that on the head count ratio of poverty. Given the conceptualization of HPI in terms of the broader aspects of deprivation, covering accessibility to basic minimum services, such large differences in rural and urban areas imply that availability of basic amenities that are virtually taken for granted in urban areas are, in fact, quite scarce in rural areas.

The inter-State differences in human poverty are quite striking. It was in the range of 55-60 per cent in the early eighties for the worse off States, namely, Orissa, Bihar, Arunachal Pradesh, Assam and Uttar Pradesh, and between 32-35 per cent in the between off States like Kerala, Punjab and Himachal Pradesh. It was only in the smaller, predominantly urban areas of Delhi and Chandigarh that had an HPI in the range of 17-20 per cent. The magnitude of HPI in early nineties had declined in all the States. However the relative positions of different States remained quite similar to the earlier period. The decline in HPI was significant in case of Himachal Pradesh Tamil Nadu, Maharashtra, Jammu & Kashmir, Karnataka and Kerala. In case of Bihar, Uttar Pradesh and Rajasthan, the decline was only marginal.

Human Poverty Index in A.P.

According to Date News Features (DNF 1998) longevity in Andhra Pradesh has risen but is behind the other three southern States as well as Punjab, Haryana and Maharastra. The difference between Kerala and Andhra Pradesh is ten years. The State ranks seventh among fourteen major States and last among the four southern states in the death rates and infant mortality rates. Malnutrition is widespread, more than half of the children being subject to wasting. The percent of households with safe drinking water is less than the all India average both in rural and urban areas and twelve of the fourteen major States. The proportion of households having access to electricity is lower than the national average in urban areas, and state's rank for rural and urban combined is the last among the fourteen major States. Sanitation facilities are accessed by a smaller percent of households in the State than the all India averages the of the fourteen major states. The literacy rate is behind the all India average.

Components of Human Poverty

The two components of human development – education and health – will be analysed in respect of Andhra Pradesh. The pyramid of inequalities in literacy in Andhra Pradesh in 1981. It shows that ST rural female has the lowest percentage of literacy. Next category having lower literacy rate is SC rural female. The next position in the hierarchy is occupied by ST rural male. Next in the order are ST urban female, AP rural female, SC rural male, SC urban female and ST urban male. Among other categories, AP urban male has a higher literacy rate than SC urban male. Likewise AP urban female has a higher literacy rate than AP rural male, which is higher than AP Literacy total rate. Thus, ST rural female has the lowest rate in 1991, the rate being less than 7 percent.

A Comparison of literacy rates, indicates that female literacy rates have improved to a greater extent in districts like Vishakhapatnam which had a low female literacy rate of 9.31 in 1961 and this improved to 42.26 percent in 1991. Likewise in Nellore it improved from 12.07 percent in 1961to 36.99 in 1991. Except Chittor, which could improve its low female literacy rate from 9.82 percent in 1961 to 36.44 percent in 1991, other Rayalaseema districts had not shown much improvement. The female literacy rates were very low in Telangana region in 1961 and thought there is and improvement besides Hyderabad, only Khammam record 30.53 percent as the female literacy rate in 1991.

The school age population (6-11 years) had increased from 42.35 lakhs in 1956-57 to 80.50 lakhs indicating a 90 percent increase in the school age population. The number of schools increased from 29,076 in 1950-57 to 49,125 in 1995-96. The number of children enrolled (6-11 years) increased from 24.54 lakhs in 1956-57 to 76.50 lakhs in 1995-96. The rate of enrollment increased from 57.94 percent in 1956-57 to 94.92 percent in 1995-96. Signifying a higher rate of enrollment. The number of children per school also increased from 84 in 1956-57 to 155 in 1995-96.

The growth of upper primary education during the period 1956-57, to 1995-96 indicates that school age population increased from 23.12 lakhs in 1956-57 to 44.95 lakhs in 1995-96 the number of children enrolled increased from 3.18 lakhs in 1956-57 to 22.35 lakhs in 1995-96. The ratio of enrollment increased from 13.77 in 1956-57 to 49.72 in 1995-96. But this enrollment does not correspond well with the enrollment in the case of primary education.

District-wise growth of schools at primary, upper primary and high school levels in between 1956-57 and 1995-96 depicts that the growth of primary schools had been relatively slow in Nizamabad district. In the case of upper primary schools, the number is relatively low for Vijayanagaram as it had only 157 schools in 1995-96. As regards high schools, Besides Hyderabad which has 510 schools,

Warangal comes a close second with 494 high schools in 1995-96. Thus though there had been growth in the number of primary schools, the growth is not commensurate in the case of upper primary schools.

The differences between male and female indicating the status of females in Andhra Pradesh in 1990's shows though infant mortality rate is lower for female being 69 when compare to 78 per males, it is relatively higher for female children in the age group 1 to 4. The percentage of under nourished children is 69 for females and 61 for male signifying a more number of undernourished children among females. While those immunized for polio is higher in the case of females, in the case of all diseases, it is higher for male than females. The longevity shows that a male lives upto 62 years while it is 59 years in the case of female. The school enrollment shows that it is 33 for females and 39 for males in classes 1 to 5. In the case of classes upto 10, it is 9 for male and 6 for female. The percent of children attending school in the age group of 5-14 indicates that it is higher for females in urban as well as rural areas, though the gap is much smaller in the case of urban areas. The employment in the state public sector is 10 lakhs for male, while it is 2 lakhs for female. Thus, females have a lower status than males in respect of most development indicators.

Poverty in Guntur District

An attempt is made in this paper to calculate the level of poverty in Guntur district of A.P. Recently, DRDA of Guntur conducted a survey in 2002 to calculate the level of poverty in Guntur District. Following are the variables chosen by DRDA.

1. Land holding size considered to solicit the data.
2. Nature and type of residential accommodation.
3. Average usage of clothing.
4. Food security.
5. Sanitation.
6. Utilization of durable consumer goods.
7. Levels of literacy.
8. Classification of labour in the family.
9. Nature of the work for livelihood.
10. Children–conditions (5-14 years age)

11. Levels of indebtedness.
12. Particulars of Migration.
13. Assistance from the Govt. programmes.

The variables were given 4 points each and totally 52 points were given to each household. The householders who got below 20 points, are considered poor, who got between 20 and 35 are considered middle and who got above 35 are considered rich. The results are discussed at length in the following pages.

Table-1: Revenue Division Wise Poverty Levels In Guntur District.

Sl. No.	Name of the Mandal	% of Poor	% of Middle	% of Rich
1.	Guntur	48.64	37.50	13.86
2.	Narasaraopet	46.58	35.28	18.14
3.	Tenali	52.26	31.99	15.75
	Total District	**49.16**	**34.92**	**15.92**

Source: Records of DRDA, Velugu, Guntur, 2004.

There are 771635 house holds in Guntur district (2001 census). DRDA, Velugu estimated the levels of poverty in Guntur District. According to its reports there are 49.16 percent of poor peoples, living in Guntur District. 34.92 percent of the households comes under middle category. The estimates reveal that about 16 percent people are rich in the district. (Table-1). It can be observed from the table that in both Guntur and Narasaraopet, poor people are less compared to the District average. More than half of the people in Tenali revenue division are poor.

Table-2: Mandal-wise poverty levels in Guntur District Guntur Revenue Division

Sl. No.	Name of the Mandal	% of Poor	% of Middle	% of Rich
1	2	3	4	5
1.	Bellamkonda	66.68	26.71	4.61
2.	Atchempet	64.07	26.04	9.89
3.	Amaravathi	39.11	31.67	29.22

(Contd...)

1	2	3	4	5
4.	Thulluru	43.20	43.46	13.35
5.	Mangalagiri	50.49	31.96	17.54
6.	Tadepalli	52.12	34.80	13.08
7.	Pedanandipadu	52.33	45.94	1.73
8.	Rajupalem	49.36	41.68	8.96
9.	Krosuru	48.13	41.74	10.13
10.	Pedakurapadu	54.63	34.11	11.26
11.	Tadikonda	54.83	24.09	21.09
12.	Pedakakani	36.32	50.97	12.70
13.	Vatticherukuru	40.65	47.41	11.95
14.	Prathipadu	44.34	48.61	7.04
15.	Muppalla	54.83	32.03	13.14
16.	Sattenapalli	33.68	42.53	23.79
17.	Phirangipuram	57.03	29.33	13.64
18.	Medikonduru	32.41	35.19	32.40
19.	Guntur	49.97	44.32	5.71
	Total	**48.64**	**37.50**	**13.86**

It can be noted from table 2 that 48.64 percent of people in Guntur division are estimated to the poor, 37.50 percent of the people are treated as middle class and 13.86 percentage of the people fall under rich category. There is a lot to be done to the poor people in this division.

Table-3: Narasaraopet Revenue Division

Sl. No.	*Name of the Mandal*	*% of Poor*	*% of Middle*	*% of Rich*
1	2	3	4	5
20.	Chilakalurpet	57.42	37.07	5.51
21.	Narasaraopet	37.62	37.84	24.54
22.	Rompicherla	56.15	28.12	15.73
23.	Ipur	34.57	63.80	1.63
24.	Savalyapuram	45.57	28.62	25.81
25.	Nuzendla	42.97	41.96	15.07
26.	Vinukonda	35.97	19.03	45.00

(Contd...)

1	2	3	4	5
27.	Bollapalli	48.48	40.96	10.56
28.	Karampudi	58.76	25.62	15.62
29.	Durgi	50.71	18.09	31.20
30.	Veldurthi	49.32	37.47	13.21
31.	Macherla	48.01	34.44	17.55
32.	Rentachintala	53.19	26.14	20.67
33.	Gurajala	43.98	21.07	34.95
34.	Dachepalli	54.20	22.64	23.16
35.	Machavaram	39.68	55.27	5.06
36.	Piduguralla	32.06	39.86	28.08
37.	Yeddalapadu	49.12	43.29	7.59
38.	Nadendla	44.66	50.04	5.30
39.	Nekarikallu	49.10	34.36	16.55
	Total	**46.58**	**35.28**	**18.14**

Table 3 reveals that 46.58 percent of people are considered poor and 35.28 percentage of the people are treated as middle class in the Narasaraopet division, duly 18.14 percentage of people comes under rich category. It can be noted that the district authorities have identified the poor people as their target group.

The percentage of poor, middle and rich people in Tenali revenue division may be seen from the above table. More than 50 percent (i.e. 52.26 percentage) of the people are living under poor conditions and this is above the poverty levels of the district nearly 32 and 16 percentage of people are considered as middle and rich class respectively in this division. The District authorities have to implement anti-poverty programmes and employment generation activities to the above target group i.e. Poor. (Table 4)

Table-4: Tenali Revenue Division

Sl. No.	*Name of the Mandal*	*% of Poor*	*% of Middle*	*% of Rich*
1	*2*	*3*	*4*	*5*
40	Duggirala	52.33	33.11	14.56
41	Kollipara	45.76	29.69	24.55
42	Kolluru	48.96	26.70	24.34

(Contd...)

1	2	3	4	5
43	Bhattiprolu	53.68	30.46	15.87
44	Repalle	50.94	29.13	19.93
45	Nagaram	63.83	26.51	9.67
46	Nizampatnam	67.86	24.75	7.40
47	Karlapalem	52.83	40.10	7.06
48	Bapatla	62.84	24.88	12.28
49	Kakumanu	48.87	44.14	6.99
50	Tenali	41.94	37.52	20.54
51	Vemuru	57.35	30.38	12.27
52	Cherukupalli	51.59	38.93	9.48
53	Pittalavanipalem	47.31	36.05	16.65
54	Ponnuru	37.74	43.04	19.22
55	Chebrolu	56.93	24.40	18.67
56	Tsundur	45.72	31.84	22.44
57	Amarthalur	54.27	24.25	21.48
	Total	**52.26**	**31.99**	**15.75**
	Total District	**49.16**	**34.92**	**15.92**

Human Poverty Index

Human Development Report – 2002 constructed human development index for developing countries and for some selected OECD countries. In our study, we have followed the same method to calculate human poverty index in the study area.

The Human Poverty Index for Developing Countries (HPI-1)

While the HDI measures average achievement, the HPI-1 measures deprivations in the three basic dimensions of human development captured in the HDI:

- A long and healthy life - vulnerability to death at a relatively early age, as measured by the probability at birth of not surviving to age 40.
- Knowledge – exclusion from the world of reading and communications, as measured by, the adult illiteracy rate.
- A decent standard of living – lack of access to overall economic provisioning, as measured by the unweighted

average of two indicators, the percentage of the population without sustainable access to an improved water sources and the percentage of children under weight for age.

Calculating the HPI-1 is more straight forward than calculating the HDI. The indicators used to measure the deprivations are already normalized between 0 and 100 (because they are expressed as percentages), so there is no need to create dimension indices as for the HD.

Originally, the measure of deprivation in a decent standard of living also included an indicator of access to health services. But because reliable data on access to health services are lacking for recent years, in this year's Report deprivation in a decent standard of living is measured by two rather than three indicators – the percentage of the population without sustainable access to an improved water sources and the percentage of children under weight for age.

Calculating The HPI

1. Measuring Deprivation in a Decent Standard of Living

An unweighted average of two indicators is used to measure deprivation in a decent standard of living.

Unweighted average = ½ (population without sustainable access to an improved water source) + ½ (children under weight for age)

2. Calculating the HPI

The formula for calculating the HPI-1 is as follows :

$$HPI\text{-}1 = [1/3\ (p_1a + p_2a + p_3a]^{1/a}$$

Where:

P1 = Probability at birth of not surviving to age 40 (times 100)

P2 = Adult illiteracy rate

P3 = Unweihted average of population without sustainable access to an improved water source and children under weight for age.

Table-5: Human Poverty Index

Area of the Respondent	P_1	P_2	P_3	*Index*	*Average*
Narasaraopet	30	65	76	30.15	30.04
Guntur	30	70	72.5	30.40	
Ponnur	15	68	79	29.58	
Velpur	15	65	76	23.76	27.73
Mandapadu	07	70	70	29.40	
Duggirala	16	60	80	30.04	

Human Poverty Index for the study known in the table 5. It can be observed from the above table that Human Poverty is high (30.04%) in Urban areas when compared with rural (27.73%) areas. It is striking to notice that Guntur city has more poor when compared to other survey areas and Velpur has few poor though it has dry lands.

Suggestions

The development of Guntur district depends on the development of agriculture as it is basically an agricultural district. The Principal crops are paddy, chillis, tobacco and cotton, turmeric etc., Employment even in urban areas of Guntur district is also based ,to a large extent , on agro-processing activities and trade including storage , transport , of agricultural products. Strengthening of agriculture will go a long way in increasing employment not only in rural areas but also in urban areas.

The following suggestions are made to tackle the problem more effectively:

1. There is a need to have a fresh look at all poverty alleviation programmes and plug the leakages and to reorient the programmes to help increase the real wages and man-days.
2. Public investment in rural infrastructure should be increased. Special attention needs to be paid to augmenting water resources. Irrigation facilities have to be strengthened. Power supply has to be increased and regulated .

3. The government should take necessary legislative as well as administrative measures to check adulteration of agricultural inputs like seeds, fertilizers and pesticides and also regulate their distribution.

4. The farmers should be encouraged and also assisted financially to diversify farm activities like horticulture, floriculture and sericulture etc., credit flow should be increased and regulated so that it is available in time in adequate quantity. Micro-regional planning should be taken up more effectively to cover the entire gamut of economic activities to generate more employment.

5. Rural industrialization should be given priority and agro-based industries particularly those related to agro-processing should be promoted as this would result in reducing the burden on agriculture and also raise the income levels because of value-addition to products.

6. Literacy programmes may be strengthened and made time-bound. Emphasis may be laid more on functional literacy and imparting of productive skills required in the local job-market. This would ensure mobility of labour from one activity to the other depending upon the demand situation.

7. Public investment in health should be increased and made more accessible to the poorer sections Communicable deseases should be controlled. Through effective distribution of medicines. Awareness should be increased through health education involving NGOS. Infant mortality can be reduced.

8. Sanitary conditions may be improved by construction of public lavatories and also giving cent per cent subsidy for construction of latrines in the houses of poorest of the poor. Collection and disposal of garbage may be done effectively through strengthening the mechanism. Drainage facilities may be improved so that malaria, cholera etc., may be controlled. All these measure would help enhance life-expectancy at birth in urban areas

9. Midday meals Schemes may be directed not only towards raising enrolment but also towards supply of nutritious food to the children to prevent underweight and sickness.

10. There is every need to rope in Panchayat Raj institutions people representatives, experts, institutions etc., to identify people below poverty line and provide the asset based assistance and guidance to use them in a proper way. Decentralised.

Participatory approach is essential to secure appropriate results from poverty eradication projects and schemes.

8

"GLOBALIZATION"
A "BOON OR THREAT"
TO GOVERNMENT DEPARTMENTS

M. Venkateswara Rao*

The thought of developed nations, to expand their business in form of diversity and development created a shape for the concept of Globalization. The Multi National Corporations (MNCs), the large companies which buy, produce and sell goods and services all over the world are become the big players in the world economy and they become the factors for Globalization. In the light of Globalization all countries irrespective of developed, developing and un-developed started looming their policies to face the challenges. If any country is to achieve higher growth, then its economic institutions and policies need to undergo major changes. India, after attaining her independence in 1947, initiated bold steps towards speedy/rapid industrialization to promote balanced regional development through PSUs. India is a country of enormous potential. Economic reforms in India still remain an unfinished task. With the right set of economic policies, India can be a major player in the global economy in the next century. Though, the PSUs promoted for a Noble cause, in course of time these are effected to the maximum extent due to low productivity, poor project management skills, over-manning, lack of technological up-gradation, inadequate attention to R & D and low priority to human resource development. If, the reforms implemented

* Legal Dept., The Cotton Corporation of India Ltd., Guntur.

in all areas of the country at full length, no doubt that, the contribution of these departments will grow much more than the present to meet the global situation and thereby "the Globalization will become a Boon for the Department Enterprises in India".

Introduction

Globalization is, in fact, a very old process, in some sense as old as human civilization itself. The Roman empire, the ancient Greeks, the ancient Chinese, the Hindu kings, the Mesopotamians, the Arabs, the Mongols, the British, the Dutch.... the list goes on and on – all rose to prominence via their cultural and economic linkages with outside societies.

The 18th century and 19th centuries saw a dramatic transformation in the political organization of human beings, as traditional feudal, royal, and tribal systems gave way to civil states. This transition continued through the 20th century. Nothing is more closely associated with globalization than 20th century developments in transportation and global communications.

The thought of developed nations, to expand their business in form of diversity and development created a shape for the concept of Globalization. In recent times the UN and the WTO are increasingly called upon to manage world political affairs and world economies. The Multi National Corporations (MNCs), the large companies which buy, produce and sell goods and services all over the world are become the big players in the world economy and they become the factors for Globalization.

Consequent upon these situations, The United Nations made "Globalization" the central theme of its 10th annual Human Development Report in 1999, presenting the concept as both a promise and a threat to the world's six billion people. Marking the symbolic close of a thousand years of history, this was a timely occasion for such a reflection on what the future held for human society and culture. In other words, "Shrinking space, shrinking time and disappearing borders are linking people's lives more deeply, more intensely, more immediately than ever before.

In the light of Globalization all countries irrespective of developed, developing and un-developed started looming their policies to face the challenges, which may arise out of Globalization concept. India, has also introduced many economical reforms to tackle the situation globally.

India is a country rich in natural and human resources. It has an impressive entrepreneurial base, growing capital markets, and an agricultural sector with food self-sufficiency. It has a diversified industrial structure and excellent centers of advanced education. The central objective of economic policy in India should be human development, poverty alleviation, and improvement of the infrastructure. India is a country of enormous potential. With the right set of economic policies, India can be a major player in the global economy in the next century. Economic growth and development of India can alter the fate of a large section of the poorest people in the world. While India has recently made considerable progress in its economic performance since the balance of payments crisis of 1991, economic reforms in India remain an unfinished task. If the country is to achieve higher growth then its economic institutions and policies need to undergo major changes. Although the authorities in India took stabilization measures and structural reforms to transform the country into a more market-oriented economy, the authorities lack well-defined goals, a popular mandate to carry out reforms, and the political strategy for implementing reform measures.

Public Sector Undertaking (PSU)

India, after attaining her independence in 1947, initiated bold steps towards speedy/rapid industrialization to promote balanced regional development. The emergence of public sector was expected to play a pivotal role in the economic and industrial development in the country.

The Government evolved the Industrial Policy Resolutions in 1948 and 1956, which paved the way for bestowing importance to the public sector. All strategic, key, vital, cores, infrastructure industries were reserved for the public sector.

The Government was expected to display initiative in the establishment of public sector enterprises, irrespective of the risk involved or long gestation periods. The public sector enterprises were specifically brought into existence as mere instruments of social welfare and to bring about desired social change in the society. The then need of the hour was to provide social justice through equal employment opportunity to everyone.

After independence, India subscribed to the "Mixed Economy" model with a strong emphasis on central planning and a big role for Government owned public sector enterprises (PSEs) that were established to control the "Commanding Heights" of the economy.

The major objectives of setting up of public enterprises as envisaged originally were broadly:

1. To help in rapid economic growth and industrialization of the country and create necessary infrastructure for economic development
2. To earn a return on investment and thus generate resources for economic development
3. To promote balanced regional development
4. To create employment opportunities
5. To assist the development of small scale and ancillary industries and
6. To promote import substitutions, save and earn foreign exchange for the economy.

Accordingly, India has set up as many as 300 Departmental Enterprises to develop Indian economy in various fields as a possible constructive critique of Government Policy.

Departmental Enterprises

State Owned Enterprises (SOEs) or Public Sector Undertakings or Enterprises (PSUs/PSEs) are government majority held companies, statutory Corporations set up by an act of Parliament and fully owned by government and its parastatals, or even the so called departmental enterprises. In India they constitute an important segment of the economy and account for more than 50% of the gross domestic capital formation. India very strongly went in for SOEs, seeing them as (controlling) the "commanding heights"; as a tool for 'social development', and in industrial transformation itself. The following are the important sectors wherein the Government established Departmental Enterprises:

- Banking & Financial Institutions
- Universities
- Joint Ventures
- Tourism & Hospitality
- Independent Departments
- Co-operatives
- Scientific & Research Institutes
- Indian Missions Abroad
- Independent Offices
- Cultural
- Public Sector Undertakings (PSUs)
- Sports
- International Organizations in India

India is an agricultural state and agricultural sectors in India constitute an important segment of the economy and account for a lion's share of the gross domestic capital formation. The agricultural marketing system in India operates primarily according to the forces of supply and demand in the private sector. Indian Government intervention is limited to protecting the interests of producers and consumers and promoting organized marketing of agricultural commodities. Hence, the Government of India has set up many organizations as Departmental Enterprises for the development of Agricultural Produces, Marketing of the agricultural produces and Infrastructure development. Among them the following are the main Departmental Enterprises set up for the development of agricultural sectors.

Boards

- Tobacco Board
- Tea Board
- Spices Board
- Rubber Board
- Coffee Board

PSUs

- Cotton Corporation of India Ltd.,
- Hindustan Vegetable Oils Corporation Ltd.,
- Food Corporation of India Ltd.,
- National Jute Manufacturing Corporation Ltd.,
- Jute Corporation of India Ltd
- National Textile Corporation Ltd.,
- Spices Trading Corporation Ltd
- Tea Trading Corporation of India Ltd.,

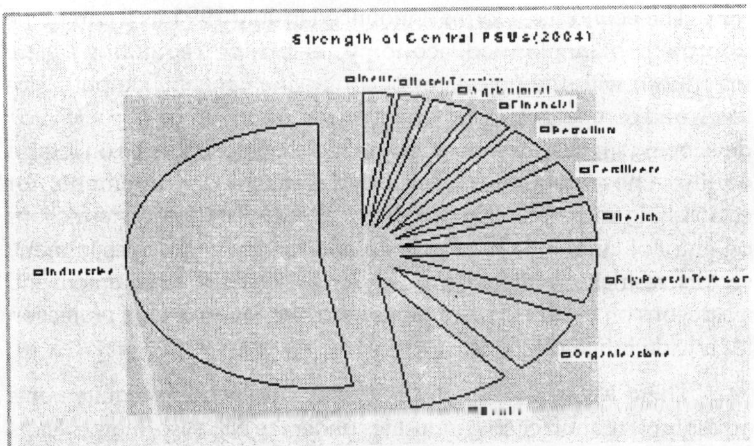

Source: Bureau of Public Enterprises.

Though, the PSUs promoted for a Noble cause, in course of time these are effected to the maximum extent due to low productivity, poor project management skills, over-manning, lack of technological up-gradation, inadequate attention to R & D and low priority to human resource development.

India's fiscal situation is precarious. Higher domestic borrowing finances the state expenditure, which is increasing. However, the rise in state spending is not financing public programs to support social and capital expenditure. Instead the high level of state expenditure is subsidizing loss-making public enterprises and paying the state's wage bill. The public sector losses put a heavy burden on India's fiscal condition. The fiscal crisis of the government is due to the fiscal problem of the public sector. India's large public sector is clearly not advancing the interest of the poor. The loss and the poor performance of public enterprises, public financial institutions, public insurance companies, and unproductive public spending are detrimental to economic growth. The authorities may overcome the problem of poor performance of public enterprise by privatization. To overcome this situation the Union Government initiated many measures to uplift the PSUs. In accordance to the measures the Government of India has introduced Economical Reforms.

Economical Reforms

The economic reforms announced in July 1991 as a part of the approach of a planned economy, extensive regulations were introduced with the objectives of controlling capacity, output, price levels and competition in important sectors, promoting self-sufficiency, developing small-scale industries and reducing dependence on foreign equity. These regulations included licensing requirements for establishing and expanding capacity in almost all industries, restrictions on entry of large Indian companies and foreign companies in many sectors, restrictions on foreign equity levels, licensing requirement and restrictions on import of most goods, and high levels of tariff protection for a wide range of goods.

There was a widespread relaxation of licensing requirements across most manufacturing industries under the NIP. Also, many sectors of the Indian economy were opened up to foreign direct investment, allowing foreign companies to take a majority stake in Indian companies. These changes increased scope for competition to all existing companies (including PSEs) from new domestic and foreign entrants. Over the 1990s, the import duties were decreased and import-licensing restrictions were removed for large range goods, leading to enhanced competition for domestic producers from imported goods.

In this context the Union Government has closed some unproductive Public enterprises and implemented disinvestments policy in some Government Departments.

Disinvestments Policy

As a result of reform measure initiated in 1991-92, the process of disinvestments in India began in 1992 under the aegis of new economic liberalization policy put forward by then Finance Minister, Dr. Man Mohan Singh. As the Government remained with no other alternative except disinvestments to protect the industrial environment and regional imbalances it opted the disinvestments policy as a tool in the hands of Government to improve the functioning and profitability of PSEs and also raise funds to mitigate its fiscal deficits. Disinvestments exercise over the past decade has been plagued by criticisms and controversies and has not achieved desired results for the Government because of political bickering.

The enunciated Government of India's policy on disinvestments as per Economic Survey 2001 is :

- Bring down Government equity in all non-strategic PSUs to 26% or lower, if necessary.
- Restructure and revive potentially viable PSUs.
- Close down PSUs which cannot be revived, and
- Fully protect interests of workers.

In the light of above Economical reforms, Disinvestments Policy and the present Privatization/Liberalization/Globalization scenario the Government has Privatized some Organizations in public sector, some went for mergers and with some Public Sector undertakings the Government of India entered with MOUs and reached the expected heights.

The MOU System

In order to improve the performance of the Public Sector, in 1988-89 the Government introduced the concept of a Memorandum of Understanding (MOU). Under this mutually negotiated agreement, the Government agrees not to interfere in the day-to-day affairs of the PSE and the performance of the PSEs is evaluated based on agreed parameters. The stated objectives of the MOU system were to:

- Introduce a performance improvement system that would simultaneously increase autonomy and accountability in the PSE.

- Remover the Fuzziness in the goals and objectives of the enterprise, and
- Set-up an objective performance evaluation system and introduce a performance incentive system.

Some refinements to the MOU system have been made over the years, especially in the weights in the performance evaluation measure. The emphasis has shifted from operational efficiency parameters to financial performance parameters, and there has increased weighting for MOU performance in the evaluation of the PSE Chief Executives. As a result, we found that, there has been increase in absolute output levels and in efficiency parameters in most of the PSEs.

The non-stop vilification campaign launched by votaries of the so-called "reforms" and the clouds of uncertainty hovering over its head notwithstanding, the public sector has again emerged as the star performer and proved the prophets of doom wrong.

Despite the constant bashing and allegations of inefficiency, mismanagement and un-productivity, the public sector has shown that it is alive to the nation's expectations and committed to play, even in the most adverse circumstances, the role assigned to it.

The public sector workers and managers have achieved the feat despite the general demoralization arising from the fear that there is no certainty as to when a public enterprise will be put on the chopping block to benefit the domestic or international private capital. The former have scaled new highs despite obstacles being created in their way to prevent them from competing with their rivals. An instance of it is the case of the Bharat Heavy Electricals Limited (BHEL).

The latest Public Enterprises Survey 2002-2003, conducted by the Department of Public Enterprises (DPE), reveals that the central public sector enterprises have declared a dividend of Rs 13,735 crore in 2002-03 as against Rs 8,068 crore in the previous fiscal (2001-02), an increase of 70.24 per cent. The dividend payout ratio has gone up to 42.73 per cent as against 31.06 per cent in the previous year.

The contribution to the central exchequer by way of excise and customs duties, corporate tax, interest on central government loans, dividend and other direct taxes has gone up by Rs 19,060 crore —

from Rs 62,866 crore in 2001-02 to Rs 81,926 crore in 2002-03, an increase of 30.32 per cent.

The central enterprises' contribution to the central exchequer during the last three years – from 2000-01 to 2002-03 – comes to a staggering amount of Rs 2,05,829.40 crore. This far exceeded the cumulative central government investment of Rs 1,46,102 crore, by way of equity and loan, as on March 31, 2003. It clearly demonstrates how imprudent it is to disinvest the government's equity in public enterprises in order to bridge the fiscal deficit.

According to the survey, the net profit of public enterprises has increased to Rs 32,141 crore in the year – an increase of 23.72 per cent over Rs 25,978 in the previous year. Return on equity share capital (net profit to paid-up capital + share application) was 28.64 per cent for 2002-03, which means earning per share (EPS) was Rs 2.86 as against the EPS of Rs 2.45 in the previous year. Here, one share has been valued at Rs 10.

The public enterprises' net profit before tax (PBT) rose to Rs 49,571 crore compared to Rs 38,233 crore in 2001-02, registering an increase of 29.65 per cent. Profit before tax to net worth for the year worked out to 19.69 per cent, the survey says. Profit before interest, depreciation and tax has risen to Rs 1,00,918 crore in the year as against Rs 89,550 crore in the previous year, registering a growth of 12.69 per cent. The enterprises as a whole earned a return on investment (profit before interest and tax to capital employed) of 17.45 per cent.

In fact, since the introduction of the liberalization process, the public enterprises have geared themselves to effectively meet the new challenges. This is evident from the survey that says the net profit of these enterprises has registered an increase of 607.17 per cent since 1993-94. The net profit has risen from Rs 4,545 crore a decade back to Rs 32,141 crore now. The return on investment has gone up to 17.45 per cent in 2002-03 as against 16.20 per cent last year and 11.6 per cent in 1993-94.

With the UPA government, in power, having committed to the Common Minimum Programme (CMP) which accords due importance to the public sector, it is hoped that the latter's performance will further improve. As the director general of the SCOPE (Standing Conference of Public Enterprises), the apex body of public undertakings, Dr S M Dewan says, “The phase of policy uncertainty vis-à-vis the public sector enterprises has now been resolved in the best interests of the country.” He added that “the thrust now would be on increasing competition and monitoring monopoly situations that may restrict it.”

“With managerial autonomy and empowerment of boards, the public sector enterprises would be fully geared to face up to global competition and would emerge as strong global players.

Conclusion

Within a short span of time the Government Enterprises proved them selves as potential departments by contributing a lion’s share to the economy of the country. At this early stage and with many limitations these departments achieved these targets. If, the reforms implemented in all areas of the country at full length, no doubt that, the contribution of these departments will grow much more than the present.

Hence, we can certainly say that, “the Globalization became a Boon for the Department Enterprises in India”.

9

VALUE ADDITION FOR SERVICES

A NECESSITY

Ch. H.K.S. Kumar* and **Dr. Talluru Sreenivas****

Value addition or creation or enhancement in value is to be inculcated as a strategy that allows a company offering the service not only to excel in its operations but also serve the customer base and the society at large in an efficient manner. Value addition should be viewed as an inherited attribute rather than an intentionally created one. If this quality is imbibed among the persons and organizations offering services, the level and quality of services obviously will be enhanced substantially. Constant improvement in the quality of service and delivery system is a sine qua non for the betterment of the society and quality of life. The article presents the differences between the characteristics of products and services, and indicates the bases on which categorization can be attempted. Of the nine major categories of services listed, the article goes into depth, and presents details of a few categories of services. These are financial services, education system, legal services, telecommunication services, police services and shipping services. In all these categories of services, considerations and directions for enhancing the value are highlighted.

* Assistant Professor, Dept. of Science & Humanities, Al Habeeb College of Engineering & Technology, Hyderabad.

** Reader, Dept. of Management Sciences, RVR & JC College of Engineering, Guntur.

Introduction

One can distinguish between a product and a service on the basis of their tangible and intangible elements. If the source of a product's core benefit is more tangible than intangible, it should be considered a product; if it is more intangible than tangible, it should be considered as a service[1]. The proportion of 'intangibility" attached to any service brand further complicates its marketing for the service providers. A similar opinion is: "The greater the weight of intangible elements in a marketing entity, the greater will be the divergence from product marketing in priorities and approach"[2].

To date, one can find a considerable amount of literature focusing on broad issues pertaining to a product's competitive advantage. But there is a dearth of literature examining competitive advantage in the context of the service industry. A typical categorization of the services industry could be in three core and eight supplementary categories[3]. This is based on where people, their possessions or the information sought by them is processed by the service. The core services process people, their possessions or information. The core service is surrounded by a variety of supplementary services as follows.

- Consolation and advice while making a decision,
- Taking orders from customers for delivery of the service,
- Courtesy and Hospitality,
- Security and Safety of the customer belongings,
- Special services such as problem solving, handling complaints, suggestions, compliments and restitution in a personalized manner,
- Clarity in billing for recovering amounts from the customers, and
- Ease and mode of payment to facilitate quick and easy payments.

Service is a performance that transacts an experience. It has to be experienced at the same time as it is rendered. In some situations, the person becomes an active participant in the process of delivery of a service, either by extending physical cooperation or by communicating. The employees of the servicing organizations play a vital role in the service delivery. Different service providers can provide the same service in different norms. Time plays a more important role in the delivery of a service than in manufacturing goods, as the service to be rendered cannot be stored for future use. The satisfaction of a customer lies in his experience during the transaction process. Problems with standardization and quality control of services appear because of the co productive nature of services product, the roles played by the employees in service delivery and the diffuculty experienced in measuring the service parameters.

Based on the following five specific questions, one can classify services thus :

(a) What is the nature of service act?

(b) What type of relationships does the service organization have with its customers?

(c) How much room is there for customization and judgement?

(d) What is the nature of demand and supply for the service?

(e) How is the service delivered?

The characteristics of the service industry as revealed from the above discussion are :

- An organization normally sells services directly to the user;
- In carrying out its mission, the service company has several contacts with its users. Each of these contacts provides an opportunity for either good or bad quality service and also gives rise to huge number of individual transactions,
- The service company has to be prepared to provide its service when the user needs it. Customers consider the timely availability of the service to be an element of its quality;
- The service company has to complete its assignments within the period desired by the customer;
- A service cannot be stored or transported, so its benefits are available to customers at the rate at which they are created; and
- Many services include the delivery of intangible products.

The following Table presents a classification of service organizations.

Table for Classification of a Service Organization

S. No.	Service Offered	Organizations
1.	Energy supply	Electric power supply station, Gas supply, Nuclear power plants
2.	Transportation	Air, Sea, Railway and Road transport, Private buses, Taxies, etc.
3.	Communication	Postal services, Telephone, Radio, Television, Telecommunication networks, Newspapers, Satellites, etc.
4.	Health care	Hospitals, Clinics, Ambulance services, cleaning services, etc.
5.	Social services	Fire brigade, Police, CID, Marriage bureaus, Community centers, Religious places, Parks, Parking lots, Job centers.
6.	Financial services	Banks, Building societies;
7.	Repair & Delivery	Repair services; Mail delivery, Courier services, Goods delivery agents
8.	Education	Schools, Colleges, Libraries, Universities, Professional institutes, Research bodies, Testing laboratories
9.	Govt. and Law	Political system, Parliament, Police, Courts, Armed services etc;

NATURE – *Factors of Heterogeneity*

The service sector involves emphasis on human factors. Unlike manufactured goods, a service is perishable and cannot be stored for consumption at a later date. This perishable nature of service requires that the service provider gets the service right the first time, every time, as it is not possible to conduct a final quality check. The lack of tangible attributes in a service makes it difficult for the producer to describe the service and for the consumer to ascertain its likely virtues.

As the consumer cannot see, feel, hear, smell or touch a service before it is purchased, he looks for signs of quality such as reputation, accessibility, communication, etc. The influence of intangibles such as reputation on purchasing decisions is much greater than the influence of tangible product specifications. This places a greater responsibility on the service organization to deliver right, the first time, what it promises. Customers also view the frontline staff and physical facilities, which perform the dual functions of production and marketing, as signs of quality[4]. It is often difficult to reproduce a service consistently and exactly all the time. A number of factors can affect the extent of the heterogeneity of a service[5].

First, the delivery of a service often involves some form of contact between the consumer and service provider. The behavior of a service provider influences the consumer's perception of quality. It is difficult to assure consistency and uniformity of behavior and also standardize and control it. In effect, what the firm intends to deliver may be entirely different from what the consumer receives. *Second*, service operations depend on the consumer articulating his needs or providing information on what he expects. The accuracy of this information and ability of the service provider to interpret it have a significant influence on the customer's perception of service quality. *Third*, the priority and expectations of the consumer may vary each time he uses the service. Moreover, his priority and expectations may change during the delivery of the service. The variability of service from one period to another and from consumer to consumer makes quality assurance and control difficult in a service industry. Service providers have to rely heavily on the competence and ability of their staff to understand the requirements of the consumer and react in an appropriate manner.

Usually, the customer does not prepare a formal specification of the type, amount and quality of service required, nor does enter into a contract with a supplier of the service. In many cases, the customer has little or no choice, as in monopolies such as electricity, gas, telephone and water services, where state laws, regulations and decisions determine the nature of the service received. Every day, millions of people buy services directly from sellers.

Usually, the marketer creates or performs the service at the same time as the full or partial consumption of the service takes place. The high visibility of the conversion process means that it is not possible to hide mistakes or quality shortfalls.

Differences: *between Services & Manufacturing*

Direct transactions with masses of people, large volumes of transactions, large volumes of paper, large amounts of paperwork, relatively small amounts of money per transaction, innumerable occasions for errors, extremely large-scale operations and so-on, create arguably major differences between service and manufacturing industries. These differences have an impact on the approach and substance of quality management.

One of the principal differences between a service business and manufacturing businesses is that manufacturing business operate from a large backlog of orders heavily dependent upon a few key customers, whereas service companies operate from a large customer base with many repeat customers. In the service business, more customers always mean more profit.

Because of this direct relationship, maintenance of the customer base is crucial to the survival and growth of the service business. These characteristics, as outlined above, complicate operations in the service sector as compared to manufacturing as both technical and behavioral aspects, many of which are difficult to measure, play a major role in its management.

The differences between the service sector and the manufacturing sector are outlined in the following Table.

Differences between Service and Manufacturing

Characteristics	*Service System*	*Manufacturing system*
Customer Contact	Limited	Through channel
Machine/Instrument	Moderate Large volume	Small volume of
Control Transactions	of paper work involving low amounts of money	paperwork Involving large amounts of money
Scope for making errors	More tangible	Less tangible
Tangibility	Customer does not prepare any formal specification	Detailed specifications are prepared
Customer		
Customer involvement	Direct, dynamic	Indirect
Focus Indicators	Human factor	Product quality, Quality
of quality	Customer complaints/ declining sales	standard, Specifications
Quality improvement approach	Short-term, related to day-to-day problem solving, less strategically oriented	Long-term, structured, strategic

Service Excellence: *Source of Value Addition/Creation Strategy*

In all industries, some firms are more profitable than others, irrespective of the industry's average profitability. The superior performers have something special that allows them to outperform their competitors. In strategy literature, these unique features of an organization are referred to as sources of competitive advantage. Competitive advantage can result from either value-creating strategy that is distinct from strategies used by current or potential competitors, or from superior execution of the same strategy as used by a competitor.

A firm's sustainability is achieved when skills and resources underline a business competitive advantage and resist duplication by other firms in the industry[6]. There are a number of studies that have explored the various facets under which a business sustains its Value Addition/Creation Strategy. There are four requirements for a skill or a resource to be a source of sustainable Value Addition/Creation Strategy.

- It must be valuable;
- It must be rare among a firm's current and potential competitors;
- It must be perfectly imitating and
- It must not have a strategically equivalent substitute for this resource/skill.

Unique Resources (Assets) and Distinctive Skills (Competence) are the usual two broad sources of Value Addition/Creation Strategy. Day and Wensley (1988)[7] characterize superior skills as the distinctive capabilities of a firm's personnel that set them apart from the personnel of competing firms and superior resources as more tangible requirements for advantage that enable a firm to exercise its capabilities[8]. These sources of Value Addition/Creation Strategy either enable a firm to provide service at a lower cost or lead to differentiation of its service from that of its competitor.

Bharadwaj, Varadarajan and Fathy (1993) have offered some propositions relating to sustainable competitive advantage in the service industry, which need to be validated through research on a particular industry (shipping)[9]. These propositions are based on certain factors related to a service industry-for example, Scale effects, Cost and demand synergies, Product, process & managerial innovations, Brand equity relationships, Spatial preemption, Communication, Corporate culture, Organization expertise and Information technology.

A focus on the methodology of how Value Addition/Creation Strategy works in various different services, like Financial, Educational, Legal, Telecommunications, Police, and Shipping services can be examined in the subsequent discussion.

Financial Services

In a financial company, internal operations are carried out somewhat differently from those in a manufacturing company. Managers and staff are most closely related. Job descriptions are often developed with the real possibility of the staff member becoming a manager as a natural evolution of his career in the company. Thus, in a financial service, the staff perceives itself as much closer to the management team than in the manufacturing sector. Furthermore, in a manufacturing process, the raw materials and final products are accountable for and controlled. This enables total quality control before the customer gains access to the goods.

In a financial service, the degree of intangibility of the service delivered, and intense face-to-face contact between employee and customer during the process itself, enable the organisation to control the quality performance of the service delivered before it is offered to the customer. Thus, it can be said that the primary raw material in a financial service is the customer and the primary resource is the employee.

Another area of difference is the use of statistical techniques on individual products/services. Manufacturing goods can have a statistical tolerance level imposed. However, in a banking service, a money transaction must be absolute. This means that customers will tolerate no mistake. All transactions must be 100 percent accurate. Finally, in a financial service, the customer is normally accurate as both the supplier and the buyer of services. One obvious example of this is a financial transaction in which a customer pays in cheques and credits at one end of the system, and these are processed through to ensure that the customer accounts are approximately credited at the other end.

According to Shashikant, Gururajan and Sethu (1996)[10], quality initiatives in the financial services sector differ from those in the manufacturing sector due to the following reasons.

(a) Monetary benefits have to be accurately delivered; tolerance for errors is zero[11];

(b) The product is intangible and, therefore, perceptions matter a great deal;

(c) Financial products are information sensitive and valued & priced on a continuous basis;

(d) Certain levels of service are regulated to protect investor interest, and

(e) The service centers on a series of processes in which investor participation is direct.

Financial companies concentrate on the improvement of the multiple features of service products. In the case of financial products such as equity, bonds and other financial papers, the design features concentrate on the packaging of risk, return and liquidity. In most cases, service delivery is restricted to maintenance of accurate investor records to meet statutory obligations. The fine-tuning of products on the basis of the service expectations of customers has largely escaped attention thus far. Kotler (1995) listed the value addition that have to occur in the financial services sector through quality programs[12].

He suggested the following eight steps to establish the value addition strategy:

1. Establishing a sense of urgency; examining the market and competitive realities; identifying and discussing potential crises or major opportunities;
2. Forming a powerful guiding coalition;
3. Creating a vision to help direct the change effort;
4. Communicating the vision;
5. Empowering others to act on the vision;
6. Planning and creating short-term wins;
7. Consolidating improvements and producing still more change, and
8. Institutionalizing new approaches.

Education System: *Deming's 14 Points as Applied to Education*

These points, adapted from Deming, to reflect the language of educational entities provide scope for dynamic value creation, are as follows.

1. Create consistency of purpose toward improvement of students and services. Aim to create best-quality students, capable of improving all forms of processes and entering meaningful positions in society;
2. Adopt the new philosophy. Educational managements must awaken to challenge, learn their responsibilities and take on leadership for change;
3. Work to abolish grading and the harmful effects of rating people. Cease dependence on testing to achieve quality. Eliminate the need for inspections on a mass basis (standardized achievement tests, minimum graduation exams, and so on) by providing learning experiences that create quality performance;
4. Work with the educational institutions from which the students come. Minimize the total cost of education by improving the relationship with student sources and helping to improve the quality of students coming into the system. A single source of students coming into a system is an opportunity to build long term relationships of loyalty and trust for the benefit of the students;
5. Improve, constantly and forever, the system of student learning and service, to improve quality and productivity;
6. Institute education and training on the job for students, teachers classified staff and administrators;
7. Adopt and institute leadership. The aim of supervision should be to help people use machines, gadgets and materials to do a better job. Technology frees leaders to lead;
8. Drive out fear so that everyone can work effectively for the school system. Create an environment that encourages people to speak freely;

9. Break down barriers between departments. People in teaching, special education, accounting, food service, administration, curriculum development and research and so on must work as a team. Develop strategies for increasing the cooperation among groups and individual people.
10. Eliminate slogans, exhortations and targets for teachers and students that ask for perfect performance and new levels of productivity. Exhortations create adversarial relationships. The bulk of the causes of low quality and low productivity belongs to the system and thus lies beyond the control of teachers and students;
11. Eliminate work standards (quotas) on teachers and students (for example, 'raise test scores by 10 percent'' or 'lower dropout rates by 15 percent"). Substitute leadership;
12. Remove barriers that rob students, teachers and management (principals, superintendents, and central office support staff) of their right to pride and joy of workmanship. This means, *inter alia*, abolition of the annual or merit rating and of management by objective. The responsibility of all educational managers must be changed from quantity to quality.
13. Institute a vigorous program of education and self-improvement for everyone.
14. Put everybody in the school community to work to accomplish the transformation.

Legal Services :

Legal service providers need to know not only how to produce high quality products, but also how to provide what clients perceive to be high valued legal services. At present law schools do not provide education from that point of view. The skills and knowledge that are the basis for a rewarding law practice, such as good listening skills, the ability to relate to, communicate with and negotiate on behalf of the client, are seldom taught. Blodgett (1988) presented a study conducted by S. Welch identifying the necessary requirements in the legal process[13]. Value can be implanted into the legal process by the following the steps given:

1. Defining the dynamics of a professional law practice;
2. Flow charting the steps of practitioner-client interaction, beginning with client identification and ending with the firm providing the service;
3. Identifying the most important practitioner performance issues through a group of current and prospective clients;
4. Using these surveys to estimate current client satisfaction with each area of performance;
5. Using statistics to determine a prioritized list of practitioner performance requirements and indicators that relate to each area of performance;
6. Using the prioritized list of clients' requirements as goals and standards for practice improvement, and
7. Using current satisfaction indicators as benchmarks for measuring practice improvement efforts.

Some of the important considerations for enhancing value in the legal process are :

- Considering relationships with the clients as long-term partnerships;
- Showing concern for clients as people, not cases;
- Listening to clients proactively;
- Visiting the clients' offices to meet them on their own turf and observe their operations;
- Talking to clients about their long-term business plans and strategies;
- Writing personal letters to clients after the conclusion of a case to thank them for the confidence they have shown in the legal firm;
- Proactively determining the clients' needs and making sure they are aware of the services provided, and
- Making clients aware of the value of the legal firm's expertise.

Clients look for the following inputs from legal firm.

- Prompt, personal response to inquiries;
- Self-discipline and organization;
- Creative thinking and problem solving abilities;
- Careful listening and skillful interpersonal communications;
- Empathy and genuine concern for the client, and
- A successful track record in the client's area of concern.

Clients always appreciate quick responsiveness from a legal firm. If lawyers take the initiative to meet the requirements of their clients and follow the guidelines given above, the value of legal services will certainly be enhanced.

Telecommunication Services

The department of telecommunications is a service organization that is subscriber-oriented. The system in the telecom sector includes the total environment that affects its performance, such as the internal plant and the external plant. It also includes the behavior of the staff that interacts with the subscribers. Detailed knowledge of the system includes understanding of customer requirements, understanding of processes (flow of work) that the business uses to provide those products and services keeping in view its capabilities, plus an understanding of how the business relates to the community.

Statistical knowledge is required to understand variations in output, which, in turn, indicate what type of action must be taken and whether the action has been effective. Knowledge of psychology is also required, as people are a fundamental component of the processes. From the subscriber's point of view, the value creation of telecom services may be seen to include:

- Availability;
- Connection Establishment;
- Connection Retention;
- Connection Quality, and
- Billing Integrity.

There are 15 parameters, which include the development of the performance of the system, subscriber's information and common services. Each of these parameters has been given a certain weightage, which are taken into account for calculating the total score of a system. This weightage has been worked out taking into account the present status of the network and final goal to be achieved to get the maximum performance out of the system. The performance parameters include the following main points.

- Availability 10 points;
- Accessibility 15 points;
- Reliability 30 points
- Integrity 5 points; and
- Total 60 points.

Customer satisfaction is measured by asking a set of questions to a sample of subscribers. The sample chosen depends on the population of the system. Parameters chosen for the measurement of subscriber satisfaction are

- National Subscriber Dialing Service;
- Manual Truck Service;
- Operator Assisted Services, and
- Customer Services.

The consolidated score for each telecom district is calculated twice a year. At present, this system of evaluation is being carried out in about 60 telecom districts in the country and the statistics indicate that there has been improvement in the system.

Police Services

The police department is extremely manpower-intensive. In recent times, police intervention has increased manifold and there is continuous demand for increase in police personnel by police managers. Changes in moral values, loosening of formal controls, disruption of joint families, exposure and interaction with diverse cultures, increased aspirations and general defiance of set patterns have all the law and order machinery under severe pressure. However, the basic functioning of the police in India has remained the same and not changed from the set pattern laid out in the Indian Police Act, 1858.

A police station cannot be compared with a production unit as its output and activities cannot be quantified. A sense of safety or security is a feeling. Similarly, the detection of a crime depends on many parameters, none of which can be classified. The following parameters are found to be essential for a police force that is efficient, sensitive and impartial, but conforms to the law and also meets the expectations of the people.

1. Number of Agitations/Dharnas (non-political) per month;
2. Initial investigation response time (non-raid-oriented cases);
3. Arrest index for heinous cases or non-heinous cases (non-raid-oriented cases and cases where the accused persons are known);
4. Manpower utilization index in agitations, police arrangements for different kinds of activities;
5. Summons/warrants served in a month per person (addresses are known and addresses changed separately);
6. Ratio of petitions received directly at the police station (in person and by other modes) to those received/referred from higher offices over a period of a month;
7. Number of complaints received against police personnel per month;
8. Satisfaction ratio among persons who approached the police station (to be calculated through sampling and questionnaires);
9. Prevention index for property offenses for both day and night, and
10. Prevention index for other kinds of offenses.

Shipping Services

The transportation sector is the lifeline of all global economies. It includes both passenger and cargo transportation. The transportation sector includes all such agencies as railroads, airlines, shipping, etc, used by people for the physical movement of resources. The criteria used in enhancing the value of transportation services are:

- Effectiveness of the agent in selling customer protection;
- Effectiveness in estimating transportation charges;
- Efficiency of packing;
- Efficiency of storage;
- Accuracy of a paper work, and
- Efficiency of the transportation mode.

The value addition or creation of the transportation service can be assessed by its

- Information reporting system;
- Surveillance of the process and rating programs, and
- Customer suggestions and rating programs.

In the shipping industry, the freight rate (price), rather than service, decides the fate of the company. To capture market share, companies are announcing new innovative services backed by aggressive pricing strategies. A business strategy based on competitive pricing leads to a cascading effect on the freight rate, whipping out small time players in the process and cutting profit margins for exiting companies to a bare minimum. Shipping lines have to switch business strategies from those which make technological innovations and consider internal operation issues to those dictated by profits, people, business design and external customer service considerations.

All the services offered by different shipping lines and agencies exhibit a mix of tangible and intangible elements. The customer has the ultimate say in choosing a shipping line's service depending upon the mix of service attributes it offers. Jha (2000) identified these services attributes through an exploratory survey carried out in Mumbai, which encompassed all the constituent of the shipping industry-shippers, shipping agencies and shipping lines.[11] The respondents were asked to list down the various service attributes they thought were important and should be offered by a shipping line. These are what they listed :

1. Transit Time;
2. Carting Facility;
3. Frequency of Sailing;

4. Freight Rates;
5. Port Calls;
6. Post-Shipment Container Tracking;
7. Special Equipment Availability;
8. Error Free Documentation;
9. Reliability;
10. Quick Response
11. Courtesy;
12. Crisis Recovery, and
13. Employee Competence.

These attributes were clubbed according to their tangible and intangible features. The respondents were then asked to rate the attributes in terms of their importance in choosing a shipping line. Freight rate, transit time and frequency of sailing were identified as the most important service attributes. Among the intangible parameters, reliability figured at the top, followed by quick response, employee competence and courtesy and crisis recovery.

1. Courtesy of Customer Service Representatives;
2. Ability and speed of Customer Service Representatives to solve problems;
3. Ease of Accessibility;
4. Promptness in Executing Work;
5. Quality of Food, and
6. Quality of Arrangements.

The steps initiated by the company to stimulate the employees to higher levels of participation and productivity are

- Decisions based on the basis of both employee and external customer inputs;
- Compensating customers for service failures;
- Formation of an employee task force for evaluation of service guarantees;

- Commitment to employee participation;
- Communication campaign focused on all stakeholders;
- Attention to the educational and training needs of employees;
- Formation of an independent quality group of non-management employees, and
- Internal and external customer satisfaction surveys.

The company has to write credo that all services provided by it will completely satisfy customer expectations. These could include

- Providing management reports with specific recommendations to improve a customer's on-site operations on time;
- Provide qualified, training personnel, with a specific clause in the agreement to make prompt reparations. If their performance falls below the agreed-upon performance expectations;
- Promptly correct all work that does meet the customer's requirements, at no extra cost;
- Set performance standards based on specific customer requirements, and
- Effective customer participation can increase the likelihood that the benefits the customer seeks are actually attained. A service in which customer participation is high requires that the customer perform his role effectively to get the desired output. For example, in education, active participation by students, as opposed to passive listening, increases learning significantly. Similarly in healthcare, the patients' compliance to prescribed medication, changed diet, etc, is critical for health improvement.

Conclusion

Value Addition or Creation or Enhancement is to be inculcated as a strategy that allows the company to not only excel in its operations but also as it can serve the customer-based society in most efficient manner, ultimately leads to an environment where Value Creation is viewed as an inherited activity but not an intentionally created one. If this feat is achieved, probably all the practitioners around the globe would be starting their contribution to develop another strategy, which would still improvise the system and so on.

REFERENCES

1. Berry, L.L., and Parasuraman.A., *Marketing Services – Competing Through Quality*, New York, Free Press, 1991
2. Bharadwaj, S.G., Varadarajan, R.P., & Fathy, J., *Sustainable Competitive Advantage in Service Industries: A Conceptual Model and Research Propositions, Journal of Marketing,* Vol. 57, 1993
3. Lovelock, Christopher H., *Product Plus: How Product + Service = Competitive Advantage*, New York, McGraw Hill, 1994
4. Haywood-Farmer,J., *A Conceptual Model of Service Quality, International Journal of Operations & Production Research*, Vol.8. No. 6, 1988
5. Ghobadian, A., Speller, S., and Jones, M., *Service Quality Concepts & Models, International Journal Of Quality and Reliability Management,* Vol.11, No. 9 , 1994, pp.43-46
6. Barney, J., Firm *Resources and Sustained Competitive Advantage, Journal of Management*, Vol.17, 1991, pp.99-120.
7. Day, G.S., and Wensley, R., *Assessing Advantage: A Framework for Diagnosing Competitive Superiority, Journal of Marketing*, Vol.52, 1988, pp.1-20.
8. Bharadwaj, S.G., Varadarajan, R.P., & Fathy, J., *Sustainable Competitive Advantage in Service Industries: A Conceptual Model And Research Propositions, Journal of Marketing*, Vol. 57, 1993
9. Bharadwaj, S.G., Varadarajan, R.P., & Fathy, J., *Sustainable Competitive Advantage in Service Industries: A Conceptual Model And Research Propositions, Journal of Marketing*, Vol. 57, 1993
10. Shashikant, U., Gururajan, R., & Sethu, G., *Quality Challenges In A Dynamic Context: Experiences from The Indian Financial Service Industry, WCTQ*, 1996.
11. Kotler, P., "*Marketing Management Analysis, Planning and Control*", Prentice-Hall, New Delhi, 1995
12. Blodgett, N., *Lawyers Find a Partner in Quality, Quality Progress*, May 1988, pp.83-90.
13. Jha, S.K., *Service Excellence for Shipping Industry: An Integrated Approach*, proceedings of 10th World Congress on Total Quality held at Mumbai, 2000, pp. 158-171.

10

FOREIGN INSTITUTIONAL INVESTORS (FIIS) PORTFOLIO INVESTMENT TRENDS IN INDIAN CAPITAL MARKET

Dr. Rajesh C Jampala*

The paper explains various aspects of diversification of capital markets by highlighting the advantages of international investing. In portfolio diversification, the basic premise is the broader the diversification, the more stable the returns, and the more diffused will be the risks. The core coverage of the paper is analysis of the major trends of foreign institutional investors (FIIs) portfolio investments in the Indian capital market from 1970, with more details from 1990. Considering the growth rate of the Indian economy, market capitalisation, and liquidity of stock markets; relative share of the foreign portfolio flows towards India remains marginal [3.0 per cent of Gross Domestic Product (GDP), and 25.4 per cent of merchandise exports in 2003-04].

Capital Flows to Developing Countries

The twentieth century has seen massive cross-border flows of capital. The initial thrust to cross-border flows of equity investment came from the desire on the part of institutional investors to diversify their portfolios globally in search of both higher return and risk reduction. Financial deregulation and elimination of exchange controls

* Reader, PG Dept. of Business Administration, PB Siddhartha College, Vijayawada - 10.

in a number of developed countries permitted large institutional investors to increase their exposure to foreign equities.

One of the major themes of capital market theory concerns the merits of diversification. In an efficient capital market, sensible investment strategies will include holdings of many different assets. The advantages of international investing are several. For one thing, an international focus offers more opportunities. Over two-thirds of world's stock market capitalization is in non-US companies, and this fraction is increasing over time. The expanded universe of securities available internationally suggests that possibility of achieving a better risk-return trade-off than by investing solely in one country securities. This follows the basic rule of portfolio diversification. The broader the diversification, the more stable the returns, and the more diffused will be the risks. As the barriers to international capital flows come down, and improved communications and data processing technology provide low-cost information about foreign securities, investors are starting to realize the enormous potential in international investing. Table 1 presents data regarding net capital flows to developing countries from 1970 to 2003.

Table-1: Net Capital Flows to Developing Countries

Year	*Net capital flows US $ billion*
1970	11.3
1980	82.8
1990	100.8
1995	237.2
1996	281.6
1997	324.3
1998	266.5
1999	236.7
2000	193.7
2001	206.1
2002	190.6
2003	228.2

Source: *nse news*, National Stock Exchange of India Limited, May 2004.

Capital can flow to a developing country in one or more of three ways. Developed country investors can directly purchase shares in the stock market of a developing country. Or companies from developing countries can issue shares or depository receipts in the stock markets of developed countries. Finally, indirect purchases can be made through a mutual fund which may be a specific country fund or a multi country regional fund. Table 2 gives the composition of capital flows to developing countries.

Table-2: Composition of Capital Flows to Developing Countries

(US $ billion)

Year	*FDI Flows*	*Portfolio Flows*	*Debt flows*
1970	2.2	0.0	6.9
1980	4.4	0.0	65.2
1990	24.5	3.7	43.4
1995	95.5	32.1	77.0
1996	119.0	45.88	87.6
1997	171.1	22.6	105.3
1998	175.6	6.6	57.6
1999	181.7	12.6	13.8
2000	162.2	12.6	-9.8
2001	175.1	4.4	-1.2
2002	147.1	4.9	7.3
2003	135.2	14.3	44.3

Source: World Bank, Global Development Finance, Washington D.C.

The composition of capital flows to emerging market economies have gone through significant changes over time. Bank loans were the major component of capital flows in 1970s. The FDI flows (Foreign Direct Investment Flows) which started picking up in early 1980s gained real momentum between 1987 and 1997. They have been showing an upward trend over years, though decline was noticed periodically. The portfolio flows, which were non-existent till 1980s, have become a major component of international capital flows from the early 1990s, and have come down from 1998. Debt flows moved upwards up to 1997, and thereafter declined substantially. In 2003, increase was recorded.

Globalization has forced many developing countries to open their economies and implement economic reforms. As a part of this process, Indian government implemented financial reforms, and took bold steps to integrate our financial markets with global markets. These reforms include deregulation of interest rates, reducing taxes imposed on foreign investors, allowing foreign portfolio investment, enhancing foreign direct investment limits in many sectors, allowing Indian companies to raise GDRs and ADRs in international financial markets, setting up of financial infrastructural facilities like depositories, introducing derivative products in capital markets, reducing foreign currency controls, introduction of commodities trading, electronification of financial markets, etc.

The purpose of this article is to track the major trends of FIIs (Foreign Institutional Investors) portfolio investments in the Indian capital market.

International Capital Flows to India

Since the introduction of economic reforms, India has become one of the most favoured destinations of the international capital flows. The Industrial Policy 1991 permitted foreign companies to have majority control in a large number of industries, and the trend is further relaxation in the limits. In 1992, the Government of India allowed Foreign Portfolio Investment (FPI) by Foreign Institutional Investors (FIIs). As mentioned earlier, the reforms initiated by Government of India brought about a radical transformation in the quantum and nature of capital flows to India. The net capital flows were averaging around US $ 4 billion during the 1980s increased to an average of around US 49 billion during 1993-2000. As it can be seen from Table 3, the composition of capital flows has also gone through a transformation over time in line with the global trends.

Table-3: Composition of Capital Inflows to India

Year	*Total Net Capital inflows (US $ billion)*	*Non-debt creating inflows as a per cent of total flows*	*FDI flows as a per cent of total flows*	*Portfolio flows as a per cent of total flows*	*Debt-creating flows as a per cent of total flows*
1990-91	7.1	1.5	1.4	0.1	83.3
1995-96	4.1	117.5	52.4	65.1	57.7
1996-97	12.0	51.3	23.7	27.6	61.7
1997-98	9.8	54.8	36.2	18.6	52.4
1998-99	8.4	28.6	29.4	-0.8	54.4
1999-00	10.4	49.7	20.7	29.0	23.1
2000-01	10.0	67.8	40.2	27.6	59.4
2001-02	10.6	77.1	58.0	19.1	9.2
2002-03	12.1	46.6	38.5	8.1	-10.7
2003-04	22.1	72.5	21.1	51.4	1.4

Source: Reserve Bank of India(2004), Annual Report 2003-04, Mumbai, 306.

The non-debt capital flows have slowly become a major component of total net capital flows replacing debt-creating capital flows, thereby reducing the incidental interest burden on the economy.

Foreign Portfolio Investment Flows to India

Portfolio investments broadly consist of investments in American Depository Receipts (ADRs)/Global Depository Receipts (GDRs), investments by offshore funds and investments by FIIs. In line with, the recommendations of Narasimham committee report on financial system, India has gradually opened its capital market for direct participation by FIIs such as pension funds, mutual funds, investment trusts, asset management companies, nominee companies, and incorporated institutional portfolio managers or their power of attorney holders. These investors are allowed to invest in all securities traded on primary and secondary markets including the equity and other securities/instruments of companies listed/to be listed on the stock exchanges in India. Table 4 gives the source-specific foreign portfolio investment in India during the period 1992-93 to 2002-03.

Table-4: Composition of Foreign Portfolio Investment in India

(US $ million)

Year	*GDRs/ADRs**	*FII investment@*	*Offshore Funds*	*Total*
1992-93	240	1	3	244
1993-94	1520	1665	382	3567
1994-95	2082	1503	239	3824
1995-96	683	2009	56	2748
1996-97	1366	1926	20	3312
1997-98	645	979	204	1828
1998-99	270	-390	59	-61
1999-00	768	2135	123	3026
2000-01	831	1847	82	2760
2001-02	477	1505	39	2021
2002-03	600	377	2	979
2003-04(P)	459	10,918	–	11,377

(P) provisional

* represents the amount raised by Indian corporates through GDRs and ADRs

@ represents fresh inflows of funds by FIIs

Source: Reserve Bank of India (2004), Annual Report 2003-04, and earlier issues, Mumbai.

The net investment flows by FIIs have always been positive every year from the year of their entry except in the year 1998-99. This is because of sanctions imposed by US and other countries due to testing of nuclear bombs. Table 5 presents the trends in FII investment in India. The rise in FIIs inflows into the country coincides with rise in the number of FIIs registered with SEBI. The total number of registered FIIs is 637 at the end of December 2004, and net FII Investment in 2003-04 is $ 9,949, the highest recorded so far. Table 6 presents the number of FIIs registered with SEBI.

Table-5: Trends in FII Investment

Year	Gross Purchases (Rs. million)	Gross Sales (Rs. million)	Net investment (Rs. million)	Net investment (US $ million)	Cumulative net investment (US $ million)
1993-94	55925	4663	51262	1634	1638
1994-95	76310	28348	47963	1528	3167
1995-96	96935	27517	69420	2036	5202
1996-97	155539	69794	85745	2432	7634
1997-98	186947	127372	59575	1649	9284
1998-99	161150	176994	-15844	-386	8898
1999-00	568555	467335	101219	2339	11237
2000-01	740506	641164	99340	2160	13396
2001-02	499200	411650	87552	1846	15242
2002-03	470601	443710	26889	562	15804
2003-04	1448575	990940	457645	9949	25754

* Net investment in US $ million at monthly exchange rate.

Source: *SEBI Bulletin*, April 2004.

Table-6: FIIs Registered with SEBI

As on	No. of FIIs
31 December 2004	637
31 December 2003	517
31 December 2002	489
31 December 2001	482
31 December 2000	556

Source: *SEBI Bulletin*, December 2004.

The total number of registered FIIs are from many countries with USA accounting for the largest share at 42 per cent, followed by UK and Luxemburg at 19 and 7 per cent respectively. Table 7 gives country-wise break up of SEBI-registered FIIs in India.

Table-7: Country-wise Share of SEBI Registered FIIs

(in per cent)

Country	*FIIs*
USA	42
UK	19
Luxemburg	7
Hong Kong	4
Singapore	4
Canada	3
Mauritius	3
Australia	2
Switzerland	2
Others	14

Source: *SEBI Bulletin* December 2004.

The importance of FIIs' role in Indian capital market is better understood by looking at the assets under their custody as compared to other institutions and participants. As of November 2004, the total assets held by the FIIs stood at Rs.198243 crore as compared to Rs.91084 crore with mutual funds, and Rs.42855 crore with financial institutions including banks. Table 8 gives the assets under custody of custodians for the latest three financial years.

Table 8: Assets Under the Custody of Custodians

(Rs. crore)

	2001-02	*2002-03*	*2003-04*	*November 2004*
FIIs	61753	56139	159397	198243
Financial Institutions	110824	113154	1551655	19389
Mutual Funds	32570	41368	90338	91084
NRIs	185	263	563	745
OCBs	1285	1136	1330	1523
Brokers	0	0	35	35
Corporates	13311	13498	20156	22070
Banks	17798	20814	21188	23466
Foreign Depositories	17297	15890	34636	39115
Others	15343	16593	30717	37552
Total	**31231**	**32552**	**497260**	**578222**

Source: SEBI Bulletin December 2004.

The data clearly shows that there is growing importance of FIIs, and their investment is more than the position of mutual funds in Indian equity markets. However, considering the size of the equity market capitalization of India which stood at US $310 billion in March 2004 which is 49 per cent of GDP, the total foreign investment which includes the Foreign Direct Investment and Foreign Portfolio Investment is only 3 per cent of GDP, and 25.5 per cent of merchandise exports (Table 9) during 2003-04.

Table-9: Foreign Investment as per cent of GDP and Exports

Year	*Foreign Investment/ GDP (%)*	*Foreign Investment/ Exports (%)*
1990-91	0.0	0.6
1999-00	1.2	13.8
2000-01	1.5	15.1
2001-02	1.7	18.1
2002-03	1.1	10.7
2003-04	3.0	25.5

Source: Reserve Bank of India (2004), Annual Report 2003-04, Mumbai, 94.

Net investment by FIIs rebounded from depressed levels in the preceding year to record an unprecedented surge during 2003-04. Portfolio flows were recycled to India following readjustments of global portfolios of institutional investors, triggered by robust improvement in macro economic fundamentals, financial performance of the corporate sector, and the buoyant and attractive valuations in the Indian equity markets relative to other emerging market economies (EMEs) in Asia.

In brief, reform in the external sector was meshed with reform in other related sectors, and reform within the external sector itself. Capital flows were managed keeping in view the needs of efficiency and stability in the economy.

Conclusion

A stream of attractive and high-profile public issues, robust economic growth, competitive valuations of well-managed and successful companies, the general resilience of the domestic economy to global economic and financial cycles, strengthening of regulatory framework, and establishment of other financial infrastructural facilities made India one of the attractive destinations for FIIs in emerging markets. However, considering the growth rate of the Indian economy, market capitalization, and liquidity of the stock markets; relative share of the foreign portfolio flows towards India remains marginal.

REFERENCES

1. Batra Amita, 2003, *The Dynamics of Foreign Portfolio Inflows and Equity Returns in India, ICRIER (Indian Council for Research on International Economic Relations) Working Paper 109.*
2. *Reserve Bank of India (2004), Annual Report 2003-04*, and earlier issues, Mumbai.
3. ______ (2004), *Report on Currency and Finance 2003-04*, and earlier issues, Mumbai.
4. *World Bank, Global Development Finance*, various issues.
5. SEBI website.
6. *nse news*, National Stock exchange of India Limited.

SECTION–II
GENDER DISPARITIES

11

GENDER AND THE DEVELOPMENT DEBATE

Prof. V. Bhavani*

The article brings out the areas where gender equality between men and women needs to be debated, and equal rights provided for. To talk of development without specific focus on women is seen as wasteful and self-defeating. In all issues and strategies for development, the gender dimension, i.e., what are its effects on men and women as social categories, and how far they facilitate more just and human relationships, must be analysed before policies are finalised. Specific reference is made to overall strategies to integrate women more effectively into development. Approaches relate to welfare, anti-poverty, and equity/equality. Empowerment - economic, political and social – is an important direction to strengthen the role of women. Through constitutional provisions, and social approaches, integration needs to be brought about to safeguard the role of women, and enhance their contribution to the economic well being of the society and the nation.

Introduction

In the 1950s and 1960s the growth oriented approach showed only minimal concern for the human dimension of development throughout the world as well as in India. In 1970 for the first time women's issues and development were conceptually linked. The need

* Dept. of Political Science and Public Administration, Acharya Nagarjuna University, Nagarjuna Nagar, Guntur.

for integration of women into the development process was realized world-wide since isolating half of the population from development framework would only lead to failure of all public policies. Development projects which targeted the poorest households providing access to productive and consumption resources ignored the possibility of unequal relations between men and women within the households. Men frequently were the primary beneficiaries of the development assistance and as a result women, particularly of the poorer groups found their access and control over resources actually weakened. Planners and Project Officials under-estimated women's economic and social contributions to productive and reproductive activities. Many research studies like those of Esther Boserup concluded that the majority of women's work was not recognized as an integral part of national wealth and they were being ignored by governments, planners and development theorists alike. This led to demands to take women into account, to recognize and value their existing contributions and to integrate them into the mainstream of development. The International Women's Year conference in 1975 marked the beginning of the UN Decade for women.

Since then, at national and international for a, women's role in the economic process has been a major component of all development debates.

The Debate

Central to the debate on women is the view that the major challenge for development, whether Economic, Political or Social is to recognize and make efficient use of the scarce human resources. Young and adult women, as substantial contributers to family's real income as well as bearers and rearers of children, constitute a distinctive human resource. Thus to talk of development without specific focus on women is seen as wasteful and self-defeating. Overall strategies to integrate women more effectively into development include :

1. Education, especially vocational/technical training which is seen as an essential prerequisite for women to be able to move into the development process.
2. Moving women into decision-making positions so as to oversee the allocation of funds and resources to women's projects and further hasten the integration process.

3. Making sufficient opportunities available to women to enable them to move into the market economy and thereby ensure income, access to economic and social resources and a sense of self-confidence and participation in the development process.

Within this women's development debate there are a number of approaches which stem from different economic and political perceptions of development itself. The most prominent of these are:

(a) Welfare Approach

This approach lays stress upon the importance of women's role as wives and mothers and care-takers of family welfare. The aim of this approach is to upgrade women's traditional skills (like cooking, child-care, home management etc.). This would provide essential water and sanitation services, nutritional and medical advice as well as small-scale income generating projects at home like tailoring, food-processing or handicrafts.

(b) Anti-poverty Approach

This approach recognizes the social loses due to women's absolute and relative poverty, inferior health, education and economic status. Projects aim to mobilize poor women in income-generating schemes (like our DWACRA groups) often on a Co-operative basis as well as to provide financial, technical and marketing assistance. This is expected to encourage women to take up self-employment or income earning activities. Cooperation amongst poor women is emphasized on the principle that only by organizing women together will they be able to gain recognition and acquire a place in the market economy.

(c) Equity/Equality Aproach

Central to this approach is the recognition of the important productive contribution of women not merely as actual or potential wives/mothers but as individual contributors to economic growth and development. Policy measures in this direction aim to increase opportunities to women in education, employment and also in political representation. The ultimate aim of any national policy should be to provide women their rightful place and equal position in the nation.

Interventionist measures on adhoc basis like income generating, educational or nutritional projects, while offering short term remedies to exploited women do not question the roots of discrimination, displacement and marginalization of women in society. The central argument is the structuralist view that existing economic and political relations are unlikely to enable growth in all developing countries. The argument is that the direction of development towards ecological degradation, political factionalism and violence is in itself distroted and biased against several groups including women. Full transformation of existing social and economic structures is needed before output and productivity can increase whether in industry or agriculture. Unless there is a better distribution of the benefits of growth, social groups will not prosper socially, culturally and materially. Without a better understanding of how both 'patriarchy' and economic systems promote oppression of men and women, there will be no effective means of bringing about a new order and social justice.

The feminists approach argues that true development cannot happen when the needs, talents and potentialities of half of the world's population are seen as secondary and marginal. Feminists strongly believe that gender relations determine the wider economic, social and political outcomes. The ideological bases of concepts and methodologies used in present development debates have to be anaysed from a gender perspective to bring out whether traditional prejudices are garbed in modern terminologies. Gender relations are those socially constituted relations between men and women which are shaped and sanctioned by norms and values held by members of a society. Central to these relations are culturally specific notions of masculinity and femininity of the sexs' different capacities, attitudes and predispositions. Gender thus involves sets of ideas and behaviours as to what is appropriate for men and women.

Empowerment

A consensus has been reached among both liberal and radical arguments on women's question in the advocacy of Empowerment. Empowerment has been defined as a process of gaining control over the self and the resources which determine power. It is a process which challenges injustice and attempts to transform the structures, systems and institutions. Why should women be empowered? First and foremost, they are full-fledged human beings as members of their families, communities, nations and the world at large. They are not a separate human sector but equal partners in development alongwith the men-folk. Their concerns, perspectives and visions are necessary on every issue concerning the nation-whether it is nulcerisation, environment, human rights or economic liberalization. All human issues are also women's issues.

That women are subordinated and their potentialities have been disused or misused is a universally accepted fact. Yet, when a legal and constitutional action is resorted to in order to empower them, it instigates controversies. Even within the women's movement in India, there is a divide on the issue of empowerment through reservations. An eminent activist Ela Bhatt confessed that she has her own doubts about the efficacy of reservation policies. According to her, collective and cooperative strength, a unified vision and struggle within the political parties for equal share with men are better alternatives than political reservations. On the otherhand, another academic-cum-activist, devaki Jain argues that reservation was necessary to "break the hard rock of patriarchy". She argued that women's demand for space in political structures was based on two pillars-their representation as a social category and the contribution of feminist leadership to the quality of governance and management of the state. The 73rd and 74th enactments brought about in early 90s provided for one-third representation for women in systems of local governance, both urban and rural. However, the attempts to bring them into Parliament and State Assemblies initiated first by 85th Constitutional Amendment Bill are systematically being obstructed for want of consensus among various political groups. It is often criticized that in local government bodies they act merely as proxies to their male family members and remain on the fringes. But the very visibilization of women on representative bodies is a democratic move long-delayed. It is too short a period to assess the public performance and abilities of a social group which has long been deprived of education, public exposure and a sense of self-confidence.

If we turn towards the economic sector, in the early 90s hopes were expressed by many that there will be several areas of skill development both for men and women with the onset of liberalization. Several agencies besides the state are expected to undertake training programmes for women in areas like processing of agricultural raw-materials, forest products, medicinal plants, sericulture, commercial forests etc. Gender-sensitisation programmes and strategies were developed by government as well as non-governmental organizations to help women-friendly atmosphere in development. But when the actual process of liberalization started unfolding itself, it began exploits women's labor, skills, time and sexuality. They ar trapped by sub-contractors and excluded from formal rules of minimum wages, conditions of work or any other social security measures of formal economic systems. Women in low-paid, low status and precarious jobs face more violence and harassment than their male counterparts due to physical and social vulnerabilities.

To sum up the debate, there is no single panacea for all the fall-outs of gender-discrimination. In all issues and strategies of development, the gender dimension i.e., what are its effects on men and women as social categories and how far they facilitate more just and human relationships, must be analysed before policies are finalized.

The human element should not be lost in the eagerness to bring about scientific development.

12

NATIONAL POLICY FOR THE EMPOWERMENT OF WOMEN 2001
AN APPRAISAL

Prof. B.P.C. Bose*, Dr. M. Venkateswara Rao,** and **Dr. M.V.S. Koteswara Rao*****

The development of the country depends upon mobilising every available human resource. Keeping away a substantial section of the society away from knowledge, opportunities, involvement and empowerment hampers the process of development. Indian women, who constitute fifty percent of the population, had been kept away from the production and intellectual process. Most of the attempts to draw them into national mainstream could not produce the intended results. The last and important attempt in this process was national policy for the empowerment of women. Enacted in 2001 this policy carried a number of strategies to empower women. This is divided in to seventeen sections, with each section concentrating on one area of change. Though this policy disappointed many people who had been expecting more realistic attitude in preparing the policy, it indeed a positive beginning. If we keep the point that the empowerment of

* Professor, Dept. of Political Science & Public Administration, Acharya Nagarjuna University, Nagarjuna Nagar, Guntur.

** Professor and Head, Dept. of Chemical Engineering, R.V.R. & J.C.College of engineering, Chowdavaram, Guntur.

*** Associate Professor, Dept. of Political Science & Public Administration, Acharya Nagarjuna University, Nagarjuna Nagar, Guntur.

women needs a change in the cultural milieu also, this policy and subsequent steps to implement it yield desired results.

"You can tell the condition of a nation by looking at the status of its women"

— Jawaharlal Nehru

Introduction

Empowerment of women is an on-going concern of academicians, policy makers, NGOs, Civil Society Organizations, and stake holders themselves, i.e., Women and activist groups. Both the Union and State Governments in this regard have initiated several measures covering the multiple dimensions of issues relating to women since Independence. Over the years, several expert committees and commissions have been appointed to look into the Problems and issues connected with women apart from the initiatives in the form of enactments. The focus of these expert bodies is mainly on improving the status of women through institutional arrangements, allocation of resources to specific policies and programmes, etc. These efforts, no doubt, have aimed at overcoming the limitations and inadequacies, and to strengthen and revitalize the role and status of women in the country.

However, many observers and analysts expressed the opinion that most of the efforts directed towards empowerment of women have not been translated into reality. In spite of the proclaimed commitment to the issues and problems relating to women, the post independence scenario indicates that the condition and the status of women is one of negligence, discrimination, subjugation, and marginalization. They suffer from hunger, poverty, malnutrition and poor health, lack of education, overwork, and mistreatment.

The women have become so unwanted and undesirable that according to one estimation deaths of young girls in India exceed those of young boys by over 3,00,000 each year, and every sixth infant death is specifically due to gender discrimination. Of the 15 million baby girls born in India each year, nearly 25 percent will not live to see their 15th birthday (see, *www.thp.org*/reports, p.4.). The same is proved to be correct in a study conducted by UNICEF in 1996.

Social institutions all over the world are in transition. So are the nature, role and status of women in various societies. The Indian situation is no exception to this. The paper is addressed to the efforts of empowering women in the post-Independence period in India, especially in the light of National Policy on Empowerment of Women (2001). The paper also presents the limitations of the policy.

The term empowerment has different meanings in different political and social contexts. The contextual meanings associated with empowerment include self-strength, control, self-power, self-reliance, own choice, dignity of life in accordance with one's values, capable of fighting for one's rights, independence, own decision making, being free, awakening and capability. Empowerment is of intrinsic value. It also has instrumental value. Empowerment is relevant at the individual and collective levels. There are obviously many passive definitions of empowerment. In its broadest sense, empowerment is the expansion of freedom of choice and action. It means increasing one's authority and control over the resources and decisions that affect one's life. As people exercise real choice, they have increased control over the lives. In essence, empowerment is the expansion of assets and capabilities of marginalized and disadvantaged sections of the society to participate in, negotiate with, influence, control, and hold accountable in situations that affect their lives.

Empowerment of women was sought to be achieved through several methods in several areas. They are: Electoral representation; Institutional existence and autonomy; role and status; resources etc. They can be further categorized that there are two methods of constitutional empowerment of women through conferment – namely, coordinate status and independent status. The constitutional spirit of social welfare seeks to establish a social order in which freedom, equality and social justice are the central values. Government is expected to plan and implement programmes meant for the various sections – especially the vulnerable and disadvantaged of the society.

In the post independence period, policies are being adopted through the planning process for rapid economic growth, which would ultimately result in the well-being of all citizens. In tune with the stated goals and objectives, a number of social legislations and policies were initiated. In India, recognition of the need to bring women into the mainstream of development has underpinned national policy and planning since independence. For example, as early as the late 1950s, Mahila Mandals or grass root women's organizations were promoted to ensure better implementation of welfare schemes run by the government.

The issues connected with empowerment of women come under the purview of several ministries both at the central and state levels. Institutional arrangements were made through Department of social security in 1964. Women welfare was one of the subjects assigned to it. Department of social security was redesigned as Department of Social Welfare. The same was divided in 1985 into Ministry of Welfare and a Department of Women and Child Development.

The Department of Women's Welfare and Child Development is currently located under Ministry of HRD covering the following subjects.:

(a) Family welfare

(b) Women and Child Welfare

(c) International affairs relating to women and children

(d) Promotion of voluntary effort pertaining to women

(e) Administration of SITA Act, 1956

(f) Dowry Prohibition Act 1961, Act

Various programmes were launched for the welfare of women with incremental outlays rising from the first five year plan to the current plan. Major programmes include rescue homes, protection homes, service women's homes, working women's hostels, vocational training, creches for working women, socio-economic production groups, self-help groups, DWCRA, DWCUA, etc. In spite of these efforts for the development/empowerment of women most of the stated objectives were on paper and they were not translated into concrete action programmes of reality.

Ironically men treat women as a burden, even though they work more than men. The presence of women, Mrs. Indira Gandhi, in the most powerful position for a long time did not change the position. The programmes announced for the betterment of their position, particularly from 7th Plan remained on paper. However, it was not until the sixth Five Year Plan (1980-85) that women's advancement received recognition as a specific development sector. In later Five Year Plans, there has been a gradual shift in favour of women's empowerment programmes as compared to the women's development approach of the earlier plans. The ninth Five Year Plan (1997-2002) identifies the empowerment of women and other socially disadvantaged groups as crucial to socio-economic change. The plan seeks to promote their participation in local government and in people's organizations.

A joint committee constituted to keep women's concerns under constant review and to monitor progress in pursuance of plans of action developed at national and international levels. 73rd and 74th constitutional amendments which came into effect in 1993 reserve 30% of the seats in Panchayat Raj (local Government) Institutions for women, bringing thousands of grassroots women into the country's political life. Women's Development Corporations have been set up in about 18 states of India to channel financial assistance to women's economic enterprises. In order to soften the impact of structural adjustment programmes on poor women's lives, a special fund has been established under the social safety net to offer credit to women for self-employment and for setting up micro-enterprises.

National Policy 2001

Thus, the National Policy for the empowerment of Women assumed significance, even before it was formally approved[1]. Most of the concerned eagerly awaited its declaration. The policy proposes, among their things, a system of regularly collecting sex-desegregated data on resource allocation, specializes sectoral polices and the performance of different development programmes for the advancement of women, Four Indian states, Andhra Pradesh, Madhya Pradesh, Maharashtra and Tamilnadu, have also issued policies or plans of action for women.

The national policy document is divided into 17 small sections. The introduction reminds us that the gender equality and positive discrimination were guaranteed by the Constitution. Beginning from the fifth five-year plan, informs the policy, to 73rd and 74th amendments, a number of steps were taken to build a strong foundation for empowering women and making them participate in decision making.

The first section deals with various international conventions and India's declared commitment to innumerable declarations[2] and appreciates the steps taken by non-government organizations and the spirit of the 9th Five Year Plan. This section rightly concludes that there is a wide gap between the declared goals and the situational reality in India[3]. The same section identified goals and objectives of the policy as:

(i) Creating an environment through positive economic and social policies for full development of women to enable them to realize their full potential.

(ii) The de-jure and de-facto enjoyment of all human rights and fundamental freedom by women on equal basis with men in all spheres – political, economic, social, cultural and civil.

(iii) Equal access to participation and decision making of women in social, political and economic life of the nation.

(iv) Equal access to women to health care, quality education at all levels, career and vocational guidance, employment, equal remuneration, occupational health and safety, social security and public office etc.

(v) Strengthening legal systems aimed at elimination of all forms of discrimination against women.

(vi) Changing societal attitudes and community practices by active participation and involvement of both men and women.

(vii) Mainstreaming a gender perspective in the development process.

(viii) Elimination of discrimination and all forms of violence against women and the girl child; and

(ix) Building and strengthening partnerships with civil society, particularly women's organizations" (1:11).

The second section underlines the necessity of introducing the required changes in the judicial legal system to make it gender sensitive and more responsive. Section three promises to take all measures to guarantee equal access to decision-making bodies. The fourth section talks about the mainstreaming a gender perspective in the development process. The fifth section unfolds various ideas to ensure the economic empowerment and eradication of poverty. They include micro credit, reinterpretation and redefinition of conventional concepts of work, preparation of satellite and national accounts, training the women in soil conservation, social forestry, poultry, fisheries etc. While inviting the process of globalization this section wants to design strategies to enhance the "capacity to meet the negative social and economic impacts, which may flow from the globalization process" (5:4).

The sixth section is about the social empowerment of women. Equal access to education, holistic approach to health and recognition to the traditional knowledge of women on health care etc. are stressed in this section. The problems of intra-household discrimination in nutritional matters, safe drinking water, sanitation, housing, shelter, environment etc., are given special importance. Sections seven and eight deal with violence against women and rights of girl child respectively. Section nine is on mass media and it is for using the media to portray images that are consistent with the human dignity of girls. Section ten is about action plans and the next section is on institutional mechanisms at central, state and district levels.[4] Section twelve touches upon the key issue – issue of resources and says that the necessary resources to implement the policy will have to be managed by concerned departments, society as a whole and connected/concerned institutions. It assigns the responsibility of monitoring and reviewing the implementation to Department of Women and Child Development. Section thirteen repeats the theme of second section, which deals with Judicial – legal efforts. While the 14th section deals with the need for gender sensitisation of personnel, the 15th section hopes that the 73rd and 74th amendments (reservation to women in Panchayat Raj and urban local bodies) play a key role in enhancing women participation.

The 16th section assures the voluntary organizations of appropriate support. The last section reaffirms its will to implement international obligations and commitments in all sectors of empowerment of women.

It is highly appreciable that a national policy on empowerment of women, who constitute, half of the universe, is formulated. As the document rightly put it, right from nutritious and equal share in square meal to equal status, everything is a scarce commodity to women. Though it is very late,[5] late by at least 54 years, finally we have a policy now. The wise say "better late than never".

This policy document is successful in identifying the areas where extra inputs are needed to ensure the empowerment. The importance given to the micro-credit, to prepare national account for the contribution of women in generating the domestic product warrants particular appreciation. Identifying various strata among women and exclusive attention to their problems is another novel feature of this policy because the feminist attitude of projecting women as a homogeneous group proved to be less useful to women from poorer sections (Sahell, Sabala Sangh, 1991).

However, this policy document did disappoint the people who had been waiting for it on many counts.[6] The text and spirit of the policy appears like a statement of promise. Each paragraph positively promises something or the other. Though the policies carry assurances, assurances themselves don't become a policy. A policy is an attempt to set something right or to achieve something. For that purpose it has to overcome the hurdles created, and utilize the opportunities provided by the social environment. The policy makers have to strive hard to identify the opportunities and ways of overcoming hurdles. From this flow the necessary strategies, programmes, with a thorough understanding about alternatives. Being a policy on a vital or most important segment with social consequences, a policy of this nature is supposed to be rational rather than populist or all promising one.[7]

The readers of the policy are at a loss to understand how so many wonderful changes could be possible, when nothing substantial was achieved in the 54 year history of independent India. The Policy acknowledges that a wide gap exists "between the goals enunciated in the constitution, legislation, policies, plans, programs and related mechanisms on the one hand and the situational reality of the status of women in India on the other. But did not try to identify the reasons for failure. To be polite, this is a vital overlook. One has to remember that, this policy was formulated after 54 years of experience in development effort, or 51 years of experience in planned developmental effort. The question that naturally arises is what factors prevented or downsized the expected development. The failure of the policy to address this point is a major drawback.

A fatal mistake of the policy is to treat the elders (old members of the household) an obstacle to empowerment. Consequently the policy proposed to "expand and improve" homes for the aged and disabled to ensure full co-operation of women in social, political and economic life.[8] This implies that old and disabled are a hurdle for women's participation in public affairs or productive activities. This is an erroneous conclusion. Otherwise, this leads to a situation where every other member of family is treated as a hurdle for women participation in social affairs or her empowerment. As the American experience demonstrates, breakdown of emotional relationship in the family automatically leads to the breakdown of social life, paving the way for "pleasure seeking" individualism.

The stand taken by the policy on globalisation vis-à-vis women needs a debate. There is a considerable section of academician's who feel that structural adjustment programs cause more harm to women. A good number of case studies also proved the same (Maithreyi, 1993; Krishnaswami, 1993 and Sujaya C.P., 1993).[9] Even the policy document accepts that globalisation has presented new challenges for the realization of the goal of women equality and growing global economy lead to feminisation of poverty. Still the policy assured that the "strategies will be designed to enhance the capacity of women and empower them to meet the negative social and economic impacts, which may flow from the globalisation process". The rest of the document, or later documents released by Department of Women and Child Development did not come out with any strategy till date.

The policy document is completely silent on the need for developing counter culture as an essential precondition for achieving gender equality. The existing cultural values run counter to the gender equality. It is quite natural for everybody to treat women as inferior beings.[10] Most of the religions, the education, particularly at the elementary level, perpetuate this feeling. Unless appropriate counter strategies are developed, the gender equality remains as an academic discussion. The need of the hour is for a secular outlook and an education system, which project the women as an essential subsystem of a wider social system. The realization that any injury or inadequacy of a sub system ultimately becomes an injury or inadequacy to the total system is a prerequisite for gender equality. It is the hope of this paper that a serious attention to the above-mentioned issues makes the women policy more comprehensive.

Experience during the Five and half decades from 1947 to 2003, indicates that empowerment of women has several positive and negative aspects. Positive aspects include institutional framework, raising expectations, need to establish integration and linkages, facilitation of opportunities for democratisation etc. In spite of these positive aspects, women continue to be discriminated and the issues relating to women receive low priority since a long period. The tragedy has been that these positive features have remained confined to only select areas in few states. By and large if we look at the overall picture of the process of empowerment of women and their actual impact on socio-economic situation and transformation has been dismal. While states are so keen about promoting empowerment of women they are not always equally keen to promote and support their cause. The gap between promise and performance has been widening. There is perhaps no alternative to making statutory arrangements in this regard. The establishment of a National Commission for Women and the state level commissions has, however, fallen short of the expectations.

It is to be noted that Statutory reforms on their own cannot bring in the desired changes but it is the mindset of the stake holders involved in the empowerment of women – Public, political representatives, policy makers at the state and union levels, bureaucracy and civil society organizations – play a significant role in empowerment of women. Features of the initiatives compels one to be skeptical and substantiates the apprehension that problems have really been compounded because of lack of commitment with wholesale political determination, the growing expectations will essentially widen the gulf between promise and performance.

When in opposition our political leaders are extremely vocal about empowerment of women. All major political parties have promised to empower women in their manifestoes during the election season. The moment they came to power, they change colour. It is such lip service to women that tends to undermine them. In a functioning democracy, empowerment of women should not depend on the sweet will and pleasure of the government in power. The larger interests of the society within the over-all framework of national interest should guide them. It is a fact that the empowerment of women is mainly correlated to the political game plan of ruling political parties. Experience in India shows that progress only takes place when the political executives decides, for whatever reason, that empowerment of women is important. Support of the political head is necessary and not a sufficient condition for progress. Positive and supportive guidance from the higher civil service is another necessary condition. One the whole, the available evidence points to achievements that are 'normal' or 'sub-optimal'.

In an appraisal of the achievements so far in a different context, it is noted that enfranchisement, empowerment and ethical functioning with a moral code of conduct, are the three elements of democratic decentralization. If democratic decentralization is viewed as a 'stages approach' in transformation, it can be safely asserted that India has successfully crossed the first stage of enfranchisement and has partially moved towards the second stage of empowerment with limited success. But what has been called the third wave of democratic transformation, which is the 'ethical mode of functioning', is yet to be addressed in its totality (Sundaram, 2000:298). One of the major impediments to the empowerment of women is the "dependency syndrome" created by cultural and psychological factors. A committed effort by all concerned to create a counter cultural and psychological culture is the major prerequisite to empowerment.

FOOTNOTES

1. Though this was the first ever policy, certainly not the first attempt in the direction of ensuring empowerment of women. This is just the culmination of a prolonged effort. The first attempt was made in 1974 when an official document entitled "Towards Equality: Report of the Committee on the status of women in India" was published by Department of Social Welfare, Ministry of Education and Social Welfare, Government of India. This was a report by the Committee on the status of women in India. The Ministry of Education and Social Welfare constituted this committee in 1971. There was a National Perspective Plan For Women 1988-2000, published in 1988 and Sharamashakti Report, a report on the condition of women working in unorganised sector.

2. The policy statement that "India ratified ...... Convention on Elimination of All Forms of Discrimination Against Women (CEDAW, 1993)" was not correct. In fact the Government of India did not become a party to Art. 16(1) and 16(2) of CEDAW, that dealt with uniform code of marriage and compulsory registration of marriage respectively. The Government also rejected Art 29(1), which imposed compulsory arbitration in international Court of Justice in gender discrimination cases (see Empowerment Women through Self Help Groups, a report published by the Department of Women and Child Development, 2000, p.2).

3. To be clear, the problem of empowerment of women is not only an Indian one, but almost universal. For a brilliant presentation of the status of women world over see, "Further Actions And Initiatives to Implement The Beijing Declaration And the Platform For Action" document adopted by the 23rd special session of the UN General Assembly entitled "Women 2000 : Gender Equality, Development, and Peace for The 21st Century". For the place of women in decision making process see "50-50 by 2005 : Get The Balance Right", and Sushila Ramaswami, "Women in Parliament : A Global Glimpse".

4. The Prime Minister and the Chief Minister act as heads of the Councils at centre and state levels. Besides representatives from the concerned departments, chair persons of National and State Commissions for Women, social welfare boards, representatives of non-government organizations, women's organizations, corporate sector, trade unions, financing institutions, academics, experts and social activists also serve on these councils.

5. It may be recalled that the vital issue of women empowerment had been on the agenda way back in 1942 the National Planning Committee's sub-committee on women prepared a policy note entitled "Women in planned Economy". It reminded the nation about the necessity of involving women on equal status in the economy and decision making (see Empowerment women through Self Help Groups, a report published by the Department of Women and Child Development, 2000, p.2, p-12).

6. It is appropriate to recall here that the whole nation in general and the clientele groups in particular waited for four years for this document. Inspired by the Beijing Conference (1995), a draft national policy was formulated. A series of consultations with members of parliament, State Government, Non-governmental organizations, women organizations, social activists, researchers and other experts delayed the finalization of the policy. The policy in its finalized form was sent to the cabinet around February 1998 (See, Asha Das, 1998). The political uncertainity and other factors delayed the policy announcement for two more years.

7. For a detailed discussion on this point see, Anderson, James E (1979), Anderson Walt (1975) and Easton David (1965).

8. As early as 1910s and 20s a Feminist, Alexandra Kollontai argued that child – rearing and children education is the responsibility of the state. She also argued that the precondition for women participation in collective affairs is liberating her from private responsibilities. Neither Kollontai nor feminists of her school ever bothered to make their better–halfs as equal partners in household affairs, so that private and personal remains as private and yet women get more time and space to contribute to collective affairs (see Holt, Alix 1977 and Lokaneeta Jinu, 2001).

9. There are another set of writers who argue that the structural adjustment programme helps the economic empowerment. A representative example is Sudha and LK Deshpande (1992), and Nandita Shah et al. 2001).

10. It pains to see that even the leaders of the feminist movement and academicians who champion the cause of gender equality like to be recognized by the names of their better-halfs or fathers.

REFERENCES

1. Anderson, James, E.1979. *Public Policy Making*, New York: Rinehart.
2. Anderson Walt, 1975. *Politics and Environment*, California: Goodyear.
3. Asha Das, 1998. Secretary, Department of Women and Child Development. *Statement to The Commission on the Status of Women*, U.N.O.
4. Department of Women and Child Development, 2001. Women's Empowerment Year, Delhi: Ministry of Human Resource Development.
5. Department of Women and Child Development, 2000. *Empowering Women Through Self Help Groups*.
6. Easton David, 1965. *A Frame Work of Political Analysis*, New Jersy: Prentice Hall.
7. Holt, Alix, 1977. *Selected Writing of Alexandra Kollontai*, London: Alison.
8. Krishnaswamy, 1993. *Notes on Issues Regarding Women and the New Economic Policy*.
9. Lokaneeta Jinu, 2001. *Alexandra Kollontai and Marxist Feminism*, Economic and Political Weekly, April, 28.
10. Maithreyi, Krishna Raj, 1993. *The New Economic Policy: Safeguarding Women Interests in the New Economic Policy and Women* : A Collection of back ground papers to Sixth National Conference 1993. Bombay : Indian Association for women studies.
11. Nandita Shah at.al. 2001, *Structural Adjustment, Feminization of Labour Force and Organizational Strategies* in Nivedita Menon(ed.), Gender and Politics in India.

12. Saheli, Sabala Sangh, 1991. *Development for Whom – A Critique of Women's Development Programmes* Delhi: Action India.

13. Sudha and L.k.Desh Pande, 1992. *New Economic Policy and Female Employment?, Economic and Political Weekly*, 10 October.

14. Sujaya C.P, 1993. *Effects of Adjustment : A Review of Experience.*

15. Sundaram K.V., 2000. *From Top-Down Planning to Decentralized Regional and Local Development in India – Vision and Reality : Challenges and Perspectives*, Indian Social Science Review, 2(2) : 275-300.

16. UNICEF (1996), *The Asia Engima.*

13

PRACTICAL AND STRATEGIC GENDER NEEDS

Dr. Aney Thomas*

The roles that women play are different in any society and the legislation, religious norms, economic status or class, cultural values, ethinicity and types of productive activity of the country, community and household determine their situation. Gender refers to the social relationships between women and men, not just the biological differences. It is a basis for the division of labour, which varies according to context and culture. This paper highlights the different policy approaches to Indian Women with stress on implementation and evolution procedures.

Introduction

Gender roles may be complementary, but they can involve an unequal exchange of effort e.g. of work time, resources or money. Women often have less access to resources, rewards and power, (lower incomes, less political and social influences, less control over personal and reproductive lives). The terminologies, policy, strategy, planning and organization of implementation are closely interrelated making it difficult to determine where one term ends and another begins. Policy making is the process of social and political decision making about how to allocate resources for the needs and interest of society and

---

* (Presently) Dept of RDFS, Debub University, Awassa, Ethiopia, (On lien) HOD, Dept. of Family and Community Science, M.S.Home Science College, Angamaly South, Ernakulam Dt., Kerala.

concluding in the formulation of a policy strategy. In short, policy is about what to do. Strategy is the mechanism of implementing economic, social and political decisions. Planning is the process of implementation of the policy or how to do it. The organization of implementation is the process of administrative action to deliver the programme designed often resulting in a completed product. It is about what is actually done. If development undertakings are aimed at benefiting equally both male and female members of a community then the development policies, strategies, plans and organization of implementation need to be gender responsive.

Any development efforts in the past largely misunderstood and neglected of development human dynamics. Women who are almost, 50 percent of the key elements of development sustainability were left in the slipstream and are also ignored in the mainstream. In spite of this situation still women have contributed significantly to the economic and social life of their community.

- The Management of units promoted by women entrepreneurs is beset
- Establish gender-specific objectives which challenge existing division of Labour, tasks, opportunities and responsibilities of women & men.
- Put mechanism in place to ensure that women and men are actively involved in project decision making.
- Ensure that allocations to gender-specific activities are adequate.

Check that

- Gender is consistently integrated in the project proposal i.e. at all stages.
- Adequate gender disaggregated information is provided.
- Men and women in the target group are actively involved.
- Barriers to women's participation are identified together with measures to address them
- Planned resources and activities are adequate to meet gender needs identified

Different Policy Approaches to Indian Women

Issues	*Welfare*	*Equity*	*Anti-Poverty*	*Efficiency*	*Empowerment*
Origin	Earliest approach	Original WID Approach	Second WID Approach	Third and new	Most recent approach
Period most popular	1950-70; but still widely used	1975-85; attempts to adopt it during the Women's Decade	1970s onward: still limited popularity	Post-1960s, now most popular approach	1975 onward: accele-rated during 1980s, still limited popularity.
Purpose	To bring women into development as better mothers : this is seen as their most important	To gain equity for women in the development process; women seen as active participants in development	To ensure poor women increase their productivity: Women's poverty seen as a problem of underdevelopment, not of subordination	To ensure development is more efficient and more effective; women's economic participation seen as associated with equality.	To empower women through greater self reliance; women's subordination seen not only as problem of men but also of colonial and neocolonial oppression.
Needs of women met and roles recognized	To meet PGN in reproductive role, relating particularly to food aid, malnutrition and family planning	To meet SGN in term of triple role-directly through state top-down intervention, giving political and economic autonomy by reducing inequality with men.	To meet PGN in productive role to earn an income particularly in small-scale income generating project.	To meet PGN in context of declining social services by relying on all three roles of women and elasticity of women's time.	To reach SGN in terms of triple role-indirectly through bottom-up mobilization around PGN as a means to confront oppression.
Comment	Women seen as passive beneficiaries of development with focus on their reproductive role; non-challenging, therefore, widely popular especially with government and traditional NGOs.	In identifying subordinate position of women in terms of relationship to men, challenging criticized as Western feminist, considered threatening and not popular with government.	Poor women isolate as separate category with tendency only to recognize productive role; reluctance of government to give limited aid to women means popularity still at small-scale NGO level.	Women seen entirely in terms of delivery capacity and ability to extend working day; most popular approach both with governments and multilateral agencies.	Potentially challenging with emphasis on Third World and women's self-reliance; largely unsupported by governments and agencies; avoidance of Western feminist criticism means slow, significant growth of under-financed voluntary organizations.

Source : Caroline, 1994, pg. 56-57. PGN : Practical Gender Need. SGN : Strategic Gender Need.

- The likely positive and negative effects on women's position relative to men have been assessed.
- It is clear how progress on a gender basis will be measured.

Implementation Process

- Assess & strengthen capacity of agencies, national institutions and individuals in the design and implementation of gender responsive programs.
- Help women to articulate and negotiate their development priorities
- Ensure gender objectives are addressed
- Have women have equal access with men to project resources & benefits.
- Be flexible in addressing bottlenecks to women's progress.
- Provide gender-specific targets to staff and monitor them

Evaluation Procedure

- Collect, analyse and use gender disaggregated data in monitoring review and evaluation
- Evaluate progress in relation to gender objectives
- Hire gender aware consultants
- Describe any negative effects on any group of women's or men's
- Indicate women's current workload relative to men's
- Indicate which women and which men have benefited and whether women have control over the benefits gained

SGN = Strategic Gender Need

Women are involved in food production and running of micro, small and medium enterprises. Quite a large number of them are also engaged in the informal economic sector. Though they have such an involvement and a contribution, women are excluded from economic decision-making and are low paid with poor working conditions. They have also limited employment and professional opportunities. Their unpaid work such as domestic and community work is not valued as work, it is neither measured in quantitative terms nor valued in the GDP (Gross Domestic Product).

Due to such a neglect of the complex human dynamics in development, the human kind in general and women in particular are facing the negative consequences of development including the following:

- Resources are wasted
- Sustainability is questioned
- Human needs are neglected
- Environmental problems are aggravated
- Women's access to productive resources is undermined and this marginalised women's labour from mainstream. This also decreased women's capacity to produce food.
- Daily burden of women/feminization of poverty/has become a significant trend of poverty.

In most cases development policies, strategies and plans are assumed to be gender neutral where both sexes are benefiting equally. However, from the above expositions one simply understands why this is not true.

Identifying practical and strategic gender needs

- Include gender Expertise in the design team
- Include gender in TOR for planning terms
- Analyse gender roles and responsibilities of men and women in target groups
- Do a Gender Needs assessment
- Collect/consult gender disaggregated data
- Assess national and sectoral plans determine sensitivity to and potential obstacles for addressing gender issues.
- Assess long-term effects in terms of women's increased ability to take charge of their lives and take collective action to solve problems.

REFERENCES

1. Gender Issues in Agriculture; A Reader.Department of Gender Studies in Agriculture, Wageningen Agricultural University, January 1993.
2. Gender Roles in Development Projects: A Case Book (1991), Kumarian Press, Inc., U.S.A.

3. Gender Segregation and Social Change : *Men and Women in Changing Labour Markets* (2000) Oxford University Press, New York.

4. Kimmel, S.Michael (2000). The Gendered Society Reader. Oxford University Press, New York.

5. Macdonal,Mandy,Sprenger, Ellen and Dubel, Ireen (1997). *Gender and organizational Change; Bridging the Gap Between Policy and practice.* Royal Tropical Institute, Amsterdam.

6. Mitchell, Bruce (1997). *Resource and Environmental Management.* Longman, England.

14

EMERGING INDIA
THE ROLE OF WOMEN

K. Lalitha* and Prof. G. Prasad**

The role of women in development is most intimately related to the goal of comprehensive socio-economic development, and is a strategic question for the development of all societies. Any development strategy, which neglects the need for enhancing the role of women, cannot lead to comprehensive socio-economic development. The point of priority should be to recognize the role of women as a dynamic factor and a valuable asset for the overall process of development. It is neither a burden/cost nor a mere humanitarian concession to a disadvantaged group .The position of women and their role in this context are particularly important, not only because women contribute half of the human resources in developing countries, but also because they have to bear the burden of the daily struggle for survival. Although women are not a homogeneous social group, and their position varies between and within countries there are some features which are common to all societies. Historically, their role in biological reproduction has generally restricted women's participation in the mainstream of social, economic and political processes. Thus this paper explores the untapped hidden potential in women that can be positively used for development of India as a super power.

* Principal, B.H.H. Degree College for Women, Guntur.

** Dept. of Commerce & Business Administration, Acharya Nagarjuna University, Guntur.

Introduction

It is increasingly recognized that in economic development, women along with men need to be viewed equally as agents of production and claimants of equitable share in national income. This means that the age-old tradition has captivated women in a network of social limitations forcing them to perform activities having no monetary compensation. This also created obstacles to the integration of women with the mainstream of economic activities. The role of woman as mother and homemaker determines the nature of her work. Discriminatory treatment that stems from the traditional beliefs and norms of patriarchal society precludes women's access to the social power structure. It controls women's talents, skills and capabilities.

Indian Women have diverse multi-dimensional characteristics. They have progressive as well as retrogressive, roles and values among several religious and caste groups all over India. Most of them are housewives. The urban women are better placed and have benefited from the existing opportunities for development at a faster rate than the rural women. In the field of science and technology they now play a greater role. They have many hurdles to over come yet. The emerging role of women is viewed under three broad spectrums.

- Role of Women in the Pre Independence Period
- Role of Women in the Post Independence Period
- Role of Women in Emerging India

Role of Women in the Pre-independence Period

The Pre-Aryan women enjoyed more freedom than the present day avant-garde. Pre-Aryan women lived as good as free men and were free to choose their husband and set up family, as the society was matriarchal. Even today there are several millions of Adivasis who practise this way of life. Aryans who colonized India, never restricted their women to their houses. They were more free, Independent and enjoyed several privileges equal with their male partners, and in sometime even more. The women's freedom continued to prevail up to the period of Rigveda (Circa 1500 BC) which described women as equals of men, learned, enjoyed the performance of religious rituals, and also pleasures of the social gatherings. This situation did not last long. Soon after the entry of

British rulers in India, drastic changes took place in denigration of women's status.

In the pre-independence period, the women's movement was very much a part of the nationalist movement. The liberal approaches to women's issues and over-all middle-class urban leadership marked out as significant features of the first phase of women's movement. The second phase of women's movement has pressed for equal access to economic opportunities. Access to assets and services has been considered critical including land, raw materials, credit, and financial and technical support services. The emergence of a local women's movement has made a difference. In many countries, women pressed for social recognition of public and private rights, particularly reproductive rights and equal rights in divorce, inheritance and wages.

All these efforts brought awareness among Indian women. These movements and social reforms had created awareness among women and they look to struggle for their own rights. In the freedom struggle of 1857 Maharani Lakshmi Bai, Begum Hazarat Mahal, Kasturibai Gandhi, Sarojini Naidu, Amrit Kaur, Meera Ben and many others proved that women were no less than men.

Role of Women in Post-independence Period

On August 15th 1947, India kept her tryst with destiny, and the constitution of the free nation was implemented from 26th January, 1950 as a vehicle of social transformation to realize the goals of freedom movement. The Preamble declares India as a *Sovereign, Democratic Republic; the words, Secular and Socialist* were added later in 1976. It recognizes the principle of social, economic and political justice, which the Indian women never enjoyed.

Many of the women who participated in the social reform and political activities of the 1920's, 1930's & 1940's were pleased with the constitutional provisions for gender equality. The Government asked prominent women's organizations to assist them in developing five-year plans. These women agreed with the government that economic growth was the most salient issue and shared the assumptions that women would gain from expected prosperity. The best known of the women's organizations became institutionalised as they secured permanent office buildings and libraries of their own.

They set up and continued to administer programs designed to serve, especially day-care centres, hostels for workingwomen, educational centres and medical dispensaries. Like the government with which they have been closely allied, their approach has been "welfarist".

Social reforms and political awareness during freedom struggle and subsequently constitutional safeguards along with legal framework had made Indian women socially and politically strong, but complete empowerment of women will remain a daydream as long as the economic resources are owned and controlled by men. The decision, as to how the income of family is spent, is taken by the male members of the family in majority of the cases. Non-working, non-earning and dependent women have little or no say in economic matters of the family. It has been proved by several studies, that the wishes and decisions taken by the educated and earning women in the family are respected and taken care. Women's work has become more and more visible, and women are now accepted as economic actors in their own right. The changes are most visible in the modern and organized sectors where women now appear in every field. Government tool has realized the needs and expectations of the women and made special provisions for women in each and every program of poverty alleviation and employment generation started in rural and urban areas. Some of the key features are as under :

- Under Jawahar Rojgar Yojana at least 30% jobs have essentially been provided to women.
- Under Urban Self Employment, which is a part of Nehru Rojgar Yojana, the percentage of women beneficiaries remained around 30%.
- Under Integrated Rural Development Program nearly 40% beneficiaries were women.
- Development of women and children in rural areas program, which is basically a part of integrated rural development program is indeed centralized to give opportunities for women's self employment.
- Similarly, in urban areas development programs were initiated for children and women which provide opportunities to women's self employment.

- Under TRYSEM (Training for Rural Youth for Self Employment) program, about 40% trainees were women.
- For protecting the privacy of women and providing them a respectable life provision of a sanitary toilet and healthy house is paramount necessity. Taking it into account provision has been made for the protection of the women's rights in rural areas under 'Indira Avas Yojana'. Legally such houses can neither be sold not mortgaged without the consent of wife.
- Since 1st April, 1999, IRDP, TRYSEM, DWCRA, SITRA, GKY and MWS programs have been merged into *Swarna Jayanti Gram Swa-Rojgar Yojana*. The objective of this scheme is to establish micro enterprises in the rural areas in large numbers. The people benefited under this scheme are called self-employed and not beneficiaries. This program has been designed in such a manner as to encourage the use of inherent qualities and capabilities of the poor. It has now been fully understood that the labour employment program can provide employment to unemployed but it cannot enhance the quality and skill of the poor. On the other hand self-employment programs, by enhancing the quality and skill of the labour can substantially increase the source of their income. This program can be more effective for the reduction of the poverty, generation of employment and empowerment of socially deprived including women. In this program there is a provision that at least 40% of the self-employed are women. In this way in the field of proper use of credit, repayment of loans and women empowerment, this Swarna-Jayanti Rojgar Yojana will play a more effective role.
- More than 4.5 lakhs women from destitute and marginal workers, poor families, where the head of the family is woman, have been given training in Animal Husbandry, Poultry Farming, Piggery, Handicrafts, Cottage and Rural Industries etc., for providing income generating employment that will result into the economic empowerment of women.

- The beneficiary women are imparted training from Funds received from the Development Authority of Norway. Training is imparted in the fields of electronics, electrical, computer programming, handloom, textiles, spinning and weaving, management of canteen, fashion technology etc.,
- Central Social Welfare Board is running a program of education and professional training for such women who have already left their studies previously for some reasons.
- Central Social Welfare Board provides grants-in-aid to such VO's which run the program for training of women.
- National Women Fund constituted on 30th March 1993 with a capital of Rs. 31 crores for fulfilling the requirements of poor women specially of informal sectors, gives loans and grants to self help groups and individuals by itself and through VO's.
- From 16th October 1998 a scheme with an outlay of Rs. 186.21 crores has been implemented namely 'Swashakti' which is known as a scheme for development and rights of rural women. Under this scheme to make women self sufficient, self help groups are constituted with a view to provide grants so that women can uplift their standards of living. Co-ordination is built between self help groups and lending institutions so that economic resources can be made available to the woman for earning income, rising the standard of living. By this way women will be able to establish their control over income and expenditure.

Emerging India – The role of Women

It is not surprising that the development of women in India has been the centre stage of its development planning since Independence though the concept has been evolving from plan to plan. Women need to be viewed not as beneficiaries but as active participants in the process of development and change. Her capacity to work, her knowledge and her skills are often the only resources to call upon for survival in households. Today, women have entered in diverse fields, attained success, and gained popularity starting from their landmark in education till ruling the country

The role of women can be studied under 3 special heads in the family and outside the family: namely (1) As a partner (2) As an asset (3) As a professional.

1. *Women as an Asset:* Generally there is a Himalayan Misconception that women as low grade intellect and many men mistakenly do not entrust responsibility to the women folk and mostly the decision making is done by the men. If one assess the role of women in the house in various household activities one cannot but appreciate the contribution of the women through her varied activities. Women positively is an asset to the family and to the community to which the family belongs.

   Women is the first nurse of the family. For any ailment – small or big the women as a mother attend first and when professional medical help is required she attends to it. When a member of the family is sick all the medication and nursing is done by the women of the family. In economic grounds this first aid and Medicare is in valued. Another important role for the women is an educator. The child is taught her first alphabets and also the principles of personal hygiene by the mother. As the child grows more information is also imparted by the mother. If the woman is learned and well educated the Child's education is planned and taken care of by the mother. Even in families with illiterate women the children are goaded to sit at the desk and learn. To inculcate the culture of learning in the children women's education has a great role in the family. The same applies outside the family also. Unless the light of knowledge dawns in the women force of our country, we can never join the community of developed nations. In recent times the female literacy rate of our country has increased from 12.95 % in 1961 to 54.16 % in 2001. It means that the female literacy group at twice the rate that male literacy during the same period. It is shown in the following table. For the first time, the number of absolute female illiterate has come down from 200,068,072 in 1991 to 1,89,554,886 in 2001.

Literacy Rate by Sex (1961-2001)

(in Per cent)

Census Year	*Females*	*Males*	*Male-Female gap in Literacy Rate*
1961	12.95	34.44	21.79
1971	18.70	39.45	20.75
1981	20.76	56.38	26.62
1991	39.29	64.13	24.84
2001	54.16	65.38	21.69

Source: Census of India, 2001, "Provisional Population Totals".

With the implementation of several five-year plans and extension programs and women and child welfare schemes there is conspicuous change in the awareness of women's health and understanding of the importance of maintaining health of the women in the family.

The health of the women has a direct bearing on the family and indirect influence on the nation's wealth. During the last two decades, a striking improvement is observed in the mortality rate of girl child. The Infant Mortality Rate (IMR) declined from 80 per 1000 births in 1991 to 68 per 1000 births in 2001, Child Mortality Rate (CMR) declined from 41.2 per 1000 births in 1991 to 20.4 per 1000 births in 2001. Likewise the Maternal Mortality Rate (MMR) also declined from 437 per 1000 births in 1991 to 407 per 1000 births in 2001.

2. *Women as a partner:* Women play a vital role in the family as a wife, i.e., as a partner she shares every activity of the husband, inside and outside the house. As a partner woman is a potential force guiding, advising and administering the various functions of the home. She plans the budget of the family, sets apart certain amount for providing a comfortable house to the family, proper education to the children, planning their future careers and saves for the onset of old age. All these activities are carried out with the consultation of the husband in accordance with the priorities of the family. All these activities require a high-grade intellect, understanding of

the need and administration of the family funds. So a woman as a partner in the family is of prime importance.

The potential of the women at present is not fully tapped and utilised for the community. If the woman is given her proper role in the various activities of the community, namely, social, economic and political fields women will be able to plan, mould and activate various programs for the betterment and the development of the community. She has a positive role in social welfare activities in health care, in economic progress. If the present political mindset is to be changed women must be encouraged to participate in the political activities right from the village level to national level. This is shown in the following table. If women participants in the legislative bodies many of the social problems with regard to women can be curbed or removed. Women must be made to asset herself to legislature and also through providing more opportunities in the administrative setup. The real freedom as Gandhiji dreamt will be achieved.

Details of the Female Members won and elected in the Lok Sabha

Lok Sabha	*Totai Seats*	*No. of Female Members*	*Female Percentage*
I	499	22	4.4
II	500	27	5.4
III	503	24	6.7
IV	523	31	5.9
V	521	22	4.2
VI	544	19	3.4
VII	544	28	5.1
VIII	544	44	8.1
IX	517	27	7.1
X	544	39	7.1
XI	543	39	6.3
XII	543	43	7.5
XIII	543	49	9.2

Source: Kurukshetra, August, 1998, P. No. 41.

3. *Women as a Professional:* With the expansion of the educational facilities and the reservations for the women in various professional and general courses there is vast improvement in the formation of women work force. There are several courses like Bio-Technology, Bio-Chemistry, Micro Biology, Information Technology, Auditing, Journalism in which women specialize and prove themselves even in Police Force women like Kiran Bedi proved to be good Police women with foresight and vision. Women like Kalpana Chawla have even flew into the outer space providing clearly that women can never be less than a man. If right education and a proper training are provided women can undertake any profession including the male preservers like Army. At present the employment of women in various professions is only 8.4% which is not encouraging. Where as the work participation of women is high as the following table indicates. It is necessary to draw to attract more women into various professions by providing certain special privileges like absence from duty during conception, child care centres at the work spot, and child health care by the employer. This is particularly necessary in Indian conditions as the women inspite of her training and education is home bound and the family is of top priority.

Estimate Stock of Graduates in General and Professional Education by Sex upto 2001

Year	*General*		*Professional*		*Total*	
	Males	Females	Males	Females	Males	Females
1981	5388	1498	741	665	6003	2005
1991	9689	4058	1257	1122	10811	4193
2001	15381	7351	1902	1694	17375	7559

Work Participation Ratios by Sex

S.No.	*Year*	*Males*	*Females*	*Ratio of M/F*
1.	1981	53.0	21.2	2:2
2.	1991	51.6	24.0	3:2
3.	2001	55.0	25.6	3:4

4. *Women as an Entrepreneur*: Ever since India opened its doors to liberalization in early 1990 there has been a steady transformation in India's economy. It is the time that we require a change in mindset to allow economic participation of women on an equal footing with men in society. Women need to move away to a certain extent from the traditional roles of homemakers and child rearing to more progressive roles where their economic contribution to society is regarded in a positive light.

   In the field of fashion, beauty and career counseling, many fashion designers are women with their own labels . To name a few: Ritu Kumar, known as the queen of Indian Textiles , Ritu Beri, who has had a stint in the French fashion industry and Rima Dhaka among others. Likewise the world of beauty culture has opened up many opportunities for women entrepreneurs. Women are setting up successfully small establishments as beauticians and hair stylists. To name a few: Vinita Jain of Biotique and Shahnaz Hussian of Shanaz Herbals are global brands today. In the field of education, counselors, are mostly women, primarily because men did not see it as a lucrative sector. As disposable incomes increase with the opening up of the economy, women are taking to opening up restaurants as well. Recently the Government of Andhra Pradesh decided to entrust the management of mini-hydel power stations, to tribal women groups under a Central Government scheme at 16 places in the agency areas of the State. Under this proposal, well established Mahila Samakhyas of DWCRA groups would be given the responsibility of running these projects, each with an installed capacity between 1MW and 3MW, and allowed to share the profits, women participation in economic ventures led to income generation and greater sense of fulfillment for women from all strata of society. The future will, no doubt, see women establishments bigger in their own right.

Conclusion

Thus the Indian housewife, or the Indian woman, is an amazing human being. She can do numerous things at the same time. It is this human resource which we have, but do not recognize. We do not understand the quality of our own people and do not respect our own strength. We do not recognize the strength of our own women. When a boy is born, we are jubilant and we say "O wonderful a boy is born! Great!". If a girl is born, we remark "O my god: Dowry? Marriage Expenditure etc., etc.,. ?". That is the attitude from the day the girl has to go out and work and she has to do her duties at home also. We are making a general sweeping statement to make a point. The women of India are much more involved and much more developed than the men, because she goes through much more experience than the men.

So, people in India are great as such and whether the men like it or not, we need to understand the greater strength is actually in Indian women. The 21st century may witness a new phenomenon in supporting this statement.

REFERENCES

1. Sushila Nayar & Kamala Manohar, *Women Pioneers in India's Renaissance*, National Book Trust, India, 2002, pp. – 373 to 389.
2. Neera Desai & Usha Thakkar, *Women in Indian Society*, National Book Trust, India 2001, pp. – 95.
3. Satnam Kaur, *Women in Rural Development*, Mittal Publications, Delhi, 1987, pp. – 30.
4. Kalpagam, *Women in the 20th Century*, Sebastil Raj, Quest for Gender Justice, T.R. Publications for Satya Nilayam Publications, Institute of Philosophy Centre, Madras, 1991, p. – 20.
5. Bathiwala S. *The Meaning of Women's Empowerment: New Concepts from Action*, Gita Sen et. al. (es) Population Policies Reconsidred, Health, Empowerment and Rights, Harvard Centre for Population and Development Studies.

6. Ghosh, *Rural Development and Women Benefits Ground Level Realities*, Nirnay, Vol. 10, No. 2, June 1995, pp. – 42 to 67.
7. Malini Ghosh, *Literacy, Power & Feminism, Economic and Political Weekly*, April 27th – May 3rd 2002 Volume XXXVII No. 17, P.No. 15,16.
8. Uma Chakravarthi, *Women and Electronic Media, Economic and Political Weekly*, April 29th – May 5th 2000, P.No. – WS 12 to 17.
9. Radhika Chopra, *Gender and Masculinities, Economic and Political Weekly*, April 26th – May 2nd 2003, P.No. – 1652, 1657.
10. *Women Legislatures in U.P., Background, Emergence and Roll, Economic and Political Weekly*, March 9-15 2002, P.No. 923.
11. Mary E. John, *Alternative Modernities? Reservations and Women's Movement in India, Economic and Political Weekly*, November 3, 2000, P.No. WS 22.
12. Manisha Sethi, *Women in Hindu Nationalism, Economic and Political Weekly*, April 20, 26 2002, P.No. – 1545.
13. Lella Sami, *Gender Differentials in Famine Mortality, Economic and Political Weekly*, June 29, July 5 2002, P.No. – 2593.
14. Narayana K.S., *Gender Disparity in Indian Polity; Need for Political Reservation, Kurukshetra*, P.No. 17 to 21.
15. *Rural Women Beneficiaries of DWACRA Scheme, Kuruskhetra* Volume – 47, 9, June 1999, P.No. 225.
16. Dr. H.D. Dwarakanath, *DWACRA in A P, Kuruskhetra* Volume – 47, 12 September 1999, P.No. 14 to 18.
17. Dr. H.D. Dwarakanath, *Self Employment Generation under DWACRA - A Review, Kuruskhetra* Volume – 49, 5 February 2001, P.No. 33.
18. *Women Empowerment for Gender Equality – A Functional Analysis, Kuruskhetra* Volume – 49, 11 August 2001, P.No. 33 to 35.
19. Sakunthala Narasimhan, *Womens Role in Gram Sabha, Kuruskhetra* Volume – 48, 1 October 1999, P.No. 35.

15

ROLE OF WOMEN ENTREPRENEURS IN THE INDIAN CONTEXT

Dr. D. Nageswara Rao*

The main objective of this paper is to analyse the crucial role of women entrepreneurs in the process of economic development of a emerging economy like India.

Women is half of sky, half of the earth half of the soul of the society. No one can deny this fact, because woman is indeed a pivot around whom the family, society and humanity moves on. The creative entrepreneur is the backbone of a nation industrialization and economic development. There is no gender for the entrepreneur. In a male dominated society women have been victims of social prejudices and discrimination. But in advanced countries like USA, UK, Canada, France and Germany woman entrepreneur account for not less than one third of the small business especially in the areas like retail trades and hotel making business. As far as India is concerned, women constitute, a very negligible proportion of total entrepreneurs. In India women entrepreneurs are rare, in this context the present paper attempts to find reasons as to way it is so.

Now, women are rapidly emerging as smart and dynamic entrepreneurs. They have entered almost all areas of business activities, such as textiles, engineering goods, electronics, beauty parlours, fashion designing, steel works etc. Educated women are making a land mark in the new conventional field like consultancy, advertising,

---

* Reader in Commerce, Hindu College, Guntur - 522 003.

garment export, interior decoration, textile printing, handicrafts etc. If the entrepreneurship developed among the women it leads to independent thinking, increase the foresight, improve the good organization ability, innovative skills, vision and finally the women entrepreneurs gets knowledge from her entrepreneur abilities. Thus, in current Indian context a woman entrepreneur contributes her experience in the knowledge society.

Introduction

Women is half of the sky, half of the earth, half of the blood and half of a soul of a society. No one can deny this fact, because woman is indeed a pivot around whom the family, society and humanity moves on. The destiny of a notion is crucial and inane without the service and sacrifice of woman with the advancement of science and technology the world had moved very fast, and therefore, woman has to assume a dynamic role in the changing context of the time and locale. It is indispensable that women forms an important component of the work force of the society. She shoulders the triple burden of the society and it is because of this vital role that she should be allowed to harness her energies and exploit her talents for the betterment of human life.

The creátive entrepreneur is the backbone of a nation's industrialisation and economic development. There is no gender for the entrepreneur. Even though women constitute almost half of the total world population, historically, women have played disproportionately small role in the field of business. In traditional society, they; were confined to the four walls restricted to household activities. In a male dominated society women have been victims of social prejudices and discrimination. Parents prefer the male child to the female. Women are considered to be weak, passive and dependent on others.

Women are not exposed to risks which condition adversely affects self-confidence, innovativeness and enterprising nature. But in advanced countries like USA, UK, Canada, France, Australia and Germany, women entrepreneur account for not less than one third of the small business especially in the areas like retail trades and hotel making a significant impact on all segments of economy. Women's empowerment should not restrict itself only to income generating process but include other components, such as capacity building, control over production, tools and process, conversation of natural resources, strengthening organisation and social security. According to the Ninth Five Year Plan document (Vol. II.p.313), the SHGs (Self Help Groups) would provided a permanent forum for articulating their needs and contributing their perspectives to development. The National Policy for the empowerment of women- has rightly felt that institutional mechanisms are needed to promote the advancement of women that already exist at the central and state levels.

Problems of Women Entrepreneurs

The chief objective of the paper is to highlight the problems faced by the women entrepreneurs in India and, thereby, to suggest suitable measures to resolve the problems faced by them. 'Woman entrepreneur is one who initiates, organisers and operates a business enterprise'. In developing countries like India such innovators are found less in number when compared with advanced countries.

Most of the women entrepreneurs face peculiar problems like illiteracy, fear of risk, lack of training and experience, feeling of insecurity, limited purchasing power and competition from male entrepreneurs. Most important problem faced by women entrepreneurs is that they do not get enough support from family members. Women in rural areas suffer more when compared to urban women entrepreneurs. In rural areas, Joint family system is still the norm. Some of the major problems faced by women entrepreneurs are, because they are either dependent on father or husband and children, and above all they are financially dependent on the above persons. It appears that Banks do not encourage women entrepreneurs. Women entrepreneurs face severe competition from large sized organizations and male entrepreneurs. Middlemen exploit women entrepreneurs in marketing their produces.

Further, they also face problems from legal formalities, procurement of raw material, travelling to; distant places, family bond, traditions and customs, risk bearing etc. Lack of training, late start, social conditions, family etc., are the other problems that deter the growth of women entrepreneurship. In addition, a variety of personal, social, economic, legal, resource and support system constraints, restrict women entrepreneurs in achieving their enterprise target. Efforts to identify these hurdles and carving their remedial strategies would go a long way. Further, effectiveness of the communication in every network is very essential because the women do not have access to scientific information latest know-how and supporting agencies etc.

Even though, we are in 21st century, socio-economic evils like gender discrimination and poverty are the two social banners ruling the community today. As far as India is concerned, women constitute a very negligible proportion of the total entrepreneurs.Women in India are still shy and emotionally attached to family. A majority of women entrepreneurs are engaged in the unorganised sector like agriculture, agro-based industries, handicrafts, handlooms, kitchen activities (pickles, powders and papads) and other cottage based industries like basket making etc. Therefore, it is hypothesized that several problems are faced by women entrepreneurs, whose consequences are alarming and adversely affect the standard of living of the women entrepreneurs. In the absence of such problems the standard of living of the women entrepreneurs as well as the economy of country would have been far the better. Therefore, there is a need to resolve the problems faced by the women entrepreneurs to protect the interest of all the concerned. In India women entrepreneurs are rare, in this context, the present paper attempts to find out the reasons why it is go. The following are the important factors contributing to the assumed phenomenon.

- The deplorable status of Indian Women.
- Low knowledge, skill, motivation, etc., of women to become entrepreneurs.
- Lack of support of government agencies
- Problems in running the units.
- Women do not posess in the required degree, characteristics like risk taking, innovation and economic ability to turn themselves.
- The status of Indian women is not conducive to the development of entrepreneurship among them.
- There is also the influence of social and psychological factors on women and hence, it is becoming difficult for them to enter business.

- The Management of units promoted by women entrepreneurs is beset with all kinds of problems, thus having a demonstration effect on potential women entrepreneurs.

Need and Significance

The present problem is considered to be very relevant to the present day society and country as a whole, as it reflects the various hidden issues pertaining to women entrepreneurs. One must accept the fact that entrepreneurship is not related to sex of an individual. Women can be as successful entrepreneurs as men. The entry of women in business is only recent development in the orthodox, traditional, social and cultural environment of our society. Our society has not allowed women to think independently in the past. But in the last decade, economic compulsions have led more and more young girls to take up employment and potential sources of women entrepreneurship has emerged. The following are some of the reasons for emerging women entrepreneurship;

- Not finding a job
- Unable to work in her house
- New challenges and opportunities for self fulfillment
- Proving their innovative skills
- Need for additional income

The above reasons clearly indicate that economic compulsion, family responsibilities and desire to enjoy social status compel the women to take up enterprises.

Women Development in the Current Indian Context

The Customer is Queen: From December 15, 2002 to February 2003, Maruti conducted a series of rallies for Women drivers in various cities, described as "Women Power Drive Events", and these rallies are a great success. In September 2002, Kotak Mahindra Life Insurance launched the Kotak Preferred Term Plan with lower premium rates for women below 25 years.

All this points to a very interesting trend in India. Indian women seem to be target for all. "The most visible symbol of emerging India is the fact that every manufacturer is targeting women today," Everybody from a pin maker to auto manufacturers is aiming at the women.

For generations, no one bothered to ask what were needed to women and there were much less manufacturers of products exclusively needed for women. But now, women are on a roll."

According to the latest National Readership Survey, an impressive three million women joined the urban work force between 1999 and 2002. Though few have broken into the top echelons of power, the junior and middle management levels are full of women. A look at a contemporary workplace would reveal a substantial increase in number of women working alongside their male counterparts; earning as much, often more and being a part of important decisions. Women are not just joining at the beginner's level but also occupying senior positions taking important decisions. Indian offices are full of women. Peep into PR firms, publication houses, offices of TV channels and production houses one can see young and energetic women. In the MNCs too, one sees women in large numbers. All around, women are seen making confident strides, flashing their cards, making the purchase they want, driving cars, sporting the latest mobile model or generally we can state that women are having a great time.

In the words of a Mumbai-based psychiatrist Dr. Shetty, "Women in our country have for long lived in the shadow of men, making compromises for the husband and the child. Today's woman has woken up to the fact that she needn't feel guilty about pampering herself. She gets what she wants with her money and doesn't need anybody's approval. And it's this awakening that manufacturers are cashing on by trying to woo them."

From the above statement it is clear that an interesting trend is being set for women. It's not just the working woman who's in the limelight. A recent study by KSA Technopak found a mere 10 per cent difference in spending pattern between the working woman and a housewife. Clearly indicating that housewives aren't languishing. The fact that the term "housewife" has given way to "homemaker" suggests a difference in perspective.

If we can scan the ads that either run on TV, or in magazines and everywhere we observe that women are portrayed as individuals who know what they want. Hordes of companies selling branded jewellery inundate our markets. The ads for Whirlpool, Asian Paints, and the Mera Wala Pink show homemakers who swing expensive household purchases. Clearly the old stereotype of a demure quiet woman in the background is out.

Check out the latest Fair and Lovely campaign and the one before that – a man laments that he doesn't have a son. But his daughter gets a high airhostess' job and takes him for coffee at a plush hotel – outraged many but hid an interesting message. Even the current ad – showing a young girl who becomes a cricket commentator – just proves the earlier point. Women are taking giant leaps in this country. They aim for the sky and touch it too. And TV channels are adding to the melee. Almost all channels have programmes aimed at women. The weekly serials driving the intelligentsia mad are making loads of money for the channels and the advertisers. Ekta Kapoor – asked when she plans to put an end to the never-ending "Kyonki Saas .." and "Kahaani Ghar .." – said, "I would be mad to shutdown such a successful and profitable venture. They make everyone happy such as the TV channels, the producers, directors, actors, writers and most of all my viewers." Programmes like these run on commercials, which need to cater to the viewers who throng to watch them. The manufacturers would be insane not to capitalize on a captive audience.

Hotels, travel industry and nightclubs are also going all out to make the woman happy. Five star hotels have special rooms reserved for single woman travellers to make them more comfortable and secure with women attendants, feminine knick-knacks ... Mikanos, a poplar watering hole in Mumbai, has an all woman day on Wednesday for woman partygoers to have fun. Cars, credit cards and every other conceivable product are today being aimed at women. So the customer, who for long was the king, has now truly become the queen. So hail the queen.

Women in Administration of Higher Education

In the field of education in India, one finds very few women at top levels such as Vice-Chancellors/Directors of Public Instruction/

Principals/Deans, even though there are a large number of women who choose teaching as their profession.

The reality is that women's participation at decision-making levels in any field is dismally low, considering the fact that they constitute almost half the population. The picture is the same in educational administration. It is said women constitute 30 per cent of the teaching profession. In 1984-85, in higher education there were 28 women to every hundred men. (Of course, this is an improvement over the 1950-51 figure of nine per hundred!) Among university teachers, there is one woman for every ten male teachers; in research, the ratio is 1:9; in professional colleges the ratio is 1:6 and in general education 1:4. Women lecturers in affiliated colleges are around 21 per cent while it is 11.6 per cent in university departments. It is reported that there are only two women for every hundred men who are university professors. At any point of time there may not be more than 10 to 15 Vice Chancellors, (including those heading the nine women's universities), in the existing more than 230 universities in the country. In 1992, there were seven women and 98 men as Vice Chancellors, two women and 28 men as Pro-Vice Chancellors, two women and 100 men as Registrars, and one woman and nine men as Directors of Continuing and Adult Education. As academic heads, 57 women and 603 men were Deans.

Although women have gained access to higher education all over the world, the scenario is the same, namely, that their numbers are still far below men in the management of institutions of higher education. That women are lagging behind men in taking to educational opportunities possibly contributes to the fact that women are not visible in large numbers at higher echelons in educational administration. But there are many within the profession who are very capable and could wear the mantle of leadership easily. Yet these women do not seem to aspire for it.

As a matter of fact, most professionals, men or women, such as scientists and doctors, do not like administration because it is mundane and routine. But, generalisation notwithstanding, there is greater love among men for the power and influence that go with administrative posts. The "power structure" in institutions quite often inhibits women. Men say that it is women themselves who deny themselves the chances for upward mobility. This is referred to as 'psychosocial' causes, which could include the behavioural traits and skills of women. Perhaps their attachment to familial duties, whether shared or not by their men folk, makes them less mobile and unwilling for transfers or changes of any kind. May be the situation in the home is such that women are fearful of their men folk/in-laws, and they may not want to appear as ambitious or desiring to rise in their career. Gender stereotypes and the patriarchal ethos possibly govern their thinking.

The reason why women should be in administrative positions in higher educational institutions and universities as in all spheres of activity is that they have to be treated like any human being whose rights must be upheld and whose aspirations must be given opportunities for fulfilment – this for ensuring a just and equitable society. Secondly, everywhere, in every activity of decision making, women's viewpoints and experience, as much as men's, need to be captured for the decision to be balanced and complete. We must ensure that policies are drawn up through 'women's eyes' also, which is not the case now.

Gender-friendly Environment

It is said that one of the best ways of attracting women to higher posts is to create a gender friendly environment in which sexual harassment has little or no chance to prevail. Gender sensitisation in every profession is urgent and necessary for men and women separately and in groups where they are together, so that existing practices can be reviewed by them and discussed for improvement.

As a matter of policy, a decision needs to be taken at the highest decision-making level such as the Government, the U.G.C., the National Assessment and Accreditation Council (NAAC), the universities, and colleges, that the representation of women at the levels of policy making bodies and committees should be increased.

To create a pro-woman atmosphere, the rules and regulations of an institution have also to be looked at to see whether there are any provisions needing revision or which must be made more woman-friendly. Provision of support services for the care of children in the premises of the institution or close by, transport, housing, and single women accommodation also need to be taken up on a priority basis.

Women in Business

Mammon may be the deity of choice of the corporate world but there is one higher authority to which he must pay obeisance. This is power itself. It is the ability to shape and change organisations, careers, markets, entire industries, sometimes, the lives of an entire nation. It is the deafening silence that falls upon a meeting when someone with enough of the commodity to spare raises his or her voice to make a point. It is the raw envy an individual's achievements provoke in people around. It is, in equal parts admiration, respect, influence, and it is more.

The different roles played by women can be consolidated entrepreneurs, executives, wives, sisters, mothers, and daughters inducted into the family business. Those left out women who weren't actively involved in business, but who exerted considerable influence (sometimes more than those in business) simply by being close to those in power. For examples Infosys' N.R.Narayana Murthy, Reliance's Mukesh Ambani, and Godrej's Adi Godrej are all powerful men and they are married to strong women (Sudha, Nita, and Parmeshwar, respectively) who serve, more often than not, as muse, confidant, and sounding board rolled into one.

Thus, women have developed in various fields, which leads to women empowerment and finally resulted as successful women entrepreneurs.

Measures and Suggestions for Promoting Entrepreneurship among Women

Suggestions for prospective entrepreneurs : Prospective entrepreneurs should realise that (a) family support is a very vital factor and that work at the cost of the family is not desirable, (b) careful selection and proper planning of a project is very important, (c) a fair degree of knowledge of the proposed project (acquired through experience/training /learning from family business or self study) is very important, (d) a strong determination and desire to succeed is needed and (e) adequate financial resources at their initial stage and preparedness to take financial risks are also important.

Suggestions to the government: The women entrepreneurs require the support of Govt. in the following areas:

(a) Adequate institutional support (b) timely and adequate credit of financial assistance (c) adequate marketing facility and availability of raw material (d) availability of basic infrastructural facilities (e) creating conducive entrepreneurial environment (f) assistance for modernization in technical upgradation and (h) a well-articulated and comprehensive policy for women entrepreneurs.

Leadership training: The capability of women in 'management' needs to be strengthened through leadership training and imparting of administrative skills. In addition to enhancement of knowledge about 'management' and higher education including the need to have a vision and taking people along and working alongside men with confidence and belief in one self and ones capacities.

Industrial Estates for Women: There is recognition of the role of small industry in the furtherance of economic development. A new experiment is being carried during 1950s and after in developed and developing countries for promoting the growth of small industries through Industrial Estates. Under this scheme, a separate industrial township is created with the necessary infrastructural facilities like land, water, roads, electricity, transportation etc. The entrepreneurs are encouraged to occupy the land or shed and continue their activities.

Creation of separate wing in the DIC (District Industries Centre) : Another point that must be considered seriously by the State Government authorities is to think about the starting of a separate department or wing in the DIC for women at the district level.

Making Entrepreneurship as a part of Curriculum: It is believed that entrepreneurship needs a particular kind of people and they need to have certain traits on the basis of information given by the participants of the symposium on development of entrepreneurship talent, K.J.Christopher has identified eighteen characteristics as being important in case of those wishing to be entrepreneurs. The list includes factors like perseverance, hard work, risk taking ability, high aspiration, willingness to learn, good salesmanship, adaptability, innovativeness, initiative, self confidence and determination to succeed instead of these being promoted at a late age, they can be developed from a very young age. For this purpose, the school and college curriculum needs to be changed at some stage. Right from the age of 15 women having these qualities should be identified and they may be taught certain traits, which can be cultivated later for blosoming women entrepreneurs.

Changing the Social Attitudes: It has been highlighted that the attitudes of society towards women are responsible to a great extent for their oppression in India. The growth of traditional and fundamental thinking must be curbed. The society needs to cultivate progressive outlook towards, things and encourage women to compete with men. This, we think, should start from the early days of childhood. The brought up of children must change. A rigid behaviour should not be imposed on girls. The behaviour different from that of boys should neither be rewarded nor encouraged. This is considered essential, as it sows the seeds of inferiority and dependence, leading to the demand for separate status and protection. There is also a need to educate parents on this aspect.

Responsibilities of Women Entrepreneurs: In any development programmes, much of the burden lies with the beneficiaries. Unless they are interested in the programme or activities, the promotional organizations can do a little. There is much truth in the saying that "one can take a horse to the pond, but cannot make it drink". Similar is also the activity of entrepreneurship development among women. The women must be able to come out from the cob-web created by the social norms and customs. They should be different from the rest of the world and think progressively. Instead of expecting concessions and relief from the government and other supporting agencies, they should try to seize the opportunities and forge ahead.

Women should be aware of their rights: Every women needs to acquaint herself with laws pertaining to their rights so that they could knock the doors of courts to get Justice and to understand when to approach them. Women despite excelling in education and going on to become successful entrepreneurs are facing problems on the family front, which need to be tackled effectively. Economic independence for women is essential and the 'Districts Mahila Pranganams 'across the state were imparting training in several revenue – generating allocations so that, they could take up some economic activity to create self confidence. The awareness on women's rights need to be publicised in a big way in several ways and women in distress had to be told that there was a 'Legal Services Authority' at the district level, to be contacted in case of necessity.

Conclusion

Now women are rapidly emerging as smart and dynamic entrepreneurs. They have entered almost all areas of business activities such as textiles, engineering goods, electronic, steel works etc. Educated women are making a land mark in the new conventional field like consultancy, advertising, garment export, interior decoration, textile printing, handicrafts etc. However, the women entrepreneurs form a negligible percentage of the total entrepreneurs in the country. If the entrepreneurship is properly developed among the women by training them on independent thinking, increase in foresight, improving the organising ability, increasing innovative skills, and increasing vision. The women entrepreneur can get more knowledge from her entrepreneur abilities when she successfully undertakes a venture. Thus, a women entrepreneur can also contribute her experience to the present day knowledge society.

REFERENCES

1. Akhouri, M.M.P., *Evaluation of Entrepreneurial Motivation Training Programme in Assam,* Hyderabad SIET, 1974.
2. Bhanushali, S.G., *Entrepreneurship Development*, Bombay, Himalaya Publishing House, 1987.
3. Chetana Kalbaga (Ed.), *Women and Development*, Vol.3, New Delhi, Discovery Publishing House. 1991.
4. Deepak Walakar, *Women Entrepreneurs*, Delhi, Himalaya Publishing House – 2001.
5. D. Walokor & Upadhyay R.K. 1996, *Women in 21st Century*, Delhi Hamam Publications.
6. Gangadhara Rao, N., *Entrepreneurship and Growth of Enterprise in Industrial Estates*, New Delhi, Deep & Deep Publications, 1986.
7. Garfield, Charles, Peak Performers: *The New Heroes of American Business*, New York, Avon Books, 1986.
8. Gautam Vinaysil, Enterprise and Society: *A Study of Some Aspects of Entrepreneurship and Management in India,* Delhi, Concept Publishing Co., 1979.
9. Narasimha Murthy, B.E.V.V., *Entrepreneurship in Small Towns*, Delhi, Mittal Publications, 1989.
10. Patel V.G., *Developing New Entrepreneurs*, Ahmedabad, Entrepreneurship Development Institute, 1987.

11. Prithvi Nath, T., *Indian Women*, Delhi, B.R. Publishing Corporation, 1985.
12. Singh, P.N. *Emerging Trends in Entrepreneurship Development: Theories and Practices*, New Delhi, Intellectual Foundation for Development Management, 1985.
13. Satish Taneja & S.L. Gupta, *Entrepreneur Development New Venture Creation*, New Delhi, Galgotia Publishing Co., 2001.

Articles

1. Asgharl Mohiuddin, *Entrepreneurship development among women-retrospect's and prospects, sedme*, Vol. 10, No. 1, March, 1983, pp. 1-8.
2. Gumpert, David E., *Entrepreneurship: A new literature begins*, Harvard business review, Vol. 60, No.2, March-April, 1982, pp. 50-60. Gururaj, D.S., women entrepreneurs, *Economic Times*, March 10, 1985.
3. Heggade. O.D., *A Started for Developing Industrial Entrepreneurship among Harijans, Indian Journal of Industrial Relations*, Vol. 18, No.4, April 1983, PP. 585-606.
4. Hina Shah, & Bhupatani, D.D., *Fostering Women Entrepreneurship, Nirnay*, Vol.4, No.4, December 1989, PP. 93-104.
5. Lex Donaldson, *Entrepreneurship applied to middle management a caution, Journal of General Management*, Vol. 10, No. 4,. Summer 1985, PP. 5-20.
6. *Business Today* Magazine November, 2003.
7. *The Hindu* Daily Paper, 16th September, 2003.
8. *The Hindu* Daily Paper, 8th February, 2004.

16

DO WOMEN ENJOY REAL FREEDOM IN INDIA?

Dr. A. Durga Nagaveni*

From times immemorial India has been regarded as a seat of learning and we hear foreigners like Hueinsung and Faheian had visited India nearly some 1400 years ago with a view to gaining knowledge and wisdom. Nalanda and Takshasila speak volumes of our ancient culture and tradition. However, force of circumstances had given place to foreign invasions and had brought about a change in the outlook and thinking of its people. Ethical values and moral uprightness were the key factors on which emphasis was laid and society was well organized, people were contented and society was found to be ideal in all respects.

As civilization progressed there was a change in the outlook of the people and people began to feel that they should harness the immense potential of nature to make his life better and still better. In this respect the male member of the society had to assume a superior status in the family unit of society thus relegating the lady of the house to the back ground. Coupled to this illiteracy and the present day discrimination have given women a much lower status than men, much to the discomfort of women folk. This is indeed lamentable. It is only in recent times that India as a free nation has thought of giving an equal status to women in all spheres. Laws have been passed granting eligibility to women in many a field of activity considering their inequal physical status compared to their male counterparts.

---

* Lecturer in Hindi, B.H.H. Degree College for Women, Guntur.

Despite doing a lot of the upliftment of women, there is much to be desired. Another problem that needs to be addressed is providing women with economic freedom.

Introduction

Society is based on one biological division-The male and the female, this of course is natural and essential for the progeny. Anthropologists tell us that ancient humans had a primitive out-look and were leading a very disorganized life. As Civilization progressed humans found themselves into different kinds of groups and Clans that had led to the evolution of the present family system. The initial matriarchal society gave place to the patriarchal society which has a firm footing and status to the family as a unit. We also read from text books that the existence of the Joint family system is fast disappearing due to the prevailing economic and other conditions. Ancient texts reveal that status of women in those times was on par with their male counter parts and had enjoyed equal privileges.

Over a period of time this parity lost its validity and women began to be looked down as an inferior fair sex. Greed and envy gradually gripped the chauvenistic male, which had resulted in several clashes among different societies. Pride and vanity were abused by way of baits, to attract the other women, this was found to be quite luring to a number of women, and ultimately turned out to be a profession patronized by the elite of society. However over a period of time economic changes and the then prevailing social conditions also prompted this out of wed-lock relationship.

Looking back into the past, we come to know from Indian ancient texts that women were given an equal right along with men almost in every field of activity barring very few. Men used to secure blessings from their mothers and their wives used to offer the sacred Sindhoor and Harathi to their men folk before venturing whether be it a battle field or the sea.However consequent upon the various economic and social upheavals things began to change rapidly and women were given a lower status in the name of offering them protection. Also contributing were the invasions of foreign culture both from the west and the Middle East have had a profound influence on our mental set up. We began to look more towards west and imbibed to a great extent their culture and manners. Both men and women started adopting to a noticeable degree some aspects of western culture perhaps with a feeling that the native culture was found wanting. Eventually we have acquired a lot of westernized thinking and are now finding ourselves cumbersome to readjust ourselves to our ancient culture. There if a rat race between two genders vyeing with each other to occupy positions of power.

Tracing the history of medieval times, we find often women being subjected to different kinds of harassment both physical and mental in order to satiate their thirst for their marital sex. If the latter had declined ,such ladies were further harassed by those land lords and Zamindars. Further, it is said that at times women were even commanded to share the pleasure of bed with some of their close relatives.Naturally this system gave place to a condition now commonly known as the present day flesh trade,which is considered to be the oldest profession that humanity has known.

Generally it is regarded that India is a land of Karma Bhoomi, perhaps the only one of its kind in the entire world.Many things are attributed to the Karma factor which has deep roots in our present day society also. Looking at India from an ancient angle we find that society was based on the *'Varnas'* system which was in vogue to maintain a clear cut barrier between people, and ensured a definite degree of division of labour. Literacy was confined only to the privileged and that too a very great extent for men. His female counterpart had a duel role. One to take care of the house hold compulsion and the other to continue the human race. In our epics we find women enjoying status on a par with men though it was confined to the privileged and the elite.

However, envy and jealousy among men over the possession of women gave rise to conflicts among families that had led to regular wars. Kingdoms and empires were ruined for the sake of possessing one woman, causing havoc among the society. In spite of being called the only Karma Bhoomi in the world, India has seen several storms of war knowing well that the root cause for waging the war is totally unjustified.

Such conflicts and wars and the consequent ruination had brought about a change in the outlook of men who regarded women as the treasure to reckon with. Bearing this in mind, women were isolated and were made to undergo that isolation more with a view to protect her modesty. There is a saying in our language that *'A beautiful wife becomes the first enemy to her husband'*. Taking into consideration this factor women were relegated to the background and subjected to loneliness and isolation. As times began to change, during the 18th and 19th Centuries, women began to assert themselves in several fields of activity, thereby competing with their male counterparts. The women power force gradually started emerging to the forefront and carved for itself a place to reckon with. Not only in India but also in some other parts of the world where women were forbidden to come out of doors are occupying positions of power and wielding equal authority with men. This only shows signs of change that all taking place in modern India. In spite of one professing an equal status to women in our society for a long time now, we are yet to see the day when women can enjoy an equal status in all respects with men.

The plans for promoting and uplifting the status of women in our society still remain only on paper and how and when they transform into reality is a matter to be seen and is any body's guess. In this connection, we have a shining example of how our eminent parliamentarians have failed to arrive at a consensus in giving women a 33% reservation in all positions. The real reason for their inability to arrive at a consensus rather seems to be the fear that haunts many parliamentarians that they may lose their seats in parliament, if reserved for women.

Looking at the problem from a different direction women too should fight for their rights and exercise their authority freely and fearlessly without any inhibition. French women had fought for their right to vote and won their cause. Similarly, we in India should evolve a method by which women get their rights and enjoy their freedom to exercise their authority without any male hindrance.

Further the male, female ratio should be narrowed down to its minimum and a fair balance should be struck; in order to avoid this discrimination. Further illiteracy among women should be eliminated so that they may come to know of the prevailing conditions and chalk out necessary plans to assert their rights and privileges. Being a democracy, India should be the world's polestar for the rest of the world in promoting and protecting the security and safety on one side and rights and duties of women on the other. Women also should extend their maximum possible co-operation in gaining from the government, freedom to express their views openly without any hindrance from their male members of the society. This would take a long time to achieve, but with a will to do what is required will definitely bestow the desired results. In a civilized and democratic society discrimination on grounds of religion, caste, creed ,culture and gender are unthinkable and if any such discrimination if noticed or found such acts should be condemned and curbed with all the strength at our disposal. All said and done women though they are physically weaker are nevertheless a power to count upon.

If we consider the economic basis of our country, it will be noticed that society is divided in to three categories – the lower class, the middle class and the upper class. This categorization is mostly done on one's economic status. The Government's economic policy-being what it is, we notice that greater attention is given to the poorer/ lower class both money wise and policy wise, for deriving an eventual benefit. The rich/upper class is taken care of by their money, while the middle class/common man is bereft of any help or other type of assistance from any source, thus leading to a negation of the concept of an egalitarian society. Also taking into consideration, the ever growing inflationary tendencies in our economy, the need for a second source of income is increasingly felt to make both ends meet. It is in these circumstances that women too be made to contribute their share to the family income in order to enjoy a reasonably comfortable life. To achieve this objective, both government and public sector undertakings should either reserve certain percentage of jobs or indirectly provide with income generating opportunities. Undoubtedly, this is an up-hill and challenging task, but considering the latent and untapped potential of our country it should not be as difficult as imagined it to be. Perpetual disparities in economic status lead to discontentment, which in turn may lead taking to extremism, which is being noticed today in several parts of the country. The educated un- employed among the middle class youth find it difficult to remain jobless and is dubbed as a Non-performing asset. This in turn leads to frustration, resulting in taking vengeance against society, in which women invariably are victimized.

In this regard it can also be said absence of economic freedom to women some times may cause jealousy among their spouses. While women in the neighborhood earn, their co-house wives confined to the four walls of their house remaining idle, most of the time (except doing the usual minimum) creates an inferiority complex and develop a feeling of dependence. Added to such feeling, we often hear cases of harassment by some in laws and men folk against the daughters-in-law which at times may lead to suicide by young girls.

Another type of agony women are subjected to is physical and mental harassment caused by their superior officers. It is not uncommon hear of cases where young ladies are forced to have physical contacts with them. Also they are baited to by way of offering promotions and increments for obliging their physical needs. Such incidents all to be highlighted as and when they occur preferably by lady journalists. It is also noticed though not very common, that some lady members of Municipal councils are represented by their spouses in spite of protests from various quarters. This clearly shows that women members themselves are not very keen in performing their alloted duties.

The need for preserving and protecting women's rights in rural areas lies in setting up of *local adalats* comprising women. Also it is noticed that while giving a dying declaration women suppress the actual truth, to protect their spouses and in laws. Hence, it is high time that women too take an active interest in protecting their rights and come forward to meet the ever growing needs and challenges of the day. Any number of amendments to the constitution and any amount of assurances will be of little or no use, unless women themselves take up their own cause for an effective and visible progress towards the desired goals.

However, as times have changed, the status of women too has witnessed a noticeable change in their status and their outlook.We find women increasingly occupying positions at various levels and are showing up to prove that they are no longer to be considered as an inferior sex.This situation has given rise to a sort of prejudice among men against women resulting in family jealousy, family disputes and even leading to breaking up of family ties.Daring men even go to the extent of maintaining another women to meet his biological needs.This coupled with arrogance and intolerance has resulted in cases of molestation and rape thus creating a fear psychosis in the minds of women.We are yet to see perhaps a night when a women can go alone in any street of any town or city,perhaps because of her physical insecurity and modesty she dreads to risk it.

Despite the fact that a larger percentage of females are going to school and college and taking up employment at various levels, the threat perception to have safety and security is still persisting as a menacing factor. Figures speaking crimes against women have shown an upward trend between the years 1990 and 1994, thus causing an embarrassment to our society in general and the government in particular. This atrocity against women is to be viewed more as a social evil rather than as a gender disparity. The under mentioned figures speak for themselves during the above referred period.

S. No.	*Year*	*Crime against Women (IPC Case)*
01.	1990	68,317
02.	1991	74,093
03.	1992	79,037
04.	1993	83,954
05.	1994	91,010

Source: Women in Indian Society, Neera Desai.

Atrocities against women can be broadly divided into 3 or 4 segments.

1. Rape or molestation every 26 minutes.
2. Dowry death every 102 minutes.
3. Sexual harassment every 51 minutes.
4. A criminal offence of torture or cruelty every 33 minutes.

The existing mind bogging questions are to find an answer. To cite for example will the present well knit family unit survive the mounting pressure over a period of generations or will it disintegrate and become a loosely knit family that deprives itself the moral and ethical values? Based on the presumption that India is a land of Karma Bhoomi, should we, especially the women feel that though they are elevated and given an honourable status, do they ever gain the freedom of speech to express their views and manifest their thoughts through action? Do they gain economic freedom to share and supplement the basic needs of family running. It is affirmative the haunting threat of boss-employee relationship may be put to a severe test in which more often than not the latter being the victim of circumstances.

Conclusion

In order to end this age old gender discrimination, it is high time that parents especially the men folk could realize the importance of women in society towards the betterment of families as individual units. To a great extent Illiteracy, lack of knowledge and proper understanding contribute to this malady. Steps should be taken to bring about a change in the mindset of men and women, in order to accomplish this objective. Good education and sound counselling do bring about the desired change over a period of time.

Coming to the menace of dowry death problems parents should take appropriate steps to protect the well being of the feminine folk and develop an attitude of contentment with what they have. Termination of pregnancies at an early stage that confirms the birth of a girl child after some months should be made a severely punishable offence and female infanticide should receive capital punishment. Finally, it is the attitude of the humanity that makes or mars the fate of a family which undoubtedly rests with the governing parents.

17

WOMEN POWER AS STRATEGIC STRENGTH

M. Sujatha* and Dr. C.S.G. Krishnamacharyulu**

Global competition has made business environment more volatile than before. To cope with this environment developing innovative strategies has become imperative. Money, material and machinery have lost their strategic importance, in the emergent knowledge society. Human resource alone is being viewed as the true strategic strength for the reason that people can think innovatively and act strategically, to make organisations successful.

In the recent past, when one thought of human resources it was only men in the organization that came into the picture. Women were not regarded as an important contributing force. However, the scenario has been changing. Women are emerging as partners of progress and therefore can't be neglected. When analysed it will be found that capabilities of women are not being put to their utmost use even in this information age. For instance, though the proportion of women being employed is raising those being employed at higher levels is still lower. To develop women at par with men should be the mission of our country. The processes, which promote women development are emancipation, education and empowerment. These are influenced by driving forces like materialistic culture, urbanization, media exposure and active involvement of women organizations.

* Research Scholar, School of Business Management, S.V. University, Tirupathi

** Professor & BOS Chairman, School of Business Management, S.V.University, Tirupathi

The restraining forces for women participation in the force field of development are non-recognition of women capabilities by organisations, lack of confidence among women, adherence to traditional concepts and roles and dual role conflict in families etc., Measures to promote women as a strategic partner should be broad based and sweeping, covering both society and organisations.

"There is no chance for the welfare of the world unless the condition of women is improved. It is not possible for a bird to fly on one wing"

–Swami Vivekananda

Introduction

The development process has gained pace as never before with industrialization, urbanization and globalisation. In the emergent development scenario, women have been given their long due importance. The society realized that neglected women resources in the context of economic development have a negative effect on the rate of development. Women constitute nearly half of the human resources. If half of the human resources are not used effectively then rate of development also decreases considerably.

1. The Dismal Picture

It is important to have an idea of conditions of women In India before we discuss why women development is a key factor in overall development.

(a) *Women are malnourished:* "Gender disparities in nutrition are evident from infancy to adulthood. In fact, gender has been the most statistically significant determinant of malnutrition among young children and malnutrition is a frequent direct or underlying cause of death among girls below age 5. Girls are breast-fed less frequently and for shorter duration's in infancy; in childhood and adulthood, males are fed first and better. Adult women consume approximately 1,000 fewer calories per day than men according to one estimate from Punjab. Comparison of household dietary intake studies in different parts of the country show that nutritional equity between males and females is lower in northern than in southern states." (Carol S. Coonrod, June 1998).

Malnutrition causes physical and psychological problems in women. Can physically weak women fight against unfavorable environment existing in the so-called male dominated society?

(b) *Women are in poor health:* A primary way that parents discriminate against their girl children is through neglect during illness. When sick, little girls are not taken to the doctor as frequently as are their brothers. A study in Punjab shows that medical expenditures for boys are 2.3 times higher than for girls.

As adults, women get less health care than men. They tend to be less likely to admit that they are sick and they'll wait until their sickness has progressed before they seek help or help is sought for them. Studies on attendance at rural primary health centers reveal that more males than females are treated in almost all parts of the country, with differences greater in northern hospitals than southern ones, pointing to regional differences in the value placed on women. Women's socialization to tolerate suffering and their reluctance to be examined by male personnel are additional constraints in their getting adequate health care. (Carol S. Coonrod, June 1998)

Women are always seen as unwanted part of the society. Their illness is never considered as an important issue. The main reason may be this - women seldom play the role of breadwinner in the family. Any serious ill health or even death is not considered a big harm to the existence of the family. Therefore men are given more importance in health related problems than women.

(c) *Selective abortions:* The most extreme expression of the preference for sons is female infanticide and sex-selective abortion. Women are seen as a burden to the family. The Indian perception is that bearing and giving birth to a girl child would lead to heavy economic loss to the family when the girl is married due to dowry. This resulted in selective abortions, female infanticide and declining ratio of women to men.

'A study of amniocentesis in a Bombay hospital found that 96 percent of female fetuses were aborted, compared with only a small percentage of male fetuses.

"Government officials even suspect that the disproportionate abortion of female fetuses may be a major underlying cause of the recent decline in the nation's sex ratio. In 1971 there were 930 females for every 1,000 males. A decade later this figure had increased to 934, but by 1991, instead of continuing to rise, the ratio dropped to 927, lower than the 1971 figure. This sex ratio is one of the lowest in the world."

Government has passed legislation to curb the misuse of amniocentesis for sex selection and abortion of female fetuses. Women activists have been critical of this act because of its provision that calls for punishing the women who seek the procedure. These women may be under pressure to bear a male child.' (Carol S. Coonrod, June 1998)

(d) *Women are powerless:* Legal protection of women's rights has little effect in the face of prevailing patriarchal traditions. Women are subordinate in most marriages. Exposure to and interactions with the outside world are instrumental in determining the possibilities available to women in their daily lives. The situation of women is affected by the degree of their autonomy or capacity to make decisions both inside and outside their own household.

"The position of women in northern India is notably poor. Traditional Hindu society in northern rural areas is hierarchical and dominated by men, as evidenced by marriage customs. A young Indian bride is brought up to believe that her own wishes and interests are subordinate to those of her husband and his family. The primary duty of a newly married young woman, and virtually her only means of improving her position in the hierarchy of her husband's household, is to bear sons." (Carol S. Coonrod, June 1998)

Women were never perceived as an earning member of the family. The traditional model depicts women as care takers of the household. The subordinate position given to women in the Indian system does not allow women to earn on their own applying their skills and capabilities. Though the women are allowed to work along with men, in majority of the cases the decision making power and control over earnings are exercised by men as they act a the head of the family.

(e) *Women are less educated:* Women and girls receive far less education than men, due both to social norms and fears of violence. Primary education in India is not universal. Overall, the literacy rate for women is 39 percent versus 64 percent for men. The rate for women in the four large northern states - Bihar, Uttar Pradesh, Rajasthan and Madhya Pradesh — is lower than the national average: it was 25 percent in 1991. Attendance rates from the 1981 census suggest that no more than 1/3 of all girls (and a lower proportion of rural girls) aged 5-14 are attending school.

Although substantial progress has been achieved since India won its independence in 1947, when less than 8 percent of females were literate, the gains have not been rapid enough to keep pace with population growth: there were 16 million more illiterate females in 1991 than in 1981. Lack of an educated population can be an impediment to the country's economic development. The Indian government has expressed a strong commitment towards education for all; however, India still has one of the lowest female literacy rates in Asia. In 1991, less than 40 percent of the330 million women aged 7 and over were literate, which means today there are over 200 million illiterate women in India. This low level of literacy not only has a negative impact on women's lives but also on their families' lives and on their country's economic development.

Although literacy levels are low, there has been progress

in improving educational attainment for both sexes in India over the last several decades. In 1971, only 22 per cent of women and 46 percent of men were literate (Register General and Census Commissioner (RGCC), 1977). By 1991, 39 percent of women and 64 percent of men were literate (RGCC1993). Thus; there has been a large increase in the proportion of women who are literate in just 20 years. Despite the improvements in literacy, there continues to be a large gap between the literacy levels of men and of women.

(f) *Women are mistreated:* Violence against women and girls is the most pervasive human rights violation in the world today. Male violence against women is a worldwide phenomenon. Although not every woman has experienced it, and many expect not to, fear of violence is an important factor in the lives of most women. It determines what they do, when they do it, where they do it, and with whom. Fear of violence is a cause of women's lack of participation in activities beyond the home, as well as inside it. Within the home, women and girls may be subjected to physical and sexual abuse as punishment or as culturally justified assaults. These acts shape their attitude to life, and their expectations of themselves.

The insecurity outside the household is today the greatest obstacle in the path of women. Conscious that, compared to the atrocities outside the house, atrocities within the house are endurable, women not only continued to accept their inferiority in the house and society, but also even called it sweet. (Carol S. Coonrod, June 1998)

It is every body's understanding that some initiatives and measures are necessary to charge the situation of Indian women. The following may be considered.

Strategic Initiatives

- Woman education
- Women employment
- Urbanization

- Media exposure
- Active involvement of women organizations

Hurdles

- Non recognition of women capabilities
- Lack of confidence among women
- Dual role conflict

2. Strategic Initiatives

(a) *Women Education:* Women education is the foundation for women development. It transformed the traditional out look of both women and the society. To stand on their own women need better education in various disciplines. Without education it becomes difficult to realize their capabilities. Now we are witnessing a positive and phenomenal change in this direction. Small families with two or three children could educate their girl children better than before. Women must be provided more opportunities of education to give their talents more recognition.

(b) *Women Employment:* Achieving economic independence is seen as a solution to many problems effecting women. Women who are earning are able to enjoy dignity and respect in their families as well as in the society. The subordinate role to which women were kept restricted to is being replaced with equal role because of economic independence. Career development among women is giving them recognition, self esteem and an opportunity to prove their talents. This has contributed to the overall social development.

(c) *Urbanization:* Urbanization has given many employment opportunities to women. Increase in cost of living has acted as a driving force to make use of available earning opportunities. Small family allows women to use her leisure time to take up part time or full time employment. Advancements in computer technology helped women to earn without leaving home, for instance, medical transcription.

(d) *Media exposure:* Media is capable of bringing a radical change in the society. Electronic media, is more powerful in shaping the opinions and attitudes. Unlike print media, electronic media has a profound effect on women, even uneducated. Media educates women, improves awareness of various social and economic issues. The knowledge relating to various schemes started for women welfare is well communicated to rural women using electronic media. This resulted in success of various welfare measures like family planning, women education, health care, micro finance etc. undertaken by the government.

(e) *Active involvement of women organizations:* Women Organizations, Non-Government Organizations and Government Departments working for women welfare act as catalysts in women development. There are actively involved in women education, health care, micro credit etc. and also training women in various vocations. They also fight collectively for victims of dowry, harassment and abuse. This helped women to build confidence in themselves and made them feel that they are not alone. Self help groups are gaining prominence among women.

3. Hurdles

(a) *Non recognition of women capabilities:* Society does not consider women as intelligent as men. Therefore women are given secondary, and subordinate functions only. Organizations hesitate to give key functions to women, which involve decision making. But this situation is changing owing to pursuit to higher education by women. Now women are equally qualified to take up challenging positions in various fields. This trend must be encouraged.

(b) *Lack of confidence among women:* Most of the women are not aware that they can accomplish challenging tasks. They do not realize their hidden potential. They hesitate to accept challenging positions, because of fear of failure. Confidence level among women is lower. Society makes them think that they are less capable than men. This attitude among women must change.

(c) *Dual role conflict:* Married women are expected to balance both career and family responsibilities. But this is not easy and is a cause of conflict. Taking care of children would not allow women to focus on career. They have to sacrifice their career advancement to a certain extent for children. This might be a reason why women do not prefer jobs demanding much time, effort and travel.

4. How to leverage women power for organizational success?

- Providing equal opportunities for women at all levels of organizational hierarchy.
- Women should be preferred for positions where women can perform better than men.
- Flexible working hours and leave facilities help to reduce stress and dual role conflict among women.
- Work from home facility gives an opportunity to balance dual responsibilities.
- Creative, artistic and designing talents in Indian women are in plenty. These talents should be incorporated in their work.

Conclusion

What we have seen so far is that women have come a long way crossing many hurdles. Still they face many challenges in career as well as personal life in this fast paced world. Women need more skills and right attitude to cope with changing times. They should also create good support system for themselves to fall back in times of crisis. Society needs to be more sympathetic towards women problems and think progressively to leverage women power.

REFERENCES

1. Carol S. Coonrod, June 1998, *Chronic hunger and the status of women in India*, www.thp.org.
2. Victoria. A. Velkoff 1998, *Women's education in India*, www.census.gov.

SECTION–III
INFORMATION TECHNOLOGY

18

THE ROLE OF INFORMATION TECHNOLOGY IN EMERGING INDIA

V.V. Suresh Babu* and **M. Kishore Babu****

Information Technology is one of the greatest boons of science to humanity. It is revolutionizing life on earth in a way that no other technology has done in human history. It has a deep influence on the economy, communication, culture, educational system, and social interaction in all countries, bringing them closer in a world transformed into a Global Village and laying the foundation for a new civilization. India, as the cradle of civilization, is poised to become a major IT power in the coming years and contribute to the realization of its many promises for our own benefit and for global good.

Information is critical to the social and economic activities that comprise the development process. Telecommunications, as a means of sharing information, is not simply a connection between people, but a link in the chain of the development process itself. The report entitled *A Phone in Every Village,* included plans to provide every rural Indian village with access to a telephone by 1999.

Information technology, when designed for the right job, can be deployed even in regions that lack adequate water, food, and power. Technology can be effective for many tasks, not the least of which is

* Lecturer, Department of Computer Science, Mahatma Gandhi College (PG), Guntur.

** Head, Dept. of Business Studies, Mahatma Gandhi College (PG), Guntur - 522 019.

human and economic development. In fact, technology is often indispensable in meeting basic needs. While the information revolution may threaten to increase inequity, it also provides tools to reduce poverty. An agenda for technology — improved access to education, health care, and information — is increasingly possible for the rural sector in India.

This article emphasizes on the technological issues regarding the IT industry, telecommunications and rural development with innovative thoughts.

Introduction

The success of Indian IT entrepreneurs and professionals – those in India as well as the ones working abroad – have created a new wave of hope, excitement and self-confidence among our talented young men and women. This combination of aspiration, knowledge and enterprise is laying a robust foundation for India's accelerated progress in the new century.

India has been often praised as the main development center of Global Software skills. Some people attribute this to the genetic factors in the Indian race and some to the strong English based, memory dependent education system. We often talk of India becoming a global super power in the IT industry. The move of the New Jersey State to stop its vendors by law importing BPO services from foreign companies should set the Indian IT companies thinking about their future business strategies.

Information is critical to the social and economic activities that comprise the development process. Telecommunications, as a means of sharing information, is not simply a connection between people, but a link in the chain of the development process itself. The report entitled *A Phone in Every Village,* included plans to provide every rural Indian village with access to a telephone by 1999.

Information technology, when designed for the right job, can be deployed even in regions that lack adequate water, food, and power. Technology can be effective for many tasks, not the least of which is human and economic development. In fact, technology is often indispensable in meeting basic needs. While the information revolution may threaten to increase inequity, it also provides tools to reduce poverty. An agenda for technology - improved access to education, health care, and information - is increasingly possible for the rural sector in India.

This article emphasizes on the technological issues regarding the IT industry, telecommunications and rural development with innovative thoughts.

Information Technology is one of the greatest boons of science to humanity. It is revolutionizing life on earth in a way that no other technology has done in human history. It has a deep influence on the economy, communication, culture, educational system, and social interaction in all countries, bringing them closer in a world transformed into a Global Village and laying the foundation for a new civilization. India, as the cradle of civilization, is poised to become a major IT power in the coming years and contribute to the realization of its many promises for our own benefit and for global good.

In a very short span of time, India's IT industry has earned global recognition and established itself as the fastest growth sector. The successes of Indian IT entrepreneurs and professionals – those in India as well as the ones working abroad – have created a new wave of hope, excitement and self-confidence among our talented young men and women. This combination of aspiration, knowledge and enterprise is laying a robust foundation for India's accelerated progress in the new century.

We are determined to remove all the hurdles of policy and implementation in the path of rapid expansion of telecom and the Internet in India. It is our endeavor to create a proper harmony between the traditional economy and the IT-driven New Economy, so that each strengthens the other to achieve balanced development of all sections of our diverse society and all regions of our vast country.

India's new focus on IT has naturally opened up tremendous opportunities for foreign IT companies and professionals for investments, joint ventures, R&D, and import and export of goods and services. Not only the Central Government, but also all the State Governments are creating a supportive framework to facilitate domestic and foreign investments. Information Technology is emerging as a powerful tool to serve humanity. We in India are conscious of the tremendous opportunities that IT offers to improve the living conditions of the people. With this in mind, we are looking towards using the power of IT to unleash opportunities for the development of the poor and deprived. Having missed the industrial revolution our endeavor now is to ensure that the benefits of a knowledge-based economy are harnessed to eradicate hunger and poverty.

With large English speaking population and a huge pool of technical and scientific human resource, we are today poised to realise the goal of making India the most preferred destination for developing tools for an IT led economy. 'Advantage India' brings out some of these efforts, initiatives and schemes along with the policies that are in place.

The Information Technology (IT) sector is amongst the fastest growing in the country. IT professionals work in all major markets around the world. Indian technology products and solutions are accepted globally. The first year of the new millennium has been a year of turbulence, tragedy, terrorism and slow-down in the world economy. The Indian IT software and services industry has weathered this storm well.

It is indeed creditable that the IT software and services industry in India has reasonably continued its robust growth of about 28 per cent during the year 2001-02.

Meeting the Global Competition - A Challenge for Indian Software Companies

India has been often praised as the main development centre of Global Software skills. Some people attribute this to the genetic factors in the Indian race and some to the strong English based, memory dependent education system. We often talk of India becoming a global super power in the IT industry.

There is no doubt that these thoughts have emerged out of the past observations and performances of Indian software professionals in the Silicon Valley and else where. Every top IT Company in the world including Microsoft, Oracle or Adobe would acknowledge the contribution of Indian software engineers to their success.

A time has come however for top management personnel in the Indian industry and NASSCOM in particular to reflect if the past glory of Indian software industry is any indication of the future trend.

It is also necessary to reflect what would be the consequences on the Indian Economy when say an Infosys and Wipro start sliding down the stock markets like the many glorious manufacturing companies in India during the last decade.

The first threat India has faced is the emergence of China, which has similar manpower strength like India. What China lacked is the penetration of English in the population and the IT education. Thanks to the short sighted policies of NASSCOM and also some of our IT Educational giants including NIIT, India is itself contributing to the empowerment of China as a competitor in the global market. After the September terrorist attacks on USA, the security concerns have risen several notches all over the world and this is the second threat to the growth of Indian software industry. Today, no American Company would trust a non-American Company for the development of critical software, in a manner in which they used to do in the past.

Despite the software skills, Indian software industry will therefore face some hurdles in continuing to make progress in the International Software development business.

Perhaps the recent ill treatment of Indian software professionals in several parts of the globe like Malaysia is an indication that Indian software skills are no longer considered indispensable. This should be taken as an early warning of the future trend.

The third and one of the most threatening aspects of the current development is the emergence of the IPR consciousness in the market place. The impact of this has not yet dawned on the Indian Software industry in full. The IPR regime will affect the Indian software industry in three ways.

1. *Super Power...How?* The contract work which Indian software companies will undertake for their International clients will all be now one time "Fee Based Coding Work". Once a "Solution" is developed for a Client based on his brief and his needs, the IPR in the product goes to the client. As a result if Indian software industry has Rs.30, 000 crore revenue in a year, this will represent the "IP Wealth Created by India in favour of the International Clients".

If we need to be proud of our IT achievement, then we can perhaps be proud of India being a Super Power in enriching the IPR of their International clients rather than enriching the country.

2. *Increasing Cost of IT*: The Use of software tools and software itself in India will involve payment for IPR of International suppliers creating a regular drain of Indian wealth out of the country.

   At present this impact has not been fully felt by the industry beyond the licensing of products used in Software development. If we take note of the Patents being issued on several E-Business products and the components which are embedded in many of the licensed software products, the possibility of these latent IP protected products coming out to hit the Indian entrepreneurs cannot be under estimated.

   The recent issue involving an embedded patent in Microsoft SQL server product should be an eye opener to the Industry.

   Similar threats could surface in the Trade Mark and Copyright areas also escalating the cost of IT business in India and pushing some Companies to bankruptcy because of legal non-compliance.

3. *Customers Turning into Foes:* In the coming days, aggressive pursuance of IPR will result in many customers of Indian IT companies turning their guns against them for breach of IPR. For example Banking Company in USA for whom the Indian Company has developed a Core solution may allege that the same structure or Coding pattern was used for a subsequent solution developed by the same Indian Company to an Australian Bank. In an International arbitration proceeding of this nature, it is more likely that the foreign Company with greater resources will always have an edge.

It would not be surprising if soon Indian IT Companies may be paying license fee for products part or whole of which they themselves had developed.

The Indian Company under seize may even find it difficult to carry on its regular business since the Dmitry Skylarov, Senthil Kumar and Arun Jain's incidents will make it difficult for the CEO s and top executives of the Company to travel freely beyond the boundaries of India.

As a result, the Indian IT Companies will not be able to develop more than one client in a given industry. There is therefore an automatic locking on of the business growth of the IT Company to the success of their clients.

The solution to all these emerging problems lie in a total revamping of the Marketing outlook of Indian Software Companies.

The approach should be to:

1. Develop own Intellectual Property and license it to the clients in the solutions as embedded components.
2. Develop Products, build Brand Property, harness and protect the Brand property in the global market.
3. Shift focus from contractual software development with maintenance to providing "Turn Key Services" on fee basis.

It is stated that today the share of products in the revenues of TCS and Infosys is around 5% to 7 %. If this is the trend in the top Indian companies, the industry average could be only around 3 %. This indicates that 97 % of Indian Software business is exposed to the risk of continued patronage from the Clients without any IPR protection.

This is an alarming situation for an industry hoping to be a "Super Power".

We therefore need some quick action by Indian IT majors so that over a period of next three years, at least the top 10 IT Companies should increase the "IPR Protected Component of their Business" (Whether as full products or as Reusable Components) to at least 25 %.

New Jersey Bill and the Future of Indian IT Companies: The move of the New Jersey State to stop its vendors by law importing BPO services from foreign companies should set the Indian IT companies thinking about their future business strategies.

If a developed economy like US is concerned about the employment loss and resorts to regulatory methods to protect its economy, should the Indian Government not be more concerned? Is it not necessary to think what the Indian Government and the IT industry can do to secure the long term interests of the Indian IT industry?

In the light of these developments, it is time to debate some of the strategies that Indian regulators and Indian IT Companies should adopt to protect the growth of IT industry in India. Leaving the regulatory aspects to a future article, we can focus on some of the initiatives that the Indian IT Companies should contemplate to ensure their continued success in the coming days. As a first step in this direction, it is necessary for Indian IT Companies to start devoting more attention on their marketing strategies. At present all IT Companies tend to focus on "Projects on Contract Basis". Many of these contracts are for low skill, high volume jobs similar to Y2K projects. Many IT Companies feel more pride in setting up development centers abroad which only replicate what their Indian offsite centers can do more effectively, than setting up "Product Marketing Cells" either in India or abroad.

Data Processing jobs and Migration work fill the financial balance sheets of companies in the short run but have very little long-term benefit for the Company. Such jobs neither create any reusable information assets or even skills. They may only build up the IPR of their principal clients. There is therefore an urgent need for Indian IT companies to switch attention to "Branded Product Development". It is only when Indian Companies build products on which they have the IPR and build a brand around it that the future of the Indian IT industry will be secured.

It is true that "Brand Building" and development of IPR backed products requiring "Research" and "Original Thinking" has a cost. It is possible that small companies with limited resources may find it difficult to pursue the policy of "Products" as against the easy option of "Projects".

But larger companies who have already established some reputation in the market place have no reason to fight shy of the responsibility of building own brands.

However, transforming a Company's marketing strategy from "Project Orientation" to "Product Orientation" is not an easy task. It requires both an employee re-orientations as well as some "Organizational Changes". These have HR implications as well to the HR sensitive industry which IT industry is.

While a detailed analysis of this "Transformation Strategy" is out of the scope of this article, certain salient features of the strategy can be highlighted for immediate attention.

1. *Accountability for Identifying Product opportunities :* In order to systemize the process of developing "New Product Ideas", the IT Company needs to assign duties of "Market Analysis" to a specific department. Some Companies seem to create a post of a "Business Analyst" for the purpose for different SBUs. This could be a good starting point but a better option would be a "Cross SBU Marketing Team" which can look at the synergies that can be used between different business segments.

   A senior marketing person who looks not only at the market opportunities from the perspective of "Product Planning" but also from the point of view of balancing the Client portfolio with "Country Risk", " Industry Risk" etc and also tries to even out the project implementation bottle necks arising out of bad planning would add a lot of value to the organization.

2. *Accountability for Identifying IPR Opportunities:* In order to spot opportunities of IPR arising out of the normal business processes and special research projects, a senior person with necessary understanding of the patent process should be available to keep a watch on the developments within the Company. Some times there will be opportunities to offer certain project functionality's in the form of "Reusable Components" on which the IT Company can claim IPR rather than passing it on to the project client by default.

   There will however be certain sensitive issues involved in this process, which have to be handled properly if the "Project Clients" should not misunderstand the IPR strategy.

It would be interesting to know the extent to which Indian IT Companies is using the above strategies.

A Phone in Every Village: Taking Telecom to Rural India

Information is critical to the social and economic activities that comprise the development process. Telecommunications, as a means of sharing information, is not simply a connection between people, but a link in the chain of the development process itself.

The British government introduced telecommunications services in India in the late 19th century as a means of providing defense, law and order, general administration, and revenue collection. Since that time, telecommunications has played a critical role in shaping India's march toward progress, and the importance it holds for the future of India cannot be overstated. This article :

- Reviews India's telecom policy.
- Discusses guidelines and drivers for developing telecom infrastructure in India's rural areas.
- Make recommendations for private sector involvement.
- Highlights some relevant technologies for rural telecom infrastructure build-out.

A Phone in Every Village

In 1989, the Telecom Research Center, under the auspices of the DoT, introduced guidelines for the rural telecom sector. The report entitled *A Phone in Every Village*, included plans to provide every rural Indian village with access to a telephone by 1999. The NTP, however, pushed the target date for implementing "a phone in every village" back to 1997 — a goal which the government has been unable to meet.

At the time the National Telecom Policy was drafted, only one-third of the existing 600,000 villages had access to a telephone. The DoT has divided India into 319 telecom districts, which are further divided into group centers. Telephone traffic in rural areas is primarily confined to those villages within the same group center or separate group centers within the same telecom district. The result is reduced long distance traffic and revenues, which makes the expense of rural telephone deployment that much more difficult to justify. Consequently, long distance service has to be subsidized by the provider — no doubt, a heavy burden. It is obvious that higher long distance call traffic and rates cannot be expected until all rural villages have access to telephone service.

Clearly, there are many reasons for the government to have a more active role in defining and implementing rural telecommunications policy.

1. Continued rural economic development requires a reliable infrastructure of enhanced telecommunications. Participation in the information economy by rural and poorer segments of society should be a strategic priority for both social and economic development reasons.
2. Special transition policies are a fair and equitable way to help rural India adjust to the new global telecommunications marketplace.
3. Rural residents deserve an equal opportunity to participate in the national economy and to determine their own destiny. Particular emphasis should be given to the role of telecommunications technology in enabling rural citizens to integrate effectively in the Indian economy and the global economy.
4. Successful systems require more than appropriate technology. Other elements - policies, people, processes, incentives, institutions, and infrastructure -must also be present and work well. The establishment of agencies such as the Telecom Regulatory Authority of India (TRAI) is necessary to solve disputes between public and private operators and to monitor the privatization process.

Technology for the Rural Sector

Information technology, when designed for the right job, can be deployed even in regions that lack adequate water, food, and power. Technology can be effective for many tasks, not the least of which is human and economic development. In fact, technology is often indispensable in meeting basic needs. While the information revolution may threaten to increase inequity, it also provides tools to reduce poverty. An agenda for technology -- improved access to education, health care, and information — is increasingly possible for the rural sector in India.

The Telecom Research Center has evaluated and recommended several technologies, which would work well in India's rural regions.

Fiber Optics: As a communications highway from one metropolitan area to another, fiber optics could be used to connect intermediate stations to the main highway by branch routes and drop-and-insert systems. The intermediate stations could be used as collection centers for village telephones within distances of 10 km, 15 km, or even 40 km.

Rural Cordless Telephones: Rural cordless telephones are simple and inexpensive, and they could be used in areas where villages are widely dispersed and the terrain is rather difficult. In such areas, one cordless telephone in each village would serve the purpose, and an equal number of transceivers should be provided at the base station, i.e., the telephone exchange. The number of phones in an exchange area would be limited by the available frequencies, and the signal strength, terrain, and topography would limit the distance.

Radio Sharing System: This is a radio frequency sharing system with two frequency pairs serving 15 village telephones. The ratio of village telephones to radio channels is 7.5. Even though the system is defined as two radio channels for 15 phones, there is built-in expandability to 32 if actual traffic density is lower. All phones connected to the system have individual line terminations in the telephone exchange.

Line Sharing System: A metallic pair passing by a number of villages could be used on a "line sharing" basis and provide telephone connections to every village on the route. The common pair, serving as an omnibus telephone line, is different from parallel connection of telephones on a line. This system provides for termination of all the village telephones on a manual trunk switchboard, with individual station designations for every phone. Every village telephone retains its individual identity, so it could be called selectively from any place.

Wireless Local Loop (WLL): Frost & Sullivan forecasts that WLL transmission equipment will eventually constitute nearly 30% of all new lines. This technology will assist in more rapid installation of the network and is ideal for both urban and rural areas. Very small aperture terminals (VSATs) and low earth orbiting satellites (LEOs) are also being touted as intriguing technological solutions for rural telecommunications. None of these technologies is a panacea, but each of them will satisfy the demands of rural telecommunications. Different technologies will be more or less appropriate based on specific circumstances. It is most likely that a mix of these technologies will provide the ultimate solution.

Some of the challenges to discuss are

New Technology, A Nightmare for the Police?

A Fantasy coming true? Is how you can perhaps describe the latest invention by two Japanese firms where high bandwidth data transfer can be effected when two humans shake their hands?

The technology, developed by Nippon Telegraph and Telephone Corp. and its subsidiary NTT DoCoMo Inc., uses the body's conductivity for data transmission at 10 megabits per second, comparable to the speed of a broadband Internet connection. According to the inventors, a device attached to a PDA can send and receive weak electrical signals through people, with human bodies as communications circuits. Apparel and handbags have their own conductivity, allowing an electrical connection to a PDA that can remain in one's pocket according to them. In this way, people can exchange e-mail addresses, names and phone numbers while shaking hands, with the data automatically written into both their PDAs. The technology can also allow data communications through doorknobs, switches, desks and chairs. No doubt this is an exciting development, which must have a high potential in many fields not the least the medical field where embedded devices in a human body need to be communicated with.

A thought however crosses one's mind that if the technology is as good as it is claimed to be, its early application could be by terrorists to pass on vital information to their contacts under the watchful eyes of the security personnel. While security agencies keep tapping the telephones and internet signals to look for communication leaks, the innocuous looking handshake can do all that the terrorist wants to transfer information from one member to another. Similarly, it may be used for transfer of information by betting agencies with players during a cricket match or for drug traffickers and other anti social elements.

Perhaps the Law Enforcement Agencies need to study the possible ways by which the technology can be applied by criminals and train their security personnel to spot any unusual handshakes. It is reported in some circles that the Department of Post plans to create a database of the Indian population in view of the massive marketing value attached to it.

According to the report a senior official in the DOP on the condition of anonymity, is reported to have quoted "Our aim is to compile a 100 percent database of households and businesses in each city with key demographic and business details. On an average, a single post office serves around 5,500 people. With this reach, we are the best when it comes to collection of data."

There are supposed to be over 133000 post offices in the Country which has the potential to participate in this massive "Postal Census (?)" and the sheer power to collect data which is of value to the marketers is unquestionable. However while the world over concerns are being expressed on the "Right to Privacy" and "Right not to publicize personal preferences", the current move of the Postal authorities appears to be ill conceived. While the postal department would conduct surveys in their locality to gather the necessary information or use short cut methods of snooping on the mails, depends on the honesty and integrity of the staff at the local level. If the postman records that a particular individual gets parcels containing Viagra on a regular basis, it would be a vital market information for many other manufacturers of similar products. But would the addressee be happy with such information being systematically collected and disseminated?

If Indian Post can trade on the information that comes to it because of its status as a Government body, why not the Census departments itself expand its scope of collection of information and sell it to MNC s and make money?

We presume that the intended move of the Department of Post is not a considered decision and needs to be re-traced. Otherwise it would amount to misuse of power and violation of basic right to privacy of an individual.

Blocking of Terrorist Sites by ISPs Today, Al-Queda websites are back in Cyber space, some of them in different names.

As the world continues its war against terrorism, there is a renewed need to discuss the measures to control the proliferation of websites that are considered as pro-terrorists.

The establishment view is surely to "Block Such Sites". At the same time there will also be a cry from the "Human Rights Activists" that the voice of dissent if any against any establishment should not be arbitrarily curbed. There is some truth but not whole truth in the claim of the Human Right Activists and Freedom lovers.

The answer to the dilemma obviously lies in between the two extreme measures. This means that there should be "Content Monitoring" of some kind that satisfies the human right activists and at the same time also addresses the concerns of the law enforcement.

Balancing Viewpoints

Naavi.com had suggested the following action to handle some sites, which fall as border cases between free expression and anti establishment.

1. Sites, which are said to contain "Politically Objectionable material", are reviewed by a virtual committee of experts and voted for or against being declared "Objectionable for Viewing by the Indian Government".
2. Based on such a verdict delivered through digitally signed e-mail confirmations from the virtual committee members, the Controller can issue a notice to ISP s in India to do the following.
3. Whenever a request for an objectionable site is received from a surfer, an "Objection Notice" to the following effect is displayed in a pop up box.

"The site requested by you contains information considered Objectionable" by the Government of the Republic of India vide GO No xxx of xx.xx.xx. The reasons for objection can be found here. (Hyper linked Document) A List of sites presenting a counter viewpoint can be found here (Hyper link to list of "Counter view point sites")

The moment a site is declared "objectionable", the Government should notify the same on the internet and invite the public to register their site or Pages containing counter viewpoints. These can be reviewed and if found suitable, added to the list of "Counter View Point Sites".

This strategy will enable the Government to use the public resources to produce content, which will neutralize the objectionable material.

Conclusion

Our conclusion is that Information technology is playing the vital role in achieving sustainable development, it is essential that people in outlying areas - representing the bulk of Indian society - are given the opportunity to participate in and benefit from the global information revolution. The focus on some of the initiatives that the Indian IT Companies should contemplate to ensure their continued success in the coming days is presented. After this we have focussed on Internet criminals who are very dangerous and harmful, and pointed out that secure our websites information from other intruders and hackers should be given higher priority. The final solution to providing service to rural areas in India will require a delicate blend of appropriate technological choices in combination with management and financing mechanisms, initiated at the governmental level, for supporting the development of rural providers. No time should be wasted in moving ahead with the proposed plans. The success of IT can be attribute to the genetic factors in the Indian race with the strong English based, memory dependent education system.

19

EVOLUTION AND GROWTH OF CYBER KNOWLEDGE

B. Syamala*

The success of India's information technology industry and related businesses has produced such a euphoric and exuberant reaction that some of its more enthusiastic celebrants have already declared India a 'knowledge-based society' and 'information superpower' which qualifies it for special global status. This 'knowledge-based' description sounds odd, to put it mildly, in a society in which almost half the population is illiterate, the general level of skills very low, and transmission of knowledge severely restricted by the hierarchies of class, caste and gender. India's computer software export boom has admittedly been an impressive success story, with annual growth rates of 40 per cent or more over the past decade. It has contributed significantly to India's foreign exchange reserves.

This paper deals with the growing cyber users coupled with knowledge in Andhra Pradesh. It also briefs the various fields in which computers are used in intense manner. This paper also sketches about the growing cyber crimes and with reference to cyber law.

Introduction

The success of India's information technology industry and related businesses has produced such a euphoric and exuberant reaction that some of its more enthusiastic celebrants have already

* Lecturer, Department of Economics, Hindu College, Guntur.

declared India a 'knowledge-based society' and 'information superpower' which qualifies it for special global status. This 'knowledge-based' description sounds odd, to put it mildly, in a society in which almost half the population is illiterate, the general level of skills very low, and transmission of knowledge severely restricted by the hierarchies of class, caste and gender. India's computer software export boom has admittedly been an impressive success story, with annual growth rates of 40 per cent or more over the past decade. It has contributed significantly to India's foreign exchange reserves.

Information and Technology

IT certainly contributes in growing measure to the Indian economy, but it remains an 'island' phenomenon. It cannot drive the entire country into another epoch or 'stage' of development. There are three reasons for this –

- First, the computer software business remains extremely (80 percent-plus) export-dependent. This is even truer of information technology-enabled services (ITES) like call centers and medical transcription, and business process outsourcing (BPO), which are now growing at twice the speed of software exports. The best or most informed estimate of the size of India's indigenous information technology sector, including hardware and domestic software is that it accounts for less than 2 per cent of GDP. By contrast, trade and hospitality alone account for 15 per cent of GDP. Even in external sector accounts, software exports ($7.2 billion) still contribute less than remittances, mainly from poor workers in the Gulf ($8.1 billion). Even if the ITES/BPO business grows five or eight-fold over the coming five years, as optimistic projections estimate, its contribution to India's GDP will remain relatively small.

- Second, despite their meteoric rise, most IT companies are puny even by Indian corporate standards, with their sales turnover usually within some hundreds of crores of rupees, or in the top range, a few thousand crores — as compared to tens of thousands for manufacturing sector majors. It is only now, this year, that India's largest IT company, Tata Consultancy Services, joined the 'One

Billion Club,' with revenues exceeding Rs 4,800 crores. Other IT giants, like Infosys and Wipro, have even lower revenues (Rs 3,323 crores and Rs 4,334 crores respectively). Only four IT companies figure in *The Economic Times* list of India's top 100 corporations (rated by sales). IT companies' profits are high, share prices stellar, and market capitalisation spectacular. But their economic size and influence are rather limited.

- And third, the geographical distribution of India's IT business is extremely uneven. The maldistribution bears no relationship to the uneven spread of literacy, education and other human development indicators, or to infrastructure development. For instance, of the total exports of computer software and electronics hardware, the south alone accounts for over 50 per cent, with the north coming a distant second (26 per cent), and the east lagging at a pitiable 2 per cent. If Delhi and adjoining parts of Uttar Pradesh and Haryana are excluded, the north's share falls to an embarrassing 4 per cent.

In the year 1988 – 89, the information technology industry earned revenues of Rs.24,781 crore. This was a growth of 32.2 % over the revenue of Rs.18,662 crore in the year 1997 – 98. In India, spending on information technology is currently less than 1 percent of GDP. But in USA, it is more than 3.5 percent of GDP. However, the Government of India is resolving to increase the spending on information technology in the coming years. It is expected to increase by 2.5 percent of GDP in the next two years. In this world, which is led by knowledge, the role of the state is very important. The Information Technology Industry is the fastest growing segment of the Indian economy. The Information Technology Sector has grown in size from Rs. 5,450 crores in 1994-95 to about Rs. 64,200 crore in 2001-02 contributing 0.59% and 2.87% to G.D.P. growth respectively in the corresponding periods.

IT has topped the sectoral performance on sales growth for nine months ended in December 1999 with a sales growth rate of 39.3%. Globally, IT led services have emerged as a US $75 billion industry with an annual growth rate of over 20% and estimated business in the IT enabled services is over US $3 trillion.

World of Computers

In this world of electronics, computers have become part of our daily life. The most significant plan for computerization is from the National Informatics Center (NIC). NIC works for various ministries in the whole country. It assists even Andhra Pradesh state in the development of information systems. Computer network called NICNET has some branches in various parts of the country. The main branches are at Delhi, Bhubaneshwar, Pune and Hyderabad. Now a days there is no area where the use of computer is unavailable. Computers have become the basic requirement of our day-to-day activities.

There is always a debate as whether computer education is labour killing or employment generating device. Computer education gives qualified jobs and increases the efficiency as well as productivity of the country. Many courses based on computer education have emerged in the country. There are both regular as well as diploma courses in this field. Andhra Pradesh stands second in imparting standard computer education. Computer education has become a regular subject in most of the schools and colleges in the present world. Many of Indian computer educated professionals have migrated to foreign countries for a desire to have better carrier in computers and earn better scales abroad. In fact in US nearly 70 percent of the computer experts are form Andhra Pradesh. Computers are useful now a days in various fields.

Uses of Computers

Some of the common uses of computers are listed below –

- Communication through e-mail
- Research work
- Defence and security
- Find scams
- Information of bank account
- Information on stock exchange
- Espionage
- Cryptography – study hidden information and prevent modification and unauthorized use

- Awareness.
- Booking in railways and airways.
- Distant education
- For data
- Entertainment etc.

Some of the areas of its intense uses are mentioned below.

Employment Opportunities: The employment opportunities for the educated spurred up with the revolution in information – technology and increasing demand for computer professionals. The employment created in both public and private sectors for the country are immense. The computerization of several government departments paved the way for government jobs and registration of information technology units from 23 in 1997 – 98 to over 1100 units in 2000.There is an exhausting list of areas where one can find jobs with computer qualification. Some of them are listed here - Computer education gives jobs in various areas like in – schools, companies, colleges as lecturers, exam boards, railways – in ticket booking, airways – for information and ticket booking, e-seva for various information and services, LIC, banks for projects, for research work, in the libraries, electricity boards – for billing, etc. There are many other sectors, which are generating employment for the computer professionals. The main achievement that has been made in the field of employment in the computer area is the removal of gender inequalities. In fact women are given higher importance in this sector than any other sector in the country. The women employed in this sector are more than any other sector because of the working conditions and the salaries. This marks a good signed in the gender equity and economic development of the country.

Computer Education: Computer education has been a must for all the youngsters seeking white collared jobs in top companies of the country. As already mentioned there are various courses in computer education given by various educational institutions of the country. Now a days loans are been provided by various financial institutions for higher education in computers. The following discussion gives a brief sketch about the way computers can be used in imparting education to the students..

(a) *Helping the blind:* Visually impaired students can now learn any language with the help of a new computer-based technology developed in India. The teacher uses a "talking keyboard," which talks aloud whatever is being typed and the print of the text also appears in Braille on a mini printer given to each student. This equipment is operational at the country's first Braille Language Laboratory (BLL) in Ahmedabad. The Braille lab, set up by the Lodge Fellowship of Ahmedabad, a community that follows universal brotherhood, is capable of teaching in any language, though teaching has been introduced in English and Gujarati at present.

(b) *Helpful in libraries:* The world of libraries and information centers has been witnessing a sea of change during the past few decades due to the information explosion and the emergence of new technology and other scientific gadgets. Computers are very helpful in the libraries in various ways like – for information explosion, for new techniques of studies, to have depth of contents and analysis, for specialized information and for research purpose. These are only few uses that are been listed, there are many more in reality. To get the nascent information services to the researchers, a National computer network has been established in India under the name of INDONET. It is integrated information management, with distributed data processing facility spanning the entire country. Under this project a computer network was set up with computers at Mumbai, Calcutta, Delhi, Chennai and Hyderabad. The use of computer is very common in most of the libraries in these cities.

Internet Banking

- ICICI bank has already entered in providing internet banking services in major cities in India. It is planning to spread its mobile banking network in the rural areas also.
- The Hongkong and Shanghai Banking Corporation Ltd. (HSBC) to commence Internet Banking in India by the year 2000 end.

- Sony Corporation, Japan is also planning to enter Internet banking services by next year. Towards this direction, Sony has started agreements with a US Investment bank JP morgan & Sakura bank ltd. in India.
- UTI launched Internet banking services viz., *Connect Net Banking*. In this service, an account registered person can access through all his recent updates including demat accounts around the clock from any part of the globe.
- Kerala based Federal bank ltd. started Internet based banking services branded as 'Fednet on Infosys' bank-away platform. Initially customers in 20 of its 406 branches are able to avail such service and the system would be expanded to cover 150 more branches by July, 2000.

Internet Service in the e-services Market

HCL Infosystems Ltd., entered in providing B2B (Business to Business) & B2C (Business to Customer) Internet services viz., HCL Infinet, in the e-service market. It offers access VPN (Virtual Private Network), ASP (Applications Service Provider), hosting, networking & e-commerce. The services would be launched in 40 major cities of India within a few weeks.

Internet Marketing

Six major Airlines (Air France SA, AMR Corp., American Airlines, British Airways Plc, Continental Airlines Inc. & UAL Corp.'s United Airlines) formed as an Internet market to link carriers worldwide with goods & services vital to the business, joining a growing list of industries that have set up B2B (Business to Business service) consortium. This Internet market would cover fuel & fuel services, air-frame, avionics & engine components & maintenance services.

Computerization of Postal/ Communication activities

- Computerization of registration sorting work at Delhi, Mumbai, Chennai & Hyderabad has been started in 1996. It is extended to 10 more cities in 1996-97.
- TMOs (Transit Mail Offices) were also computerized during 1996-97 at Delhi and Mumbai. Six more TMOs in India were computerized in 1997-98.

Internet Telephony: It allows computer users with Internet connecting to talk to people with the same facility anywhere in the world without any additional expenditure. The Union Government is planning to legalize the Internet telephony.

Cyber Vigilance: NASSCOM proposed setting up of a National Cyber Cop Committee to help Indian Government agencies & companies tackle hacker attacks. The committee would draw specialists from the IT world and representatives from agencies like the police. This would include creation of corporate firewalls as well as specialized cyber vigilance.

Information Technology and Cyber Situation in Andhra Pradesh

Hyderabad and Information Technology have become a synonymous with the growing conglomeration of multi-national companies. It is no doubt to be called as *Cyber bad* or the *Silicon Valley of India*. It had a phenomenal rise as one of the three important centers of Information Technology in the country. The Blue chip revolution has brought Hyderabad on the center stage and the brightest pool of talent is coming from these twin cities. It has made the giant IT companies like Microsoft, IBM and Oracle to reach destinations overnight. InfoTech has gained momentum with establishment of companies like Satyam computers, and recently opened Hi –Tech city and Indian Institute of Information Technology.

- Hi Tech city – Cyber bad
- Indian Institute of Information Technology
- Andhra Pradesh Technology Services
- Ramadevi Software Private Limited

Andhra Pradesh has a dream to be the best IT destination in the world. The State has made significant strides in transforming this dream into reality. All this has been possible due to abundant availability of highly skilled IT professionals, low cost of real estate and manpower, pleasant climate, good technical and social infrastructure and a pro-active Government. Andhra Pradesh, particularly Hyderabad, has become an ideal destination for major IT companies looking at expansion and new investment plan. Andhra Pradesh has decided to leverage Information Technology to attain a position of leadership and excellence in the information age and to transform itself into knowledge society. Andhra Pradesh has been using computers in each and every department of administration and non- administration areas. Computers have become part of daily work in various Government offices.

IT Policy

Andhra Pradesh has announced its IT Policy around two years back. The main objective of IT Policy can be categorized into three main categories-

(i) Economic development

- Export - targeting software export worth Rs. 2700 crores.
- Employment - to provide employment opportunities to 60000 people annually
- Investment in IT sector

(ii) Quality of Life

- To use IT in education
- To use IT for healthcare
- To use IT for Rural Development

(iii) Good Governance

- High internal efficiencies
- Anytime, anywhere citizen services

Andhra Pradesh is using Information and Communication Technology (ICT) for SMART Governance. ICT is being used for high quality citizen services, high internal efficiencies, better enforcement of law, HRD, Poverty alleviation etc. The State has adopted three-layer strategy for implementation of IT projects in the State. These are-

(a) Technology Framework - Information and Communication Technology (ICT) architecture.

(b) Resource Framework - IT projects require large amount of Investment. As most of the State in India facing financial problems in implementing its various projects, Andhra

Pradesh is also passing through same phase. In most of the IT projects, Andhra Pradesh is following Public-Private Partnership (PPP) model for resource generation. Various types of models like BOO (Built, Own and Operate), BOOT (Built, Own, Operate and Transfer) are adopted for various IT projects in the State.

(c) Implementation Framework - For successful implementation of IT related projects, Andhra Pradesh is following a model called 6 C model. In this model, emphasis is made on Contents, Competencies, Connectivity, Cyber Laws, Citizen Interface and Capital. For implementing local languages, AP Government has made a provision of Rs. 10.00 lacs for C-DAC to develop local language interface in two years.

AP Government is not recruiting new personnel for its IT projects. Private entrepreneurs are engaged for maintenance and development of the hardware and software. Existing manpower is also being trained for the operational purpose. Private sector institutions like, NIIT, APTEC, Tata- Infotec are engaged in departmental training's. Top leadership of each department in fully involved in the implementation of the IT projects. Each department has setup three level of personnel for their projects.

They are-

(a) Chief Information Officer

(b) Data Processing Officers

(c) Data Entry Operators

A project has been started in Andhra Pradesh for computer education. The main highlights of this project are gisted below.

Project Objectives: To provide basic computer literacy to students studying in class VI to X and access to Internet and thus create school communities interlinked through Web based communication systems.

Project Description: In the year 2000-2001, one Government school was identified in each of the 23 districts, for setting up computer training facilities. The project is now being expanded to cover 1000 high schools including around 300 residential schools. Optic fiber technology is likely to connect the project up to mandal level.

Cyber Law

Cyber law is a field of law dealing with computers and the internet,. Including such issues as intellectual property rights, freedom of expression and free access to information. Cyber law legislation is to provide the legal framework for electronic commerce and to enable electronic governance in the country. Various technology policies and acts have been past in the recent years, some of them are listed below.

- Information Technology Act 2000 – The Information Technology Act 2000 was passed by the parliament and received the assent of the President on June 9, 2000. It is an Act to provide legal recognition for transactions carried by means of electronic data inter- change and other means of electronic communication (e-commerce) that involve the use of alternative to paper based methods of communication and storage of information.
- ICE Act of India 2000 – The rapid coverage of the broadcasting, telecommunication and Internet technologies has made information technology act less relevant and gave birth to another act called Information, Communication and Environment (ICE) Act of India, 2000. It is meant to promote and encourage investment and growth of broadcasting and communication sectors, which are based on the development and use of technologies that maximize user control over carriage of information. The objective is to maximize the facility to make available the facility to the largest number of the citizens of the country.

Cyber Crimes

Cyber crimes have become common in many parts of the country. Cyber crimes are those crimes, which are connected many with mishandling the information available in the Internet or browsing prone websites. Experts say hackers are constantly attacking both government and private sector computer systems, sometimes with a specific aim a to commit crimes, but often as a sort of intellectual test. Software that enables hackers to break into private networks is widely available over the Internet itself. These days some institutions are giving training to students in hacking field. This has become a profession in some parts of the country.

Cyber talking is the act of threatening, harassing or annoying some one through multiple e-mail messages, as through the Internet, especially with the intent of placing the recipient in fear that an illegal act or an injury will be inflicted on the recipient or a member of the recipient's family or household.

Cyber theft is the act of using an online computer service, such as one on the Internet, to steal someone else's property or to interfere with someone else's use and enjoyment of property. Hacking into a bank's account records to wrongfully credit one account and debit another or interfering with a copyright by wrongfully sending protected material over the Internet. There are many other types of cyber crimes. Porn watch on the net is one of the most common and fast growing cyber crimes, now a day. Tampering with computer source documents is one more type of cyber crime, which is developing, in the recent years. Hacking the computer information is a wide and most common of the types of cyber crimes. Publishing of information, which is obscene in electronic form, is another fast growing crime. If the criminal is caught in committing such a crime he/she can be imprisoned for 5 years or fined to the extent of one lakh rupees.

Where the Computer is a Tool for An Unlawful Act

This kind of activity usually involves a modification of a conventional crime by using computers. Some examples are:

1. Financial Crimes
2. Cyber pornography
3. Sale of illegal articles
4. Online gambling
5. Intellectual Property crimes
6. Email spoofing
7. Forgery
8. Cyber Defamation
9. Cyber stalking

Where the Computer is the Target for An Unlawful Act

It may be noted that in these activities the computer may also be a tool. This kind of activity usually involves sophisticated crimes usually out of the purview of conventional criminal law. Some examples are:

1. Unauthorized access to computer systems or networks
2. Theft of information contained in electric form
3. Email bombing
4. Data diddling
5. Salami attacks
6. Denial of Service attack
7. Virus/Worm attacks
8. Logic bombs
9. Trojan attacks
10. Internet time thefts
11. Web jacking
12. Theft of Computer system
13. Physically damaging a computer system

Cyber Crimes in Hyderabad

Hyderabad has pioneered 'cyber crime police station' is all set to file the first of its charge sheets. The cyber crime police station functions within the Crime Investigation Department of Andhra Pradesh Police. So far it has investigated 11 cases and arrested four accused. The cyber crime police station has jurisdiction over all of Andhra Pradesh and deals with cyber offences under the Information Technology Act, 2000. The cyber crime police station has registered eight cases since December 2002. Besides, three cases of cyber crime, registered by the Hyderabad City Police, have also been transferred to the cyber crime police station for investigation. In a case, the cyber crime police arrested a food and beverages manager of a luxury hotel in Chennai, for sending obscene emails to a lady IPS officer, who is working as an inspector-general of police in Hyderabad One person was nabbed for stealing source code and another was arrested for sending obscene emails to the executives of a US company.

As per the IT Act, cognizable offences under Section 65 (tampering with computer source documents) are punishable with imprisonment up to three years or with fine up to Rs. 200,000 or both. Offences under Section 66 (hacking computer systems) are punishable with imprisonment up to three years or fine up to Rs. 300,000 or both. Similarly, offences under Section 67 (publishing obscene information in electronic form) are punishable with imprisonment up to five years and fine up to Rs. 100,000 for the first conviction and prison term up to 10 years and fine up to Rs. 200,000 for the second conviction.

Conclusion

Computer is no doubt an important device in our day-to-day life, but if it is used in an unlawful and illegal way then it is a demon of first order, which can spoil both life and career of a person. If the computer is used as a device that can provide information and to improve one's knowledge, no better device is there in this world to make one's career shine like the sun. Growing cyber knowledge that is imparted by the Educational Institutions should be careful in educating their students in rightful way that can improve their knowledge and help them to make bright career.

REFERENCES

1. www.rediff.com/news/2003/jul/11praful.htm
2. www.comp.edu\TwincitiesBBS- Information Technology.htm
3. www.\comp.edu\ap it\APTS.htm
4. www.comp.edu\Compu%20trn.htm
5. www.comp.edu\Compu%20trn.htm
6. *The Tribune* Nov. 23, 2003
7. *The Hindu* July 23, 2001 and December 24, 2002.
8. *Economic Survey* – 2002–03
9. *Yojana*, August 1998.
10. *Hindu* – A book on Information and Technology, 2003.
11. Shakil Ahmed Syed and Rajiv Rahheja, (2001), *A Guide to information technology*, Capital law house, Delhi.

20

CAREER OPTIONS IN IT ENABLED SERVICES

B. Murali Manohar*, C. Subba Reddy** and **Dr. L.S.N. Prasad*****

The ITES (IT Enabled Services) sector has emerged as the high-growth sector for the Indian industry. Over the last few years, NASSCOM has made considerable efforts to position India as an attractive destination and has identified this sector as a major opportunity for employment and earning foreign exchange for India. For the thousands of hopefuls joining the ITES sector, their major source of insecurity is the short-lived career promises of the industry–a stop-gap option before the great career dream materialises. It is also one of the factors that have in no small measures contributed to the high rate of attration. ITES players have, in fact, been making assiduous efforts to dispel this mindset and chalk out long-term career streams for their employees. This trend has increasingly been on the rise, as evident from the recent Nasscom-Hewitt salary survey findings which state that there has been a 14 percent increase in the number of companies offering a formalised career path to its employees. Hence, the authors of this paper wish to bring out the possible career options for young aspirants and also bring out the possible threats in this arena.

* Asst. Professor, MIS, Debub University, Awassa,Ethiopia.

** Sr. Lecturer, Dept. of Economics, GHR&MCMR College,Guntur

*** Associate Professor-Economics, Debub University, Awassa, Ethiopia.

Introduction

The Information Technology Enabled Services (ITES) industries are being recognized as the largest contributors to incremental market capitalization in India. However, it is still small in terms of contribution to GDP-especially when compared to other large sectors in the economy like agriculture and manufacturing.

This is likely to change quite substantially over the next six years. As per the NASSCOM-McKinsey study 2002, by achieving its long-term potential, the industry will dramatically boost the Indian economy. If the industry achieves its long-term potential, it will become one of the largest sectors in the Indian economy. The share of the Indian IT and ITES industries in the GDP growth between now and 2008. the ITES sector has emerged as the high-growth sector for the Indian industry. Over the last few years, NASSCOM has made considerable efforts to position India as an attractive ITES-BPO destination and has identified this sector as a major opportunity for employment and earning foreign exchange for India. As per NASSCOM estimates, the Indian ITES-BPO industry grew by 59.1% during 2002-03 and is likely to grow by about 54% to reach US $ 3.6 billion by 2003-04.

Enormous Employment Opportunities

Also, the industry will create enormous employment opportunities in the country. The IT industry which currently employs 0.5 million people, will employ over 2 million people directly and create indirect employment opportunities for at least an additional 2 million people by 2008. in ITES exports, some of the segments creating the greatest number of jobs will be customer care (contributing 370, 000 to 390,000 jobs), HR (contributing 140,000 to 160,000 jobs) and administration (contributing roughly 80,000 to 100,000 jobs). Similarly, IT services will create employment for 450,000 people; the products and technology services opportunity will contribute around 140,000 jobs and the domestic market will employ about 650,000 people. Not only, will the industry provide direct employment to 2 million people, it will also create significant entrepreneurial and employment opportunities in support services. Training, food/canteen, transport, housekeeping and security will be come of the biggest areas.

The Indian ITES-BPO industry continues its strong upward spiral on service lines like customer care, finance, HR, administration, billing and payments services, etc. Revenues from Customer care doubled during 2002-03 registering a growth of 102%. Similar trend was witnessed in payment service, which grew by over 90% during 2002-03. Other service lines like finance, HR and administration are also expected to grow significantly over the next few years.

So, far the sector has generated 100,000 jobs and the trend is expected to continue in the coming years. While the employment potential is homogeneous, one needs to remember that with the exception of the first two letters ITES is remotely connected with IT. ITES does not fall in the ambit of traditional software or hardware development, testing and maintenance. To equate the two and celebrate the upsurge in ITES as an indicator of IT recovery would be erroneous and misplaced. Rather the for any IT majors into the BPO sector is a sign of desperation born out of a need to rev up revenues in the face of sharply falling margins from IT investments. Simply put ITES is the delegation of one or more IT intensive operations (Example of IT intensive operation Food World chains using computers for billing) to an external provider, who in turns administers and manages the selected business process based upon defined and measurable performance metrics. These outsourced operations cover an entire spectrum of remotely managed activities which are business critical but not essentially core operations of the organization. These include services such as call centers, finance and accounting services, HR services such as managing payrolls, staffing, datasearch itegration and management, networking services management and web services.

By realizing its long-term potential, the Indian IT and IT-enabled services industry could be one of the most powerful drivers of India's economic growth. Murali in his article has brought out the various ITES offered by Indian organizations.

The Constant Pay Changes

The salary structure is a derivative of multiple factors process complexity, experience, productivity goals and special domain or process expertise. "Increasingly salary comprises of a base element of compensation with a significant variable component that is linked to defined productivity norms and is paid out at regular intervals (quarterly and monthly). The wage differential between India and the Western World (US and UK) remains significant and the rapid pace of salary growth in India is unlikely to impact the country's competitiveness as India's labour rates remain one-tenth of global rates in Western countries.

Balanced Salary Structure

Companies will be reviewing the compensation across skill levels and within specific expertise provide for differential amounts for those with higher tenure: "For example there will be some element of salary differentiation based on the tenure of the person on the job, specifically on complex processes, considering that his or her learning curve will have stabilized over a 12-18 month time frame on that process". Balanced compensation structure has key components such as salary, loans, retrials; conveyance, housing and variable pay (performance pay/incentives).

Variable Pay

"In this industry, performance can be accurately measured and an agent can know it at the end of the day. At the higher levels this does not hold, for instance, a team leader has to look after the quality, attrition rate, customer satisfaction. An agent touches the customer, while a manager interacts with the client, "states Baksi.

Career Growth

So, it is important to be able to discuss career path and related compensation element in a defined horizon.

Issues of Concern

1. For the thousands of hopefuls people joining the ITES sector, their major source of insecurity is the short-lived career promises of the industry-a stop-gap option before the great career dream materializes. It is also one of the factors that have in no small measures contributed to the high rate of attrition. ITES players have, in fact, been making assiduous efforts to dispel this mindset and chalk out long-term career streams for their employees. This trend has increasingly been on the rise, as evident from the recent Nasscom-Hewitt salary survey findings which state that there has been a 14 percent increase in the number of companies offering a formalized career path to its employees.

2. The recent anti BPO bill approved by the US President has little or no impact on the ITES industry, as the law can ban the outsourcing of ITES by US Govt. but not the private sector. Hence, the impact of this law will be very limited impact on ITES organizations in India. Most agree, however, that as the issue is in the purview of WTO and may be amended in the years to come.

Conclusion

So, to conclude ITES will provide the career opportunities for millions of English educated India's in the years to come, but these youngsters need to choose the right sector and organization as their career choice. As the demand on skills is ever changing and the young graduates need to upgrade their skills on continuous manner to be in this industry. The laws on outsourcing ay not have immediate impact on the opportunities as it is a matter of WTO. So, the authors of the form belief that ITES will fuel the economy in the years to come and make India a developed state as dreamed by the President and Prime Minister of India.

REFERENCES

1. B. Murali Manohar, *Competitive Advantage of ITES*, Dr. P. Jagadish Gandhi and G. Panesan (Ed.), *Services Sector in the Indian Economy*, Deep & Deep Publications, 2002, Delhi, pp.33-40.
2. http://www.nasscom.org
3. http://www.economictimes.indiatimes.com
4. http:/www.assureconsulting.com
5. http://www.thehindubusinessline.com (Sep 28,2003)
6. http://www.expreecomputeronline.com

21

INFORMATION TECHNOLOGY FOR RURAL INDIA

CHALLENGES

A.V.V. Siva Prasad*

The idea that the Internet and related technologies might have an important role in aiding developmental efforts has captured a central place in international policy debates. At present many statements affirming the need to close the so called 'digital divide' between social groups with and without access to the Internet were made through several UN agencies, at the G-8 summit, and at meetings of development organisations around the world. In South Asia, where most rural populations lack running water and sanitation systems, where electricity is still a scarce and intermittent resource, where roads are poor and education luxury, these technologies really are, on first impressions, far removed from the everyday concerns of the poorest section of the countryside. Hence, there is an urgent need to examine the catalytic and enabling role to be played by the government in ensuring that IT provide new opportunities for the 40 per cent of the people who are living below the poverty line, so that they may move above it. This paper critically examines the problems and possibilities of digital development in order to reveal the larger impact that ICTs might have on rural economies and societies.

* Lecturer, P.G. Dept. of Business Admn., Akkineni Nageswara Rao College, Gudivada.

Introduction

Our Prime Minister during his address on the eve of Independence Day 2002, declared that India would become a Developed Nation by the year 2020. The tenth five- year plan also focuses on an economic growth of 8 per cent and an employment potential of one hundred million. In recent years, technology has come to play a dominant role in improving the quality of life. Technology is the engine capable of driving a nation towards growth and prosperity, and giving it the necessary competitive edge in the comity of nations. Information Technology is one of the areas where India has an expertise and competitive edge. The significant contribution of India's economic growth comes from this sector. The software and service industries now account for 16 per cent of the country's overall exports, an employment of five lakh professionals and $ 1.5 billion in investment. Information Technology, thus has an important role to play in transforming India into a developed country.

The idea that the Internet and related technologies might have an important role in aiding developmental efforts has captured a central place in international policy debates. At present statements affirming the need to close the so called 'digital divide' between social groups with and without access to the Internet were made through several UN agencies, at the G-8 summit, and at meetings of development organisations around the world. But if a computer cannot benefit someone earning less than a dollar a day, remains a serious challenge to any attempt to ameliorate social and economic disparities through Information and Communications Technologies (ICTs). In South Asia, where most rural populations lack running water and sanitation systems, where electricity is still a scarce and intermittent resource, where roads are poor and education luxury, these technologies really are, on first impressions, far removed from the everyday concerns of the poorest section of the country side. This paper critically examines the problems and possibilities of digital development in order to reveal the larger impact that ICTs might have on rural economies and societies.

Emergence of the Information and Communication Sectors in India

As is well – known by now, India's IT sectors took – off in the early – 1980s with the establishment of off-shore development centers.

Relatively cheap English-speaking engineering and technical talent were employed at centered in Banglore and Chennai, then Hyderabad, and now in the suburbs of New Delhi (NOIDA). Since the liberalization of the Indian economy in the early –1990s, the Indian government has relentlessly promoted the IT sector as the harbinger of the nation's economic aspirations. The initial euphoria surrounding India's successful software export industry has given way to a new introspection into the reasons why these intellectual and human resources have not been applied towards the development of India's public and private institutions, education systems, and infrastructure. These reasons are not hard to find:

1. The Indian software industry solves small components of larger problems for international clients;
2. This work is usually protected by confidentiality agreements;
3. Many Indian software professionals and companies compete for the same international contracts;
4. The opportunity costs of working of Indian versus international clients is very high;
5. Low teledensity, computer usage, literacy, the inadequacies of regional language software interfaces, and other obstacles of India's developing infrastructure, coupled with regulatory hurdles, inhibit such ventures.

Despite the on-going deregulation of India's telecommunications sector, its national teledensity has improved very slowly, from .06 in 1990, to almost 3 today. Voice over Internet Protocol (VoIP), and Wireless-in-Local-Loop (WiLL or WLL) technologies, now appear set to offer a cheaper and lighter form of telecom infrastructure, that should improve rural access exponentially. With some important exceptions, the export-oriented software industry has yet to take full advantage of the opportunities presented by the newly networking home market. The still-unexplored synergies between the infotech and telecom sectors represent the best opportunity for an ICT-driven social and economic revolution in rural communities across India.

The Feasibility of Technology - Driven Social Change in India

The problems and potential for ICT-driven projects in India are truly enormous.It hosts an extraordinary concentration of new technology-driven companies, tech-savvy administrators and managers, a political class suddenly aware of the possibilities of IT, social entrepreneurs and NGO institutions structures that could all come together to bring the benefits of networked technologies to rural and disprivileged groups.

A common objection to IT initiatives is, why should we consider this expensive and elitist form of infrastructure, when more fundamental developmental needs remain unmet?

This criticism assumes that there is a standard sequence of hierarchy for development: first a society must adequately manage its nutrition and healthcare, then it must address education and achieve total literacy, then it must provide electricity to all its villages, then it must install telephones, and so forth. In fact, post-colonial societies in Asia, Africa and the Americas have repeatedly shown that they can be successful in one or another dimension of human, social, and economic achievement, without necessarily replicating a normative European trajectory of industrial development. Diverse social and infrastructural needs must be addressed more or less simultaneously to ensure a nation's future growth and prosperity.

Information and communications technologies can compensate for other kinds of infrastructure limitations. For example, if on-line work, trade, or payment were to become available for members of a village community, the poor quality of roads to and from that village becomes less of an obstacle to earnings and employment. Finally, and most importantly, if capital were to become more readily available within a village community through such networked systems, it would then be in better position to finance the basic infrastructure that it needs, including roads, dispensaries, water and sanitation systems.

Infrastructural Bottlenecks

The three basic infrastructural requirements for rural ICT initiatives are, (i) electricity, (ii) Telephony (or its equivalent), and (iii) Network Connectivity. The problems with these inputs must be recognized as inherent features of the landscape, and tackled as an integral part of the implementation process.

1. Electricity: In many rural areas, electric supply may be restricted to only six or eight hours a day. When electrical power is available, its voltage and frequency may vary outside the acceptable limits of most hardware. Finally, there is often no earthing provided.

2. Telephony: Landline telephones are still not available in many villages in India. Where they do exist they may be down for weeks at a time, and there may be other kinds of incompatibilities, which prevent data transfer.

3. Connectivity: Internet subscription is not always available in rural and underdeveloped sections of India. Even when it should, in theory, is available; long distance calls to nearby towns may be required in order to achieve true connectivity. Poor telephony ensures that modem speeds are restricted to 28.8 kbps or slower. The wireless-fax systems in Pondicherry runs even slower, at fewer than 14.4 kbps.

Overcoming Infrastructural Bottlenecks

1. For most rural ICT projects, battery back-ups and Uninterrupted Power Supply (UPS) are mandatory. In some cases, multiple tractor batteries have been connected in parallel to create a mammoth UPS that can withstand daylong powercuts.

2. Several different kinds of short-term solutions are possible to circumvent low teledensity in rural areas. A project in Pondicherry has implemented a wireless system for relatively slow data transfer using fax protocols. The Gyandoot project in Dhar, on the other hand, initially chose its target villages on the basis of their telephone access, and their location relative to proposed Optical-Fibre Cable (OFC) routes.

3. WILL technologies will soon be able to provide simultaneous and continuous voice and data connectivity in local areas; computer kiosks in villages can also be

designed so as to require only limited connectivity. Projects in Pondicherry and Warana, for example, allow users to access offline content, which is updated several times a day in brief bursts of data.

Focus Areas for Developmental ICTS

Technology & Infrastructure developments: The three major hurdles to the use of Information Technology in rural areas of India have been: (i) inappropriate software (ii) expensive hardware and (iii) weak infrastructure. In each of these fields, the landscape is slowly changing.

The Center for the Development of Advanced Computing (C-DAC) has been working on Indian language fonts and software for over a decade. Most State-sponsored IT initiatives, as well as many rural ICT projects, now use their fontographic standards, if not their text-processing software. In another significant development, a machine language translation project based in Hyderabad called Anusaraka promises to allow Indian language users translation between various Indian languages, as well as access to English language resources on the Web.

Wireless-in-Local-Loop (WILL) and related technologies have emerged as a cheaper, smarter form of telecom infrastructure, in comparison with traditional wire telephony. The TeNet Group at the IIT-Madras has been at the frontline in developing applications and incubating companies that seek to develop telecommunications infrastructure in rural areas.

Rural connectivity: Several projects are now attempting to provide information and services to rural citizen-consumers via human-mediated Intranet systems. These include the Village Centers Project in Pondicherry, the Warana Wired Village Project in and around Warana, and the Gyandoot Project in Dhar. Important lessons remain to be learnt from each of these initiatives, concerning, for example: the appropriate role of NGOs, the private sector and the State, the financial and entrepreneurial models which can make such infrastructure development feasible, and the socio-economic impact of such projects upon the village communities in which they are located.

The Sustainable Access in Rural India (SARI) project in Madurai is a newer, more ambitious project in the planning stages. It seeks to wire up all 1,000 villages in the district using WLL technology developed out of IIT-Chennai. Tarahaat is a new company seeking to build branded computer kiosks in relatively prosperous rural areas. The NIIT 'Hole-in-the –wall' and kiosks Project consists of unattended point-and-click devices in urban slums

E-governance: Some of the rural ICT projects mentioned above offer limited e-governance functions or services. With the exception of the Gyanadoot project in Dhar, these remain very rudimentary, and may be restricted to printing out standard government forms. Several state governments have announced high-profile projects to put their land records online, including Karnataka (Bhoomi) and Andhra Pradesh (CARD). The computerization of land records is an extremely labour-intensive process, the rewards of which are very long in the coming. Computerised land records are available on an experimental basis for a number of districts in these two states.

Wired Microcredit/ Microfinance/ Micro-ecommerce: There is no doubt that the computerization of microfinance and microcredit records could result in savings of time and effort, and generally facilitate the maintenance of these accounts. However, the real transformative effect of this technology will be seen only once microcredit accounts come to be used for online or distance transactions amongst or within village communities at the grassroots. This will allow rural entrepreneurs and craftspersons the same savings of time, travel and effort that the Internet has afforded individuals and institutions in the industrialized world. These possibilities have not yet been charted in any rural ICT project. The Swayam Krishi Sangam project is recording transactional information on optical ID cards for microfinance, as well as for education and healthcare.

IT – enabled artisanal industries: In addition to facilitating the flow of capital across rural areas, online financial and commercial systems could also provide the capital and infrastructure for new kinds of IT-enabled industries, in fields such as regional language data entry, Computer-Aided Design (CAD), and Computer-Aided-Manufacture (CAM). These applications of information technology, of course, will only become possible on a large-scale once rural ICT projects are better established in the landscape. The Asian Center for Entrepreneurial Initiatives (AsCent) has made as early attempt to introduce CAD/CAM technologies to artisans in north Karnataka, alongside online advertising and sales.

Computer training and IT-enabled education: So far, computer-training and IT-enabled education has been distressingly conflated and confused in the understanding of administrators and policymakers as well as the general public. Pratham, Akshara and the e-Learning Centre together represent the most important attempt to create IT-enabled learning software for underprivileged children. In Karnataka, 1,000 rural schools are to be computersied by private operators, including NIIT. School Net India, the educational infrastructure Leasing and Financial (IF&FS), is building multingual education content online, as well as CD-ROMs for use by teachers as a supplement to classroom education.

eGurucool and Zee Interactive Learning Systems represent commercial attempts to provide online educational resources coupled with products ranging from in-class instruction to interactive CD-ROMs, to cable-TV programmes. These products are predominantly in English, although regional language translations are sometimes possible.

Tele-health: Computer-based and online expert diagnostic systems could enhance the quality of healthcare and diagnosis available to rural citizen-consumers in many remote parts of South Asia. The real benefits of these systems may be the collation of more comprehensive public health information. In addition to tracking the case study of an individual patient, therefore, such systems could also collect data on public health in a region, for further epidemiological study. The George Foundation has experimented with an expert diagnostic programme on a freestanding PC in Dharmapuri district of Tamil Nadu. Other initiatives by privately-run hospitals are in the planning stages.

Research, advocacy and consultancy resources: Non-profit industry groups such as India's National Association of Software Companies (NASSCOM) have served as advocates against policy regulations that might inhibit the growth of bandwidth and connectivity in India. Their website hosts important statistics and information on

India's Internet economy. The NGO Voices serves as a research and capacity-building resource for community radio, and is beginning to experiment with interface between Internet and radio. Mahati.org, a branch of the NGO Samuha, provides IT-services for NGOs in the Banglore area.

Potential impact on Rural Economies and Societies: Development of ICT projects, therefore, have attempted to assist rural communities by providing them news, information, advice and knowledge which has hitherto been inaccessible to them. These kinds of inputs have allowed rural citizen-consumers to make more informed economic decisions: farmers can decide whether to sell their produce locally or transport it themselves further afield; landless labourers have been able to negotiate their daily wage more effectively; tractors, threshers, cattle and motorcycles have all been traded across towns and villages.

Despite the economic promise of ICTs, their social benefits may not emerge immediately. According to a preliminary estimate prepared by the Centre for Knowledge Societies – Banglore, immediate impact of ICT projects upon their rural contexts will be far from equitable. Rather, ICT access is likely to increase socio-economic opportunities for dominant caste landholding elites, relatively disprivileging non-elite, non-landholding artisanal communities. There are several reasons for this :

(a) Access to capital resources

(b) Literacy and education

(c) Social and educational access

(d) Agricultural technologies

The net effect of all these factors will be that most of the new entrants into Indian middle classes will come from rural landowning communities. Artisanal groups, Dalits, adivasis and other disprivileged groups will be relatively disabled from taking advantage of the opportunities offered by emerging technologies. It is therefore of the utmost importance that rural ICT projects be carefully designed with a view to enabling and including the very rural non-elite non-agricultural communities which are most likely to be left out.

Conclusion

Although many states in India are eager to establish networked initiatives in rural areas, there remains considerable uncertainty about the appropriate administrative, regulatory and economic models for such project to work. Rural ICT projects are to effectively position themselves as a vehicle for online commerce and a mechanism of employment for village communities. The first step in this direction would be to put rural Self-Help Groups and other Micro-Credit/Micro-Finance Initiatives online. This abstraction of cash money onto an online financial system would lay the groundwork for a new kind of rural e-commerce, which could prove extremely enabling for many communities, especially non-agricultural artisanal groups. Entrepreneurs and small-scale industries might then be able to regularise existing off-line trade relationships into online systems that track raw materials, designs, quality control and delivery mechanisms. New kinds of banking and finance systems in rural areas would make investments in rural infrastructure as well as new businesses more easily available. It seems likely that the rural initiatives most likely to succeed would integrate the State, the private sector and non-governmental organizations strategically, so as to maximally utilise their respective strengths and expertise. In order to do so, it is important that digital pioneers working in rural areas from experiments in digital development that have already been implemented. Notwithstanding the extreme hyperbole that always accompanies new technology on the one hand, and the extreme skepticism of the uninitiated on the other, emerging information and communications networks remain an unparalleled opportunity for effecting economic development and social change across rural India.

22

e-SEVA
A CASE STUDY OF CHITTOOR DISTRICT (ANDHRA PRADESH)

Soujanya Vamsi*, Md. Ziana Shireen** and **K. Lavanya Latha*****

Through a network of computerized integrated citizen service centres (ICSCs), e-Seva introduced in Andhra Pradesh in 2001 provides an integrated window offering a variety of services relating to the public and private sectors. Not only does it provide services under one roof but also allows access from anywhere in the state through any of its counters. E-Seva at present provides 46 services. In all, it is functioning in 126 centres in Andhra Pradesh at present. Proposal is to increase the number of centres to 216 in the near future. The study analyses the performance of operations of e-Seva centres in Chittoor District from September 2003 to January 2004 (5 months). Services covered in the analysis related to four organizations – (1) Andhra Pradesh State Road Transport Corporation (bus reservation), (2) Commercial Taxes Department (payment of bills), (3) State Road Transport Authority (licences and payment of tax), and (4) Southern Power Distribution Company (power bills). The number of transactions increased from over 10,000 in September 2003 to 68,600 in January 2004. Based on an analysis of these transactions, conclusions and suggestions are presented in the article.

*, ** MBA (F), Sri Padmavathi Mahila Visvavidyalayam, Tirupati.

*** Faculty, Sri Padmavathi Mahila Visvavidyalayam, Tirupati.

Introduction

The ancient Greek Philosopher Aristotle opined, "The best form of Governance is the one which interferes the least". Transposing this to our present times, we may para-phrase & it as, the best form of Governance is one which causes the least inconvenience. Keeping this in view in ever-expanding utility of all passive Information Technology, the Government of A.P. has visualised the concept of Electronic-Governance. In consonence with the best principles of efficient management of time, the Government has encapsulated access to its various services under one roof, in a normal program termed e-Seva.

Through a Network of computerised Integrated Citizen Service Centres (ICSC), e-Seva provides an integrated window offering a collage of services relating to public and private sector. e-Seva is a path breaking approach providing diverse services under one umbrella with ease and efficiency. It was first started in August 2001 in Hyderabad with 31 centres. Through ICSC and internet at www.esevaonline.com.

e-Seva facilitates the processing of financial transactions between the public and various organs of the Government with special reference to payment of charges duties and taxes and issue of certificates for a wide spectrum of needs. Not only does it provide services under one roof but also allows access from any where in the state through any of the counters. This has been setup with the responsibility shared between the Information Technology of Communications Department, Government of Andhra Pradesh and Private sector partners, viz., M/s CMS Computers, United Telecom Limited and M/s Ram Informatics Ltd. The services e-Seva is providing at present is 46. Director, Municipal Administration has identified 229 sites in all the 117 municipalities in the state. Proposal is for 216 centres and 129 centres are functioning.

Vision

"Andhra Pradesh will lever Information Technology to attain a position of leadership and excellence in the information age and to transform itself into a knowledge society". The Government of Andhra Pradesh has a clear vision to create a knowledge society by using information Technology in all aspects of development and governance.

Pioneering efforts are being made to reach the benefits of Information Technology to the citizens - urban and rural, rich and poor, literate and illiterate. The Government is conscious of the dangers of the digital divide and is making special provisions for reaching the 'information have-nots'.

Purpose

e-Seva is one of the most significant citizen centric initiative taken up by the Government of Andhra Pradesh. e-Seva is fast becoming an international role model for the electronic delivery of information and services to citizens.

The main purpose of e-Seva is

- to provide convenience and comfort to citizens.
- to serve all government services through electronic media to people under one roof.
- to avoid disturbances like waiting in a queue for long time.
- integration of departments - central and state government
- integration of services
- integration and expand
- efficiency, Reliability, Transparency, Scalability and accountability are the watchwords at e-Seva.

Objectives

- to provide citizen services
- to provide information citizen services
- to educate the citizen on Andhra Pradesh Government

Role of e-Seva

- 129 e-Seva centres(with 1032 service counters) spread over the Andhra Pradesh.
- All service counters are facilitated with an electronic queuing system.
- Operating from 8.00 a.m. to 8.00 p.m. on all working days and 9.00 a.m. to 3.00 p.m.on holidays (Second saturdays & sundays)

- 'One-Stop-Shop' for over 66 G2C and B2C services.
- No jurisdiction limits - any citizen in the A.P. can avail the services at any of the 129 e-Seva service centres.
- Provides real time online transactions.
- Any service at any centre at any place in the state.
- It saves time and money. 30 seconds per technical transaction and 30 seconds per practical transaction. The payment transaction is completed with in or less than 60 seconds.
- Likely to expand to all parts of the state.
- Online services : eforms, efiling, epayments
- Payments by cash/cheque/DD/Credit card/Internet.

Current Status

The real objective of e-Seva goes more for development of user-friendly governance where citizens feel convenient and comfortable through e-Seva centre easily reachable by them. The present study is undertaken to ascertain the role of e-Seva, Chitoor District, A.P. and to analyse the performance of e-Seva in different services in Chittoor District.

Methodology

For the purpose of achieving the above objectives, Primary data was collected through discussion with Mr.K.Narasa Reddy, Administrative Officer, e-Seva, Chittoor District. And the Secondary data was collected through internet, Manual of e-Seva and from Official records.

Table-1: Andhra Pradesh State Road Transport Corporation (APSRTC) Department and all centres collections for the period September, 2003 to January, 2004

Centre Name	*September 2003*	*October 2003*	*November 2003*	*December 2003*	*January 2004*
Municipal Premises, Tirupati	943.00 (2)	3526.00 (15)	2770.00 (16)	2350.00 (16)	2496.00 (14)
Bairagipattada, Tirupati	0.00	0.00	0.00	0.00	0.00
CTM Road, Madanapalles	0.00	0.00	0.00	0.00	0.00
Patel Road, Madanapalle	0.00	0.00	0.00	0.00	0.00
Gremspet, Chittoor	0.00	0.00	0.00	0.00	0.00
Municipal Complex, Chittoor	0.00	0.00	0.00	0.00	0.00
Total	**943.00 (2)**	**3526.00 (15)**	**2770.00 (16)**	**2350.00 (16)**	**2496.00 (14)**

Source: Records of e-Seva, District Data Centre, Tirupati.

Brackets indicates number of transactions.

The table No.1 indicates that there is a gradual increase in number of transactions of APSRTC Department in Chittoor District from past 5 months i.e. September, 2003 to January, 2004. This service provides the Reservation facility at any counter of e-Seva. In September, 2003, the transactions made were 2 only at Tirupati e-Seva centre, Municipal Premises. But all other centres at Tirupati, Madanpalle and Chittoor had no transactions.

Table-2: Commercial Tax Department (CTD) and all Centres collections for the period September, 2003 to January, 2004

Centre Name	*September 2003*	*October 2003*	*November 2003*	*December 2003*	*January 2004*
Municipal Premises, Tirupati	435218.00 (17)	4999.00 (9)	80349.00 (6)	3933.00 (2)	1163.00 (2)
Bairagipattada, Tirupati	5050.00 (11)	129950.00 (9)	0.00	0.00	0.00
CTM Road, Madanapalle	0.00	650.00 (1)	0.00	0.00	0.00
Patel Road, Madanapalle	0.00	0.00	0.00	0.00	525.00 (1)
Gremspet, Chittoor	0.00	75000.00 (1)	0.00	0.00	0.00
Municipal Complex, Chittoor	0.00	0.00	0.00	0.00	0.00
Total	**440268.00 (28)**	**25590.00 (20)**	**80349.00 (6)**	**3933.00 (2)**	**1688.00 (3)**

Source: Records of e-Seva, District Data Centre, Tirupati.

Brackets indicates number of transactions.

The Table No.2 indicates that there is a gradual decrease in number of transactions of CTD in Chittoor District from past five months i.e. from September, 2003 to January, 2004. The transactions undergone in the Municipal Premises, Tirupati which is the DDC (District Data Centre) of Chittoor District are in decreasing order. The other centre in Tirupati is at Bairagipattada where the transactions had a good beginning but slowly reduced and became zero from the month of Novermber, 2003. At Madanpalle the e-Seva centre located at CTM Road had undergone only one transaction in the Month of October and further there were no transactions. The another centre is at Patel Road, Madanpalle where no transactions took place and at Municipal complex also no transactions took place. At Gremspet, Chittoor we can see that only one transaction took place. As overall result CTD service had a low performance report.

Table-3: Road & Transport Authority (RTA) Department and all Centres collections for the period September, 2003 to January, 2004

Centre Name	*September 2003*	*October 2003*	*November 2003*	*December 2003*	*January 2004*
Municipal Premises, Tirupati	2405351.00 (737)	4926015.00 (1730)	259593.00 (787)	1533493.00 (482)	1163.00 (2)
Bairagipattada, Tirupati	1109433.00 (407)	2375294.00 (957)	825586.00 (336)	954407.00 (353)	0.00
CTM Road, Madanapalle	0.00	541076.00 (207)	240286.00 (84)	183810.00 (73)	0.00
Patel Road, Madanapalle	0.00	21020.00 (9)	2648.00 (3)	4170.00 (5)	525.00 (1)
Gremspet, Chittoor	1350.00 (1)	388441.00 (140)	11964.00 (5)	14735.00 (4)	0.00
Municipal Complex, Chittoor	76712.00 (28)	0.00	817170.00 (263)	671489.00 (230)	0.00
Total	**3592846.00 (1173)**	**10224671.00 (3773)**	**4493584.00 (1478)**	**3362104.00 (1147)**	**1688.00 (3)**

Source: Records of e-Seva, District Data Centre, Tirupati.

Brackets indicates number of transactions.

Table No. 3 indicates data regarding the transactions of RTA service provided for public at e-Seva centres in Chittoor District. RTA service had a good start and it had reached a high peak from 737 transactions to 1730 but suddenly from the month of November it again decreased and there was a continous decrease in the transactions. The other centre at Tirupati also had the same result and was zero in the month of January, 2004. The two centres at Madanapalle which had zero transactions in the month of September but further though it started having transactions it slowly decreased. The other two centres located at Chittoor also had the same result. The transactions were undergoing till the month of December but had a very poor performance in 2004 January.

Table-4: Southern Power Distribution Corporation Limited (SPDCL) Department and all Centres collections for the period September, 2003 to January, 2004

Centre Name	*September 2003*	*October 2003*	*November 2003*	*December 2003*	*January 2004*
Municipal Premises, Tirupati	2804278.00 (5669)	6524363.00 (10333)	4881431.50 (9323)	8662583.00 (15077)	7697442.50 (17082)
Bairagipattada, Tirupati	734306.00 (1433)	1423168.00 (2473)	1925605.00 (3604)	2160925.00 (4178)	3416691.00 (7605)
CTM Road, Madanapalle	397936.00 (761)	940506.00 (1835)	1670549.00 (3162)	1515672.00 (2739)	1714826.00 (3826)
Patel Road, Madanapalle	3967.00 (2)	680387.00 (1414)	1185371.00 (2522)	1457982.00 (3405)	1657665.00 (4662)
Gremspet, Chittoor	357203.70 (576)	602124.00 (1450)	791734.00 (2108)	1252766.00 (2658)	3339977.00 (15455)
Municipal Complex, Chittoor	255522.00 (443)	615638.00 (11370)	784669.00 (1690)	959112.00 (2094)	3473453.00 (12228)
Urban Police Station, Kalahasthi	0.00	0.00	0.00	0.00	33901.00 (93)
Total	**4553212.70 (884)**	**10786186.00 (18642)**	**11239359.50 (22409)**	**16009040.00 (30151)**	**21333955.50 (60951)**

Source: Records of e-Seva, District Data Centre, Tirupati

Brackets indicates number of transactions.

SPDCL Department is a Department concerned with electricity where in electricity bills can be paid at any e-Seva centre. This is one of the service which is highly utilized by public with ease at all centres. At Municipal premises, Tirupati, which started its transactions from 5669 in the month of Septermber has reached to 17082 by 2004 January. At Bairagipattada, Tirupati in month of September the transactions recorded were 1433 and has reached to 7605 in 2004 January. CTM Road, Madanpalle the transactions recorded were 761 and increased to 3826. AT Patel Road, Madanpalle which started with only 2 transactions in September, 2003 and had drastical increase of 1414 in October, 2003 and so on increased to 4662 in January, 2004. At Gremspet, Chittoor, in Septermber, 2003 number of transactions were 576 and 15455 transactions in January, 2004. In Municipal complex, Chittoor which started with 443 transactions and had a drastical increase of 12228 transactions by January 2004. But in Kalahastri, the transactions started only from January. Overall, it has increased from 8884 to 60951 transactions.

Table-5: All Centres collections for the period September, 2003 to January, 2004

Centre Name	*September 2003*	*October 2003*	*November 2003*	*December 2003*	*January 2004*
Municipal Premises, Tirupati	5645800.00 (6426)	11503894.00 (12087)	7560480.00 (10132)	10202359.00 (15577)	14182799.00 (19568)
Bairagipattada, Tirupati	1848789.00 (1851)	3928412.00 (3439)	2751191.00 (3940)	3115332.00 (4531)	6707438.00 (8956)
CTM Road, Madanapalle	397946.00 (762)	1482232.00 (2043)	1910835.00 (3246)	1699492.00 (2813)	2659600.00 (4197)
Patel Road, Madanapalle	3967.00 (2)	701407.00 (1423)	1188019.00 (2525)	1462152.00 (3410)	2779915.00 (5185)
Gremspet, Chittoor	358553.00 (577)	1065565.00 (1591)	803698.00 (2113)	1267501.00 (2662)	4378338.00 (15874)
Municipal Complex, Chittoor	332234.00 (471)	2588463.00 (1867)	1601839.00 (1953)	1630611.00 (2325)	9654680.00 (14541)
Urban Police Station, Kalahasthi	0.00	0.00	0.00	0.00	505291.00 (275)
Total	**8587289.00 (10089)**	**21269973.00 (22450)**	**15816062.00 (23909)**	**19377447.00 (31318)**	**40868061.00 (68596)**

Source: Records of e-Seva, District Data Centre, Tirupati.

Brackets indicates number of transactions.

This table gives the data regarding the collections of all centres for the period September, 2003 to January, 2004. At Municipal Premises, Tirupati in September, 2003, the number of transactions were 6426 and in January, 2004 reached to 19568. At Bairagipattada, Tirupati, the transactions undergone were 1851 and increased to 8956 by January, 2004. All other centres as a overall result had an increase. The overall transaction in September, 2003 in Chittoor District were 10089 transactions in September 2003 and has increased to 68596 transactions by the end of January, 2004.

Conclusions

1. APSRTC Department had a low rate of performance as only one centre among 6 centre had transactions and at all the centres it recorded NIL.
2. The services given by CTD was not utilized by public as the transactions show decrease in the rate day by day.
3. The third service provided by e-Seva is the RTA. Here the transactions were not uniform and there was a sudden fall by the end of January, 2004.
4. The fourth service is SPDCL that is the Electricity service which gives the highest record of transactions and is utilized at all centres. Its growth rate is still continuing.
5. e-Seva is a Unique concept aimed at re-defining citizen services providing a platform for easy access to Government.
6. e-Seva has ushered in a new dimension in citizen-Government interface.
7. e-Seva, the novel concept will be a role model fit to be enumulated by other Governments across the state and the world.

Suggesstions

1. It can be depicted that the overall performance is good but departments like APSRTC, CTD and RTA had no uniform transactions. This needs a proper promotion to make the public aware about the services provided by e-Seva.
2. The scope of e-Seva may be enlarged to encompass all departments and institutions interacting with citizens.

3. Information disseminator is to be increased to create awareness among people.
4. Making a beginning is effective but the same standards of customer care and efficiencies which e-Seva seeks to provide should be maintained.
5. Higher Officials of Government should co-operate in making e-Seva programmes still more successful.

REFERENCES

1. www.esevaonline.com
2. Official records of e-Seva, District Data Centre (DDC), Tirupati.
3. Manual of e-Seva.

23

INFORMATION TECHNOLOGY IN HOSPITALS

Dr. B.K.S. Prakasha Rao* and **Dr. Talluru Sreenivas****

The main purpose of this paper is to explore the importance of the information and its techniques in hospital industry. The hospital, a major social institution, offers considerable advantage to both the patient and the society. If the hospitals are managed properly, there would be expansion in facilities in medical care with least possible costs. The hospital of today is no more a simple institution. It has become a very dynamic and complex organization humming with activities for patient care.

The revolution in information technology is fast spreading and covers many areas in the business and day-to-day life of the individual. The convergence of telecommunications and computer paved the way for information technology and has changed almost everything. Thus, the world has a paradigm shift from industry to information society. The information technology has an important role to play in public services like railways, insurance, banking etc. Hospital is no exception, as it is required to collect, process and store huge amounts of information about people utilizing the public services. Hospital is one such public service where usage of information technology can help in providing fast and reliable service. Hospital Information

* Reader, Department of Management Sciences, RVR&JC College of Engineering, Guntur.

** Reader, Department of Management Sciences, RVR&JC College of Engineering, Guntur.

Technology (HIT) provides the required information to each level of management at the right time, in the right form and in the right place, so that the decisions are made effectively and efficiently. HIT improves the patient care by giving relevant data from time to time. This paper tries to discuss different issues related to implementation of information technology in hospitals and its impact on health care.

Introduction

India has a rich, centuries-old heritage of medical and health sciences. The philosophy of Ayurveda and the surgical skills enunciated by Charaka and Shushruta bear testimony to our ancient tradition in the scientific health care of our people. The approach of our ancient medical systems was of a holistic nature, which took into account all aspects of human health and disease. The allopathic system of medicine has, in a relatively short period of time, made a major impact on the entire approach to health care and pattern of development of the health services infrastructure in the country.

Health has been described as "the state of complete physical, social, and mental well being and not merely the absence of disease". A number of health problems require intensive medical treatment and personal care which normally are not available at the patient's home or in the clinic of a doctor. The hospital, a major social institution, offers considerable advantage to both patient and society. It is the place where a large number of professionally and technically skilled people apply their knowledge and skill with the help of world class expertise, advanced and sophisticated equipment. Thus the first and foremost function of a hospital is to give proper care to the sick and injured without social, economic or racial discrimination. Of late, hospitals are being set up with a motto to serve all sections of the society. The only function of these hospitals is to care for the sick. In addition, some of them are also engaged in promoting medical education, training and research. The development of health care facilities is influenced not only by opening of hospitals but also by their management. If these hospitals are managed properly, there would be expansion in facilities in medical care with least possible cost. The traditional concept of managing the hospital services cannot serve today's purpose. The hospital Management should insist on time honoured structural transformation.

In a developing country like India, resources are scarce and more so for health sector. Management concepts and techniques have, therefore, special relevance in the Indian situation. Though we have medical professionals and specialists of international standards, our supportive management systems have remained under-developed and neglected.

In general, when we think of hospitals and the personnel manning the hospitals, we think only of the clinical side of it. But a well managed hospital can give better clinical results. The hospital of today is no more a simple institution. It has become a very dynamic and complex organization humming with activities for patient care. Apart from the patient care, big hospitals are also acting as centers for education in medical sciences and training of medical, nursing and other para professionals, house-keeping and sanitation staff. This extremely heterogeneous group forms the team which is responsible for patient care, education and training as well as the various research activities that are carried out in the center. The hospital is a labour intensive organization and employs a very large number of manpower for its functioning. Such an organization looking after the sick and the wounded, needs a very high degree of proficiency in Management in general and suitable hospital information system in particular.

Now a days, in a hospital, Hospital Information Technology (HIT) gives solution to a number of multi-faceted problems, in order to make the hospital powerful in terms of both qualitative and quantitative aspects. It helps in rendering hospital services to all segments of the society at full length. The application of HIT makes possible quality medical services to all the sections without discrimination. It is a well known fact that the potential users face the problem of a communication gap of getting right information in right time. The proper implementation of information Technology in hospital industry tries to motivate the potential users and helps in transforming into actual users. The hospital is a social institution where the behaviour of doctors, nurses, paramedical staff and other administrators with the users of services play an effective role. We knock the doors of a hospital when all other measures are exhausted. This situation necessitates the introduction of information technology. Particularly in a developing country like India, the general masses are found disinterested in maintaining the defined norms for physical fitness. Well-managed information systems increase the health consciousness of the patients, relatives and visitors to the hospital.

Moreover, a hospital obviously has many organizational and operational elements in common with hotels, industrial organizations and educational institutions. However, a hospital is a unique institution as it includes all activities present in each of above mention groups. The difference between the hospital establishment and other organizations can be attributed to the existence of the following conditions.

1. The hospital renders service to the people who are mentally and physically ill and these services can be given only within four walls of the hospital;
2. The customers in hospitals come with individualized and highly personalized attention.
3. The hospital provides wide range of supporting services along with medical services and these are round the clock services.
4. Some of the employees (for eg. nursing staff) must accept direction from both matron and physician. The human relations in such situation are very delicate and complex.
5. Resources with which to operate the hospital functions are becoming increasingly scarce.

These above mentioned peculiarities of hospital management call for a high degree of professional competence to do justice to the job. Hence, the management of hospitals needs the same care and consideration which is essential for running a business.

In this context, this paper tries to discuss different issues related to computerization in a hospital. A hospital conducts a wide variety of activities in which application of information technology may be of great use. Computers will create new patterns of decision making or introduce new types of decisions that could never have been made before the advent of computers, by reducing redundancy of information while improving its accuracy and timeliness. Computerization provides a tremendous opportunity for hospitals to improve productivity at low costs. The introduction of information technology in the hospital environment has paralleled an increased need for timely and accurate data from various sources. Computerization results in the physician getting relieved of routine documentation and other clerical functions. It effects a reduction in paper work thus leaving more time to professionals for patient care. Computerization reduces errors. To ensure accuracy in the transmission and storage of data for subsequent use, a computerized medical information system can establish consistent standards and continuously monitor all transactions. Information technology also provides easy access to valuable medical information. The physician can have direct access to all the information, tests, results etc. of his patients through the use of remotely located terminals. It is not surprising, therefore, that more and more hospitals all over the world are now introducing computerized hospital information systems.

Information Technology – Background

The revolution in information technology is fast spreading and enveloping many areas in the business and day to day life of the individual. The new era is being increasingly referred to as the information age. The information explosion has influenced everyone, every trade and every process. The convergence of Telecommunications and computer has paved the way for Information Technology and has changed almost everything about the life styles, the business and the governance. Nothing else has changed the world in such a short span as the Information Technology. Thus, the world has a paradigm shift from industrial to information based society. It is anybody's knowledge how IT has been casting its spell. Information Technology has emerged as the core of the new changes.

What is Information Technology?

Information Technology embraces the application of computing, communication and associated technologies to capture, store, retrieve, process and disseminate information in various forms including voice, video, text and data. High speed data transfer links, are electronic mails, public networks, satellite communication, and video conference are some of the examples of the rapid transformation of communication. The transfer of data across the globe is possible within a fraction of a second and accessing of database across the continents is a reality today.

Computer and communication systems combined have to be called as information technology. With the opening up of the economy the business environment has become more competitive. In this competitive situation, it is imperative to highlight a company's strength and weakness in collecting the business information about the company's operation and innovation in rest of the globe. Hence, information technology and its management are the priority sector earmarked by the companies to march ahead in the competitive race of information collection. The globalization of market place and the means of accessing the same through the national and global info super-highway have given a new dimension to the concept of information.

The information technology has an important role to play in public services like railways, postal services, banking, insurance and hospitals etc. as it is required to collect, process and store huge amounts of information about people utilizing these public services. Hospital is one such public service where the use of information technology can help in providing faster and reliable health care services.

Information Technology in Hospitals

A hospital can be considered as a microcosm. A variety/range of functions are performed by large number functionaries to produce a product, which may be termed as patient care. Today, hospitals are one of the most complex organizations in our society. To perform their task in an effective, efficient and coordinated manner, functionaries need information. Computers will create new patterns of decision-making or introduce new types of decisions that could never have been possible before the advent of computers by reducing redundancy of information while improving its accuracy and timeliness. Computers provide a tremendous opportunity for hospitals to improve operations/productivity and lower the costs. The introduction of information technology in the hospital environment has paralleled an increased need for timely and accurate data from various sources technological innovation, and a growing awareness of the need to integrate all information systems under a uniform umbrella of hospital information systems.

In medicine today's computers are used for everything from diagnosing illnesses and monitoring patients at their beside to controlling the movement of robotic surgical assistants. Health care in all areas of Medical Professions has been a major element of technological advance. The trend for computerization is such that by the year 2010 most oral health practices will have adopted the technology. The technology in hospital operations represents an opportunity to implement an information system that can gather, organize and analyze, summarize data into reports, and assist in medical and administrative audits and utilization reviews. The ability to store, retrieve accurate timely and consistent data, effectively report those data, and allow transferability of data to other applications within a hospital environment is valuable for effective management of hospital and patient care.

Hospital Information Technology (HIT) provides the required information to each level of management at the right time, in the right form, and in the right place, so that decisions are made effectively and efficiently. HIT plays a vital role in planning, initiating, organizing and controlling the operations of the sub-systems of the hospital and thus provides a synergistic organization in the process. HIT can improve patient care by assisting data and making recommendations for care, and it can enable a hospital to move from a retrospective to concurrent review of quality and appropriateness of care. The management of a more complex and diversified hospital offering a broader range of services becomes much more difficult. To compound the complex problem, there continues to be a shortage of qualified professional personnel. Moreover, these qualified professionals now in the field are being heavily utilized for clerical tasks. Many health professionals and knowledgeable leaders in the medical computer field consider the introduction of the computer and management information techniques a solution to many of the health management problems which we are presently facing. Computerization results in the physician getting relieved of routine documentation and other clerical functions. It results in reduction in paper, work, thus, leaving more time to professionals for patient care. Computerisation also reduces errors.

The Objective of Hospital Information Technology

To aid a hospital in achieving greater operational efficiency and control of information-oriented task in administration and patient care areas. A well designed, integrated HIT, tailored to the specific needs of a particular hospital, can improve the productivity of the hospital staff, by allowing each department and service center to control its own information processing and contribute to the quality.

Benefits of HIT

The main benefits of using HIT are be the following.

(a) Automation of most of the book-keeping which results in more free time for the nurse's and Technician's time for clinical and technical activities.

(b) Assistance in preparation of operational documents like indents, treatment book, charge slip, etc.

(c) Tabulation of information such as the work lists for the laboratories daily schedules of nurses etc.

(d) Real time access to information from multiple points for decision making and monitoring such as bed census, casualty bed position and laboratory test results.

(e) Better response to enquiries of the visitors of in-patients, such as the current location of a patient.

(f) Providing up-to-date information on the stock position, status of lab tests, roster of nurses and doctors etc.

(g) Resource availability information such as that required for appointments.

(h) Possibility of creating statistical information through the computer system for yearly and on-request reporting.

(i) Reduction in duplication of work such as patient details not to be entered on three different documents at central admission desk.

(j) Legibility and standard formation of the information stored for posterity, such as case sheets for medical records.

Functioning of Hospital Information Technology

The major concern for an hospital is the patient. The essence of hospital lies in the service provided to the patient. There is a computer center which has a server with a standby. The entire hospital is connected through UNIX environment. All the departments, labs, store, wards etc. are provided terminals which are connected to the server. Most of the software manufactures have developed packages for Hospital Information Systems which can be run on various computers. A few hospitals have tried to develop Hospital Information Systems on their own. However, the most common strategy for a hospital is to select a package and computer which meet most of its particular needs and engage a software house to modify and install the package according to its specific requirements.

The major areas of HIT generally cover the following aspects.

1. Reservation, Admission and Discharge Module

At first the patient has to register himself in the registration counter where all the socio-economic background of the patient like name, age, sex, address, blood group etc. are entered in the system. The patient will be given a hospital number and the data is stored under the particular hospital number in the database. The computer assists by providing a ready-made format thereby eliminating the labour intensity and error prone process of data entry.

This module provides on-line as well as off-line statistical reports.

On-line Activities

- Entering patient profiles into database
- Reservation for in-patients
- Pre-admission for in-patients, emergency room patients and new born infants.
- Transfer of patients from one bed to another.
- Pending discharge of in-patients.
- Discharge of in-patients.
- Re-admission of a patient discharged by error.
- Displaying reservation for in-patients.
- Displaying of a specified physician's patients.

Displaying Patient Details by Name Enquiry

Off-line Activities

- Reservation list.
- List of patients admitted today.

- List of patients transferred today.
- Alphabetic census by patient name
- Physician census by patient religion code
- Nursing station census.
- Room-bed master list.
- Department master list.
- Professional master list.
- Daily in-patient report.
- Monthly maternity report.
- Monthly death report.
- Daily discharge analysis report.
- Death analysis report for new born.
- Death analysis report by age groups.

2. Medical Records

Under this section the details of all the patients are maintained and has the following reports.

- Daily Register
- Registration
- Credit particulars
- Case sheet issues
- Billing query

and these records will be helpful if the patient revisits the hospital in future.

3. Casualty

After registration the patient will be subjected to preliminary diagnosis by a junior doctor in casualty. If further diagnosis is required the patient will be sent to the concerned department. The junior doctor will feed the preliminary investigation findings in the record maintained under patient's hospital number.

4. Personal Registration Module

This module permits Doctors to register their entry and location in the hospital as well as their exit from the hospital and inform staff members about outstanding messages for them.

The module covers the following functions.

- Provision of menu for selecting a function.
- Registration of staff members in and out of hospital including arrival/departure of personnel enter the location and leave position.
- Display of checked-in staff member details.
- Entry of Standard messages like call hospital operator, call your office, contact-wanted in surgery/pediatrics/ emergency room/radiology/nursing unit.

5. Employee Information Module

This module provides the following reports on demand.

- to maintain an on-line computerized database on all employees of the hospital.
- to display records of employees of a specific type, on demand and
- to prepare various reports required by the hospital
- update the data for the employee record.
- Display names of all Medical Doctors of a given department.
- Display names of Doctors of given specialization.
- Display names of all Nursing Staff of given department.
- Medical Doctors Report by specialization and on Hospital departments.
- Nursing staff report sorted on Hospital departments.
- Supporting Technical Staff and Administrative Report sorted on Hospital departments.

6. Surgery Scheduling Module

This module provides an on-line facility to schedule, reschedule or cancel the surgery for patients. It provides a means of maintaining the current schedule of all operating rooms within the hospital. It is also capable of reserving one or more operating rooms for a physician or for holidays or for routine maintenance.

- Display Menu Screen for selecting a surgery scheduling module function.
- Allow patient name inquiry on the basis of sex and name of the patient and display patient name, age, admission date, attending Doctor, Type of patient, First surgery date and room-bed of the patient.
- Allow selection of a patient out of those displayed on the screen for scheduling, changing or cancelling the surgery for the patient.
- Display available time for surgery for a particular date for an operating room.
- Schedule surgery for a patient by specifying surgeon.
- Cancel a surgery for a patient.

7. Patient Care Module

This module provides reports like result summaries, departmental activity log and work to be done by departments.

- Enter order for a patient by procedure name
- Cancel and renew orders for a patient.
- Enter patient profile.
- Enter preliminary result for a patient.
- Enter results for a patient.
- Display/print diet census for one patient
- Enter details of procedure
- Verify an order
- Radiology work list.
- Laboratory work list.
- Respiratory therapy work list etc.

8. Pharmacy Module

The pharmacy module is a comprehensive pharmacy information system. The system also tests for drug-to-drug interaction.

This module carries out the following activities.

- Enter patient orders for regular drugs, compound drugs, IV's etc.
- Test drug to drug interaction.
- Change or delete pharmacy orders.
- Display/print pharmacy orders for patients.
- Confirm the administration of drugs.
- Adjust order schedule.
- Display inventory of drugs
- Maintain generic record of drugs.
- Medication schedule for patients.
- Pharmacy Inventory status.
- Unit Dose filling list.
- IV census.
- Order renewal list
- Price list
- Procedure code book
- Pharmacy Drug master list

9. Patient Billing and Accounting

This module covers the following activities.

- Enter details of charges for various services.
- Enter details of payments made by patients.
- Display details of charge and payments of the patients.
- Interim, final and on demand bills.
- Outstanding bill amounts report.
- Aged balance report.
- Bad debt accounts report.

10. Diet Planning

This module provides the following facilities.

- Enter details of various diets and their contents available in the hospital.
- Display identification details of patients of a nursing station.
- Enter details of diets for patients of a nursing station.
- A list showing ration requirements for the hospital, nursing station-wise.

Conclusion

Information Technology is not a single process. It is any type of control system that provides informational assistance to administrators, and it can be used to supplement the budgeting process. Thus Information Technology can be developed in four major areas such as programme development and control, performance analysis and control, financial planning and control, resource utilization and control. With the installation of above information exchange procedure, the organizational members can easily determine the means of analysis of existing data and organizational processes.

The slogan in industry and business, "the more the information, the better the decision" is equally valid in hospital Management, with, of course, a major qualification that the right kind of information should be available to the administrator at the time he needs it in a form in which he can use it. It is a common characteristic of almost all the hospitals that there is a serious lack of valid and reliable data in the absence of which the planning and administrators are forced to take major policy decisions on adhoc basis of their impressions and pet ideas and hunches. No wonder then if the plans go wrong and the programmes fail to achieve the objectives they were meant for. Very often it is too late to mend them. It is, therefore, of the utmost importance that all the hospitals in India should give the highest priority to the development of Hospital Information Systems for proper policy planning, monitoring, evaluation and feedback, especially in this crucial period of change and changing for better India.

24

INFORMATION TECHNOLOGY IN EDUCATION

Y. Krishna Priya*, K. Bindu Madhavi** and **Ch. K. Padmaja*****

Information Techonolgy (IT) is not only about computer, software or services. IT is a combination of all these elements or capped by a vision on how technology can help an organisation to reach its goals. Today, businesses are concentrating on their core activities in their struggle to service. Under these circumstances the need for well informed IT professional existence in every organisation is becoming mandatory. IT is very suitable for the transfer and storage of explicit knowledge. IT is booming in many fields primarly in educational sector. This paper sets forth the application of IT in Education.

Introduction

Over the last decade the Indian Information Technology (IT) industry particularly the software sector has grown in leaps and bounds. Industry revenues in this sector have grown more than ten fold from a mere US $50 million in 1997-1998 to US $5.7 billion in 1999-2000.As a result, India has been acknowledged the world over as an important base for the growth and development of IT industry.

---

*, ** Sri Padmavathi Mahila University, Tirupathi.

*** Faculty, Sri Padmavathi Mahila University, Tirupathi.

Importance of Education

One of the remarkable features of educational development in India during the post independence era has been the regularity with which in-depth reviews of educational policies have been undertaken at various levels and stages. Formulation and reformulation of policies have generally been based upon sound professional analysis of the existing system, availability of the expertise and resources, the possibility of optimum utilization of the same to meet the evolving learning needs of the learners and people and to face the new challenges emerging in a changing world. A number of committees and commission have contributed significantly to developments in the field of education. The overall achievements of India in the field of education have been significant during the last five decades. At the same time we have not yet been able to achieve a lot and tremendous amount of effort is still required to ensure such 'basics' as access to elementary education for all children, availability of learning centers within reasonable distance, provision for necessary minimum infrastructure needed for learners and proper functioning of formal or non-formal centers of elementary education.

Infact we are still far behind the constitutional mandate of providing compulsory elementary education to all children till they attain 14 years of age. But at the same time, our system of school education has responded in various degrees to new methods, new approaches and new techniques to enrich the teaching-learning process With the use of audio-visual aids, educational technology and even the contemporary information and communication technology (ICT).

The national policy on education of 1986 and the PROGRAMME OF ACTION documents brought out in 1986 and 1992 highlighted the emergence of IT and its possible role in the context of schooling and education. In a way this was a continuation of the vision and content of the kothari commission report on educational technology which now included IT. IT has the capability of localizing the globe .The potentiality of ICT is such that it can bring forth the entire globe with just a click of the young learner. It is almost a miracle.

Need

Several authors(Holt, Kozol, Conroy)have suggested that school education has lost its value as an instrument in the development of the individual .Some even suggest there is no possibility of improvement and the only hope is to replace traditional education with completely new mechanism.

If a student does not perceive what he or she is receiving from the educational system, as useful or having a purpose, he/she will conclude education is meaningless. The education system fails because it is more involved in supplying how's and lacks the ability to provide why's.

In current school environment in many places it is not usual to find 45 and even 50 student classrooms with one teacher as the only resource available to them for learning. This severely limits the ability of teachers to develop participatory approaches where students can use information to do things, instead of just hearing about them.

To comprehend the enormity of the task of teacher training, some statistics may be relevant. The sixth all India educational survey indicates that we had 1.62 million primary school teachers , 1.13 million middle school teachers ,0.83 million secondary and 0.62 million senior secondary school teachers in 1993 . These figures add up to 4.3 million. Today, with nearly 25% increase in teacher population; the number of teachers would be in the vicinity of 5 million. It has been estimated that the cost of training teachers is far greater than the cost of hardware and software. Resources have to be mobilized , plans prepared and the possibilities of training 5 million teachers who are on the job need to be explored, concretized and put to operation .So the present paper points out the importance of IT in Education and the future prospects in India.

Importance of Information Technology in Present Scenario

The integration of IT in education is a central matter in ensuring quality in educational system. There are two equally important reasons for integrating IT in education-students must become familiar with the use of IT since all jobs in the society of the future will be dependent on it, and IT must be used in education in order to improve its quality and make it more effective.

Several countries had started making their own spread networks And put different communication technologies to use, India had only contemplated a couple of experiments on pilot basis in the mid-eighties. By the mid-nineties a large number of countries were imparting skills of handling information and communication technologies as a part of their school system. India launched the first project called Computer Literacy And Studies in Schools (CLASS) in 1984 with the objective of generating computer literacy. The Programme of Action (1986) envisioned that computers would make the teaching learning process more efficient and effective on the one hand and would also encourage children to become more creative on the other. The 1992 Programme of Action pleaded for more computers and computerization, little beyond that our efforts between 1986-1992 were very limited in the established sector. A handful of private schools did move a head in this area.

The first major statement on computers in school education was proposed in the IT Action Plan of the government of India in july1998. It made several recommendations for the education sector of which the following were relevant for schools:

- Easy installment bank loans and other measures to help students, teachers and schools to buy computers.
- Employment of IT to promote distance education.
- Setting up of a national council for IT courses for various levels of education and training of teachers.
- Making computers and internet connections available to all schools by 2003.
- Initiation of a movement to help districts which have achieved universal literacy also to achieve computer literacy.

There is now a great deal of evidence about the potential of IT to enhance learning in schools; provided that is appropriately used. There are in fact several so-called educational technologies employing IT in various ways, which can facilitate learning. The various stake holders now need to agree amongst themselves that this evidence of the potential of IT to enhance learning is sufficient tom permit strategic and pragmatic decision to be made at national and local levels. Various nations and government are adopting policies to facilitate the adoption of the education technologies in learning institutions and those prepare students for the developing knowledge based economics.

Role of Information Technology in Internet

The emerging role of internet in building what is called the global village, with its almost infinite capacity for sharing and accessing information, paired with the availability of ever faster and more powerful computers and communication facilities is rendering the role of teachers as source of information , obsolete. At the same time the need for critical judgment becomes a crucial necessity, in face of the avalanche of information now available at the students fingertips. The paradox of being thirsty and unable to drink from the firemen's pipe exemplifies the new kind of needs the education must satisfy.

Role of Organisation

One of the prominent areas which has accepted ICT is that of distance education and open learning. The open university and the national open school as alert and active organizations have launched considerable initiatives for the benefits of learners even in hilly, far-flung and remote areas. Institutions like NAVODAYA VIDYALAYA and KENDRIYA VIDYALAYA made considerable input to spread IT in their schools . At the national level like IGNOU, NCERT, NCTE, NOS,NIC and CMC and others have to identify their own areas of contribution and also to ensure a cohesive and comprehensive approach. we have to make the best use of our resources.

Role of IT in Distance learning

Technology is drastically transforming information, especially distance learning in higher education. In just 3 years from1995-1998-the use of internet based courses grew from 22% of institutions to 60% more than 1.6 million students were enrolled in distance education courses in1997-1998.It is estimated that in 2002 about 85% of two and four year colleges would offer distance education programs and that by the year 2006 enrollment in distance education learning programmes would increase by 1.5 million students. These numbers clearly reveal an educational paradigm shift.

Strategic Objectives

The keywords in the educational system of the future are: production and knowledge, geographical and temporal independence, pedagogic and structural innovation.

An IT Educational Policy must Ensure

- Up to date qualifications in the information society IT skills and IT understanding are the central prerequisites for the individual, both now and especially in the future.
- The advantage of using IT is that time consuming work routines can increasingly be performed by means of the technology and time can thus be devoted instead to communicating and informing to the processing of information and the production of knowledge.
- IT opens up opportunities for a more individualized form of teaching in which students can themselves control the learning process and teacher is not necessarily present.
- An IT educational policy strategy includes a considerable extension of virtual educational courses and possibilities where physical presence is not an initial requirement.
- By means of IT education can thus be made available, outside of working hours, at the weekend, during working hours in cooperation between companies and educational institutions as well as in a completely different part of the country from that in which the teaching is taking place. Education can in this way, be said to be unlimited.
- IT creates an opportunity for a greater degree of internationalization of education, if considerate attention is given to the creation of virtual educational courses with international participants.

Areas of Action

The strategic objectives can be expressed in 5 areas of action:

- basic skills
- personal qualifications
- teaching and learning

- electronic infrastructure
- IT and examinations

Basic Skills: IT requires the strengthening of traditional as well as new skills. The rapid technological development means that knowledge is no longer something that an individual gains once and for all. It is rather an asset that must be constantly updated. Recurrent education will thus become increasingly important for young people and adults with a view to maintaining and developing qualifications previously achieved. The decisive new quality of the IT society is that young people and adults can be qualified to creatively sort, choose process and use great amount of information that IT makes available.

Basic IT Skills: Many IT systems are general in nature i.e., it is up to the user to find out how a given task is to be solved. It is thus the user who has to discover a series of operational steps leading to the solution of the problem. Quite fundamentally the users of an educational system must be helped to achieve an understanding of the tools of presentation of the technology, where text, sound still pictures and film can be combined into an integrated whole. The user must be encouraged to gain experience in the automatic handling of the information and data in digital form. It has turned out that these skills are best gained through independent use and not with the help of text books. Therefore, it is quite important that computers, networks and software be made available as an integral part of the teaching process, depending on the needs and wishes of the various sectors.

Personal Qualifications: IT has new and more effective possibilities for further strengthening the development of the personal qualifications of students such as independence and the abilities to cooperate and communicate.

Teaching and Learning: New knowledge based on the latest research and alternative interpretations of existing knowledge can be sent around the world in seconds by means of IT and electronic communication.

Electronic Infrastructure: The sitting of machines is very important for the integration of IT in teaching. The IT environment of the future should include IT-based homework cafes and multimedia workshops.

IT and Examination: The use of IT in connection with written examinations develops from year to year. Developments make new demands on the formulation of test and examination questions .IT provides new opportunities in writing, the handling of figures, design, simulation, information retrieval etc and an investigation and description of how these new opportunities can be used for examination purposes is to be determined.

Tasks Ahead

Integration of IT in education requires certain steps to be taken immediately at various levels and by various agencies. Some of these could be the following

Training and Orientation: In-service orientation of teachers, teacher educators for understanding the nature and scope and content of IT in the context of education.

Strategies: A concrete strategy to remodel pre-service teacher education programmes.

Understanding of Students Psychology: The psychological basis of man and machine interaction and the possibility of adopting learning techniques with suitable learning objectives and transactional strategies need to be explored, analyzed and documented.

Pragmatism: The strategies of introduction of change through the new technology would succeed only when the existing infrastructure, expertise, strategies and systems and fully understood in the specific content and utilized to build up on these an edifice of IT.

Management System: The management system of education designed for the 19th centaury certainly is not suitable for the 21st centaury. This really has to be transformed to overhaul the management system . Infact these two will have to adopt IT and adapt to it willingly. Theses have to be changed in the support systems.

Conclusion

The technology is not an educational panacea, but it is an important facilitator of education. The clear understanding of the role of technology in change and the implications of technology-mediated changes for education are the key to success of any innovation in education. Training of teachers to integrate the 21st century technology into the classrooms is an enormous undertaking. It is time we viewed the learning process as selective filtering of experience, coordination of information and construction of knowledge. To be able to do that is a biggest challenge of IT to education

Education must be relevant to the changing nature of work place on one hand and respond to the aesthetic requirement of the individual and also to nurture moral, ethical and humanistic values. Only such learning can promote humans to earn their livelihood and lead a value based life in an emerging society. It would be essential that earning alone does not become the objective of human life. Hence technologies must be utilized by human beings and the reverse should not be allowed to happen.

REFERENCES

1. www.education.nic
2. www.expressitpeople.com
3. www.npiu.nic
4. www.ipan.com

25

BUSINESS PROCESS OUTSOURCING

DESTINATION INDIAS

Dr. Rajesh C. Jampala* and **Dr. P. Adi Lakshmi****

Business Process Outsourcing (BPO) is the fastest growing segment in Information Technology (IT) industry, growing more than twice the rate of IT industry itself. According to the Gartner Dataquest study, the worldwide BPO industry is expected to generate a total revenue of $302 billion by 2004. This paper explores and consolidates some estimates in BPO particularly during the transition of India into a super power.

Introduction

As the industry gets ready to take off into the big league, there are some huge success stories and miserable failures in India. At present the Indian revenues from BPO is around $2.3 billion. The industry growth rate is astonishing 59.1% per annum, investment is to the tune of $1 billion, creating about 1,00,000 smart cubicles in 7.5 million sq.ft of space, and number of people employed in this sector is exceeding 1,71,000. The future expectations are also very encouraging. According to Nasscom-McKinsey study IT-enabled services in India will employ 1.1 million people and earn $24 billion

* Reader in P.G. Dept. of Business Administration, P.B. Siddhartha College, Vijayawada.

** Reader and Head in P.G. Dept. of Business Administration, Montessori Mahila Kalasala, Vijayawada.

by 2008. India's top 10 BPO firms are set to generate $100 million in revenues each in the next 18-24 months.

But, a vast majority of 310 new firms are heading for a crash. This is because they failed to understand the dynamics of this business model. They were clueless about people, processes, and technologies – which are three important elements of the BPO business. This results in major consolidation and restructuring in the industry which is good in the long run. Table 1 provides the information about the successful companies in India.

Table-1: Winners in BPO Business in India

Company	*Revenues ($ million)*	*Employees*	*Voice: Non-voice*
WiproSpectramind	41	5,000	80:20
Daksh eServices	35	4,000	70:30
Office Tiger	25	1,000	0:100
HCL Technologies BPO	N.A.	2,346*	90:10
ICICI OneSource	N.A.	2,175	70:30
World Network Services	35	2,500	65:35
exl Service.com	28	2,300	75:25
MsourceE	20	3,162	93:7
Hinduja TMT	24	1,400	66:34
Tracmail	11	1,000	50:50
Progeon	4.4	685	30:70

* includes 700 in Belfast, UK center. Source : Business World 4 August 2003 page 30.

Some of the early entrants in Indian BPO market failed because low billing rates, negative economies of scale, less knowhow on niche areas, and other organisational issues. Table 2 provides reasons for failure of some of the Indian BPO firms.

Table-2: Losers in BPO Business in India

Company	*Reasons*
Flex Packaging	Faced problems because of promoters' legal troubles
First Ring	90% is voice work, low billing rates, looking for more funds
Phoenix Shoes	A niche area (psychological counselling), had little knowhow
Icon Data	Sub-contract work; billing squeez
Renasonic	Large voice business (mainly telemarketing) was impacted by the 'Do Not Call' legislation in the US

Source: Business World 4 August 2003, page 31.

Segments of BPO Business : Customer care, Human resource, Payment services, Content development & others like animation, Administration, Banking Financial Services and Insurance (BFSI), Healthcare are the major segments in the BPO business. In India Customer care is a dominant segment with revenues and employment doubling in the last year. Table 3 provides information regarding the potential of various segments in BPO business.

Table-3: Domain Depth

Service Line	*Market Potential ($ Billion)*
Human resource	3.5-4.5
Customer relationship	7.0
Payment services	3.0-3.5
Content development & others(like animation)	2.5-3.0
Administration	1.5
BFSI	3.5-4.5
Healthcare	1.5-2.0

Nasscom

High attrition rate and growth aspirations of the work force are the major problems along with poor infrastructure facilities. The success of offshoring to India has woken up other English speaking countries such as South Africa, Australia, New Zealand and Canada. China is also fast catching up by making English as a compulsory course in schools. China could pose a challenge in non-voice businesses, if not voice-based operations.

Table-4: Healthcare BPO

Company	*No. of People*	*Processes*
Vision Health Source	600	Billing, claims adjudication
Hinduja TMT	500	Claims adjudication
Cbay	<500	Transcription, coding, billing
Lapiz	300+	Medical billing
Datamatics	300	Transcription, forms processing
Ajuba	250+	Coding, billing, revenue cycle management, insurance eligibility certification
Comat Technologies	250	Transcription, coding
Tranquilmoney	225	Billing, receivable analysis for pharmacies
Affiliated Computer Services	<200	Medical billing
Apollo Health Street	150	Claims adjudication, billing, coding
Ideal Solutions	45	Dental claims forms processing

NASSCOM

If the Indian BPO firms continue to do their job as best as expected and help their clients to reengineer their processes by adding value they can successfully withstand the competition and India will become BPO capital of the world. BPO boom has also helped to develop the ancillary industry to the tune of Rs.6,300 crore in India. About six lakh jobs could be created in support services by 2007. Catering services, Facility management, Transport and Training are some of the services cater to the needs of BPO industry.

Offshoring Outsourcing-consider the following:

- In March 2001, Guardian Life Insurance Company of America began outsourcing IT to India. The company later expanded its outsourcing scope to include help desk assistance, personal computer repair assistance, and a disaster recovery operation. The result is an annual savings of $12.5 million.
- General Motors just announced that it is setting up a $21 million technology center in Bangalore, India, to carry out computer-aided design and engineering research.

- J.P. Morgan Chase & Co. is offshoring some of its stock market and equity research to India, signaling possible new arenas for the offshore outsourcing trend. J.P. Morgan Chase expects to hire Indian MBAs who will do the heavy-duty number crunching, freeing up the Americans to focus on higher-level financial analysis and to spend more time with customers.
- HSBC plans to export 4,000 British finance jobs to India, China and Malaysia to slash costs by 2004. Lloyds TSB, Prudential and Aviva have already moved thousands of positions to Asia.

All the examples illustrate a mega-trend in offshoring oppurtunity. Sourcing work from anywhere in the world at the best prevailing prices is now becoming mainstream for a variety of business processes. Offshoring opportunities are increasing due to the availability of low-cost, educated, English-speaking manpower, and strong IT skills in countries such as India and the Philippines.

Table-5: Offshore is expected to grow faster Software : Onsite offshore mix

MIX	*1999-00*	*2000-01*	*2001-02*	*2002-03*
Onsite	9850	15900	16500	18500
Offshore	5950	10950	18500	27500
Products & Unclassified	13350	1500	1500	1500
Total	**29150**	**28350**	**36500**	**47500**

All figures in Rs crore Source: NASSCOM, Capital Market 3-16,2003

Offshore outsourcing is a subset of BPO. The offshore outsourcing model is rapidly taking hold in U.S. and European companies. The larger Fortune 1000 firms are already aggressively moving forward by offshoring to markets such as Ireland, Singapore, Hong Kong, India, China, the Philippines, Vietnam, Thailand, Hungary, South Africa, Malaysia, and Russia. Table 6 highlights the Unique Selling Proposition of various countries and their limitations. Table 7 documents the North America's dominance as far as India's BPO business is concerned.

Table-6

Country	*USP*	*Limitation*
Philippines	Understands the US market; Voice work; low attrition	More expensive than India; small talent pool
Canada, Ireland, Australia	Understand the US; High-end skills	High costs
South Africa	Time zone similar to Europe; 25% cost saving, good for niche work	Skill shortage
China	Low costs	No english capability as yet
Russia,Ukraine	Technology skills	Poor infrastructure; corruption; language
Czech Republic, Hungary	European language skills	Small talent pool; high costs
Mexico	30% cheaper than the US; Spanish skills	Good only for low-end jobs

Table-7: Dependence on North America remains high Software : Geography mix

Mix	*2001-02*	*2002-03*
North America	66.7	67.7
Europe	23.7	21.2
Japan	2.5	2
Rest of the World	4.3	5.9
Asia Pacific (excluding Japan)	2.8	3.2
Total	**100**	**100**

All figures in Rs Crore. Source: NASSCOM, Capital Market 3-16, 2003

The business process offshoring market is relatively young. As a result, different "guesstimates" often backed by vague assumptions are being thrown around. After a detailed analysis of various publications over the last two years, we isolated some of the widely quoted statistics on offshoring.

- International Data Corporation (IDC) has predicted that the global IT-enabled services market will account for revenues of $1.2 trillion by 2006.

- By 2015, Forrester Research estimates that as many as 3.3 million U.S. jobs and $136 billion in wages could be moved to such countries as India, China, and Russia.
- Meta Group predicts that offshore outsourcing will grow by more than 20% annually, pushing it from a $7 billion market in 2003 to a $10 billion market by 2005. The group also foresees all application outsourcing services, including the offshore component, reaching $15 billion by 2007.
- A McKinsey and National Association of Software and Service Companies (NASSCOM) study estimates that the information technology and enterprise solutions (ITES) market in India is likely to reach $142 billion in 2009. This estimate contrasts with the current price tag of $532 billion to provide these services in the United States. The difference of $390 billion would be the net savings for the U.S. economy due to offshoring. The ITES sector has the potential to generate job opportunities for more than 1.1 million Indians by 2008.
- According to Deloitte Consulting, 2 million jobs will move from the United States and Europe to cheaper locations in the financial services business alone. The exodus of services jobs across all industries could be as high as 4 million. It forecasts that three-quarters of leading financial institutions and investment banks will allocate tasks to Third World countries in the next five years and that India will be at the top of the list. Global financial institutions will invest $356 billion in India for outsourcing projects.
- Gartner, in its 2002 report titled, "IT Trends in India," wrote that the market opportunity for Indian vendors would grow to $25 billion by 2005. According to Gartner, the global BPO market grew by 13% between 1999 and 2000, to $119 billion, and it will reach $234 billion in 2005.
- Gartner also wrote in a report entitled "U.S. Offshore Outsourcing: Structural Changes, Big Impact" that 500,000 of the 10.3 million U.S. technology jobs could move offshore in 2003-2004. Diane Morello, the Gartner

analyst who wrote the report, estimated that one in ten software services jobs are at stake at computer vendors and 5% of technology jobs are at stake in the wider corporate world. These assumptions led her to her estimate of 500,000 jobs being moved offshore.

- India's software exports were estimated to be worth $9.5 billion in 2003, and the United States accounted for 60 percent of that total (almost $6 B).
- According to Datamonitor, offshore deals made up just 1.4% of total outsourcing contracts in 2003. However, the value of offshore contracts rose 890% from 2002 to $1.66 billion.
- According to WR Hambrecht: Offshore service represents a large market opportunity. The offshore BPO market is expected to grow at a CAGR of 79% through 2008 to a size of $24.2 billion, and the offshore IT services market is expected to grow at a CAGR of 43% to $56 billion.

Conclusion

By every estimate the size of the offshore outsourcing trend is huge. India expects to create 2 million jobs in the next decade in offshore BPO. The real competition is not within the country. Our Indian IT firms have to fight with firms outside India. One has to prepare for the challenge and create wealth for oneself and society. Government, Industry and industry associations like NASSCOM should together plan for the further growth in BPO business.

26

BPO

OPPORTUNITIES FOR INDIA

A. Maruthi Vara Prasad*

The aspect of societal interdependence has been one of the key factors in the evolution of the human race and can be seen in every aspect around us today. India is a country that can feel the pulse of the society and change its image accordingly inspite of this huge diversity. Over the last few years no industry in India has been a much a topic of discussion and debate as the Information Technology (IT) sector was widely discussed and debated in comparison with all other Industrial aspects. The IT sector has contributed much to the economy in terms of exports, employment, corporate governance, transparency, and wealth creation. Passing through the information technology phase the country has gradually transformed itself into a hub of IT and IT—Enabled Services(ITES). In catching up with the latest trends in global business no stone is left unturned. It is remodeling curriculum to suit the contemporary needs.

Business Process Outsourcing (BPO) is one of the fast growing segments in the IT industry, growing twice the rate of the IT industry itself. More and more organizations worldwide are opting for BPO and reaping its benefits. The last four to five years have seen India emerging as a favourable destination worldwide for IT Enabled Services and has the potential of becoming the major processing center for the world. The skills of vast pool of English speaking people, the

* Lecturer, P.G. Dept. of Commerce, T.J.P.S. College (P.G.Courses), Guntur.

country's main asset, must be honed. Today, the world looks towards the IT software and services industry for its good quality and high price performance. The Indian government recognizes the IT and IT Enabled Services will influence economic development extensively. The government will need to focus on three areas to help the industry realize the potential-removing regulatory hurdles especially in emerging service lines such as ITES unlocking growth in domestic market, and proactively addressing potential infrastructure and talent bottlenecks to ensure that India stay ahead of competition.

Introduction

The aspect of societal interdependence has been one of the key factors in the evolution of the human race and all that we see around us today. India is a country that can feel the pulse of the society and change its image accordingly, inspite of its huge diversity. Over the last few year no industry in India has been a much a topic of discussion and debate as the Information Technology (IT) sector. The sector has contributed much to the economy in terms of exports, employment, corporate governance, transparency and wealth creation. And even though the rate of growth has slowed down from the frenetic 50% annual growth there is no denying the fact that this sector continues to outperform not only many other sectors in India, but also the IT services sector world wide. Passing through the Information Technology (IT) phase, the country has gradually transformed itself into a hub of IT and IT – enabled services (ITES). In catching up with the latest trends in global business, no stone is left unturned. It is allowing tax holidays and providing incentives, giving benefits in imports of computer parts etc. It is remodeling curriculum to suit the contemporary needs. Business process outsourcing (BPO) is one of the fastest growing segments in the IT industry, growing twice the rate of IT industry itself. More and more organizations world wide are opting for BPO and reaping its benefits.

The concept of outsourcing dates back to Indian mythological times. What could be possibly viewed as the very first outsourcing contract is the 'deal' interaction between Hermit *Vyasa* and Lord *Ganesha* for transcribing the tacit and verbal narration of the Krishna avatar of Lord Vishnu into the explicit epic and Voluminous *Mahabarata*. The contract was struck after a perfect understanding of the needs of the outsourced service seeker *(Vyasa)* and well comprehended capability of the service provider (Lord *Ganesha*).

Over the years, organizations were also realizing the need to focus on their core competency and outsourcing the non-core activities. This increased focus on core business activities and developing competitive advantage has left companies wondering whether to spend their limited resources for non-core and less strategic processes in functional areas like human resources, accounting and finance. On the other hand, the growth role and importance of information and communication technologies in organizational activities has reengineered business process. The technology – intensive reengineered business processes can be delivered to any organization from any location thus giving organizations an opportunity to seek such services without losing their focus on core competency. This has led to the emergence of business process outsourcing (BPO) which is delegating an IT – enabled business process to third party that owns, administers and runs the IT and other activities related to the process according to a defined set of metrics.

BPO had been occurring for decades but gained attention only during the 1990s when companies began signing high – dollar agreements for total or selective outsourcing, primarily to cut costs and growing emphasis on improving business performance. The table 1 shows the changing colours of BPO over the last couple of decades.

Table-1: Changing Colours of BPO

	1970s onwards	*1980s onwards*	
	Era 1: Remote *manufacturing*	Era 2: Shared *services/BPO*	Era 3: Offshore *Business Processing*
Concept	Reduce manufacturing costs by migrating manufacturing to low -cost locations.	Consolidate back-office operations – "insourcing" model.	Goods manufactured in countries of lowest factor costs and/or areas with large local markets.
Examples	Significant reducing in manpower costs Economics of scale.	Achieve 25% savings Leverage economies of scale.	Enable companies to access highly trained manpower at labour rates less than 20% of those in the North America.

(Contd...)

Benefits	Over 80% of printed circuit board made in Taiwan.	Nearly 90% of Fortune 500 re-engineered support functions through Shared Services.	Companies like GE, Americal Express, Dell and AOL have several thousand people in India.

Source: Transworks Research Team

Major Drives for BPO

The following are the major drives for the BPO market.

- The economic downturn and increased competition are putting pressures on enterprises to reduce cost of transaction processing in non – core areas.
- Globalization is driving multinational enterprises to outsource business processes to local service providers to gain local process expertise.
- A shift in regulatory environment is leading enterprises to achieve even higher cost efficiencies to focus on their front – end processes.
- Industry consolidation continues to create opportunities for outsourcing.

Factors Moulded as a Favourable Wind

There are several factors contributed for the favourable wind of ITES in India. These include:

*Good Education System:*The India education system places strong emphasis on mathematics and science, resulting in a large number of science and engineering graduates. Mastery over Quantitative concepts coupled with English proficiency has resulted in skill set that has enabled the country to take advantage of the current international demand for IT.

*Abundant Human Resources:*Every year approximately 19 million students are enrolled in high schools and 10 million students in pre-graduate degree courses across India moreover 201 million graduates and 0.3 million post graduates pass out of India's non-engineering colleges. While 2.5-3% of them find jobs in other fields or pursue further students abroad, the rest opt for employment in the IT industry. If the flow from high schools to graduate courses increases even marginally, there will be a massive increase in the number of skilled workers available to the industry. Even at the current rates, there will approximately be 17 million people available to the IT industry by 2008.

Rich Manpower: Indian programmers are known for their strong technical skills and their eagerness to satisfy clients. In some cases, clients outsource work to get access to more specialized engineering talent, particularly in the area of telecommunications. India also has one of the largest pools of English speaking professionals.

Favourable Government Policies: The Indian Government recognizes that IT and ITES will influence economic development extensively in the future. IT is a part of the governments national agenda and all policies are driven to achieve maximum benefit to their industry.

The liberalization and deregulation initiatives taken by the Indian Government with the global economy. The reforms have reduced licensing requirements and have made foreign technology accessible. The reforms have also removed restrictions and investment and made the process of investment easier.

Quality of Services: In the past few years, the Indian IT and ITES industry has pursued the goal of attaining the highest international standards of quality. A world bank funded study conducted as early as 1992 to discuss Indian software strategies had concluded that vendors in the US prefer to get their software developed in India for its quality and cost advantage. India also boats vendor sophistication with more than 200 companies being quality accredited and serving the needs of over 255 FORTUNE 500 companies. Today, the world looks towards the Indian IT software and services industry for its good quality and high price performance.

Well – Developed Tax Structure: India has a well-developed tax structure, with the authority to levy taxes divided between the central and state governments. The central government levies direct taxes such as personal income tax and corporate tax and indirect taxes such as customs duty, excise duty and service tax. The states impose local and state sales taxes and other taxes. The tax system in India has undergone considerable reform in the past few years. Tax rates have been rationalized and tax laws have been simplified. Tax revenue as a percentage of GDP has been consistently increasing. During fiscal year 2000-01 it was 14.6%.

The above factors have led many multinationals including GE, British Airways, Dell Computers, AOL and several other *FORTUNE 500* companies to outsource their business processes to India reaping significant cost benefits. For instance, GE capital saves an estimated $ 340 mn per year through its 13,000 skilled back - office workforce in India. The cost factor included cheap labour and low costs of establishing telecom infrastructure. The large size of English – speaking work force, high literacy rate and relatively low employee turnover rates in the industry were the factors favouring India.

*India on the Winning Edge:*After the sweet success in the field of Information Technology, India now dreams of becoming the most preferred destination for BPO ahead of countries such as Philippines, Mexico, and Ireland. BPO was the only sector in India offering consistent employment opportunities since 2002. The sector hired almost 200 people everyday. The good news is it will continue to grow at a rapid rate. We have just touched the tip of the iceberg. For the fiscal year ending March 31, 2003, the industry generated revenues of $2.3 bn employing more than 1,70,000 people. According to the Nasscom-McKinsey estimates, the industry revenues are expected to increase more than 10 times to cross $ 24 bn by 2008. By then, the industry will be employing 1.1 million people.

According to a study conducted by A T Kearney, India was rated as the best offshore BPO destination among 11 most preferred countries for BPO. India was rated No.1 because of its relatively low costs and high quality workforce. A.T.Kearney has developed a quantitative evaluation tool to support companies offshore location strategies (see box: The Offshore Evaluation Tool). This proprietary tool rates countries according to there factors: Cost, environment and people (Table 2). Each factor is assigned a weight, thus establishing its importance and relative ability to meet a company's unique needs.

The Offshore Evaluation Tool

A joint team for A.T. Kearney and a Furtune 100 miltinational corporation assembled the offshore evaluation tool over a 10-week period. The team first narrowed the universe of countries using the following criteria:

- Presence of multinational corporations
- Degree of information technology and business process maturity.
- Availability of skilled labor
- Expected future development
- Scalability of operations

Eleven countries made the final cut. The team then evaluated these countries against more than 30 measurements comprising three major categories. Cost, environment and people. Team members quantified the attributes and assigned weights using detailed industry and proprietary data, cross-referencing their findings with data from industry analysts and subject matter experts.

Table-2: Criteria and Weights in Country Analysis

Category *(Percent of total)*	Country *Characteristics*	Metrics Used
Cost (40%)	• Cost of labor • Cost of management and infrastructure • Tax and treasury impact	• Blended BPO and IT labor cost • Average cost of infrastructure (occupancy, utilities, telecom, management) • Corporate tax rates, profit realization and exchange rates
Environment (30%)	• Risk (economic, political) • Country infrastructure • Cultural compatibility • Geographic proximity • Security of Intellectual Property (IP)	• Gauge political and business risk, degree of government support • Relative strength of infrastructure and investments • Cultural differences or compatibility compared to Unite States • Relative distance (in band) from United States • Relative security of intellectual property

(Contd...)

People (30%)	• BPO and IT process experience • Size of labor market • Education level of workforce • Language barriers and literacy rates • Employee retention literacy rates	• COPC and CMM SEI and quality ratings, business process expertise and offshore market share • Available total labor market • Expected per capita education level • Percent fluency in English (overall and select companies, country • Select company retention and turnover rates

Customer operations performance center (COPC) defines performance standards for all centers worldwide. Capability Maturity Model (CMM) was developed by the Carnegie Mellon Software Engineering institute (SEI)Source: A.T.Kearney

The BPO industry comes as a welcome opportunity for India. India is the top rated country in two of the three major categories, cost and people. It boasts the most highly skilled, lowest cost labor force. This is a powerful combination, particularly when its experience in offshore business processing is factored into the mix. GE Capital, American Express, Citibank, Conseco, British Airways and Dell Computer are among the many companies taking advantage of India's capabilities. India is in the lead position over the low-cost software developing countries in the globe as shown in the table 3.

Table-3: Low-cost Software Developing Countries

Leaders	*Up and Comers*
India Latvia, Lithuania, New Zealand,	Brazil, Caribbean, Egypt, Estonia, Singapore, Ukraine, Venezuela.
Challengers	*Beginners*
Canada, China, Czech Republic, Hungary, Ireland, Israel, Mexico, Philippines, Poland, Russia, South Africa.	Bangladesh, Bulgaria, Cuba, Ghana, Korea, Malaysia, Mauritius, Nepal, Senegal, Sri Lanka, Taiwan, Thailand, Vietnam.

Source: Gartner Inc.

Driven by cost advantage and competitive pressures many companies are now looking for specilised service providers to whom they can outsource their non-core but necessary business processes. Technological advances have made distance a redundant concern.

In such a scenario, India with its cost differential, educated workforce and quality of service is fast emerging as a preferred destination. Business process outsourcing is emerging as the next big opportunity for India.

Conclusion

In the new scheme of thinking BPO translates into enormous business opportunity for India. The last four to five years have seen India emerging as a favourable destination worldwide for IT Enabled Services and has the potential of becoming the major processing center for the world. India is positioned to capture a sizable chunk of the global pie in outsourcing. The reasons include cost advantages, availability of talented workforce, improving infrastructure, geographical location and the resultant time difference. The encouraging attitude of the government is another positive factor in India's attractiveness. The skills of vast poor of English speaking people, the country's main asset, must be honed. Today, the world looks towards the IT software and services industry for its good quality and high price performance. IT-enabled services are expected to be around $ 18.6 bn by 2008 employing approximately 1.1 million people.

The Indian government recognizes the IT and IT Enabled Services will influence economic development extensively. The key to success in the long-term would be in expanding the breadth of services as well as meeting customer requirements. Irrespective of the form, be it captive center or third party provider, BPO is bound to have a positive impact on the Indian economy letting thousands of flowers bloom. The government will need to focus on three areas to help the industry realize the potential-removing regulatory hurdles especially in emerging service lines such as ITES unlocking growth in domestic market, and proactively addressing potential infrastructure and talent bottlenecks to ensure that India stay ahead of competition.

REFERENCES

1. *Business Process Outsourcing in India; Gaining momentum, Analyst,* August 2002.
2. A.T. Kearney, *Where to locate, E-Business*, September 2003, pp 31-32.
3. Prakash Gurbaxani, *The BPO industry in India, E-Business*, January 2004, pp 7-9.

4. Makarand Padalkar, *Indian IT industry the second wave*, *Analyst*, September 2003, p 26.

5. Deepak V Kuriakose, *BPO:Building profitable organisations*, *E-Business*, January 2004, p 50.

27

OFFSHORE OUTSOURCING
ISSUES AND CONCERNS

Dr. P. Adi Lakshmi*

Offshore outsourcing is becoming mainstream in retail, banking, financial services, insurance, and telecom industries. Companies are more inclined than ever to move work offshore. The number of million-dollar deals, the number of five-million-dollar deals, the number of 20/30-million dollar deals - are all up this year. In this paper an attempt has been made to discuss certain offshore outsourcing issues and concerns of Indian Companies.

Introduction

Offshore outsourcing is becoming mainstream in retail, banking, financial services, insurance, and telecom industries. Companies are more inclined than ever to move work offshore. The number of million-dollar deals, the number of five-million-dollar deals, the number of 20/30-million dollar deals - are all up this year.

Consider the case of GE, a pioneer in the offshore outsourcing arena. In the early 1990s, Jack Welch, the former CEO of GE introduced a new rule that governed GE's offshore actions. It is called the 70:70:70 rule. In an e-mail to GE employees, Welch mandated that 70% of GE's work will be outsourced. Out of this, 70% will be done from offshore development centers. And out of this, about 70%

* Reader and Head, Department of Business Administration, Montessori Mahila Kalasala, Vijayawada, 520 010.

will have to be done in India. This comes out to about 30% of GE's work being outsourced to India.

GE's BPO operations in India come under GE Capital International Services (GECIS), which was set up in '97 to carry out back office operations for GE Capital's businesses. Its services offerings include ERP and Oracle database consulting, IT help desks, knowledge services, software solutions, analytics, data mining and modeling, remote network monitoring, e-learning and customer contact centers.

GECIS employs over 12,000 people and delivers over 450 processes to 30 different business units in the US, Europe, Japan and Australia. In India it operates from Gurgaon, Hyderabad, Bangalore and Jaipur. It has four sites in Gurgaon, two in Hyderabad and one in Bangalore. Clearly, for GE offshoring is one delivery method of outsourcing. The old way of thinking about offshoring was that foreign work lacks quality and is hard to supervise. These two mind-sets are no longer true.

The Benefits

The most obvious benefit to offshoring is the low cost. Compared to a U.S. call center, offshoring saves companies at least 50% in operational expenses. But there is more to why people are shipping call centers to countries such as India besides cost. Benefits such as an educated, English-speaking labor pool, low turnover of employees, and complimentary time zones all make offshoring attractive.

Let's look at India. India is home to the largest educated English-speaking population in the world. Other than language, the geographical location of India lends to a 24x7 operation. The time zone difference between the United States and India is about 12 hours. This means that a job submitted at 6 p.m. Pacific Standard Time (PST) reaches India at 6 a.m. and is completed by 6 a.m. PST the following morning. Another feature of India is highly motivated workforce. U.S. call centers often experience low morale and very high turnover, usually 40%-70% per year. Considering the time and costs associated with training new agents, it becomes difficult to maintain quality service at a low cost. Currently, Indian call centers have an average turnover rate of 5%. We expect that this number will go up.

The Concerns

As with any endeavor that offers great benefits, you always need to wonder what the catch is. Outsourcing to offshore locations exposes countries to greater risks of many different types, such as country or political instability, regional turmoil, unstable economy, poor infrastructure, lack of exposure to Western business culture, and security of data risk. All of these increased concerns need to be addressed in the partner selection phase.

India has been busy building and promoting their technology sector since the 1980s. Although it is currently safe to travel to India, tensions between Pakistan and India continue. In addition, any time a company sends it customer data to another company, there is a risk of data being misused. However, on the infrastructure side, India has recently made enormous improvements in the infrastructure in many cities that are becoming offshoring hubs, such as Hyderabad, Mumbai, and Bangalore.

The primary criteria for locating services offshore are senior management's expertise managing remote locations, the caliber and cost of labor; language skills; telecom bandwidth, cost and reliability; political stability, the enforceability of intellectual property rights and business contracts; and the general maturity of the business environment.

The following section deals with various segments of offshore outsourcing opportunities.

BPO in Finance and Accounting Services

Timely, accurate financial and accounting information is crucial for corporations hoping to maintain a competitive edge in the market. Outsourcing back-office finance and accounting (F&A) enables them to focus on their core business while cutting costs. F&A outsourcing is maturing rapidly. Whether it's entering data or running complex financial reports, external service providers can do it. They can either work with the software applications that are currently in use or build interfaces into applications in use so that companies can retain some of the sensitive data.

Leading executives continue to clamor for strategic, end-to-end F&A solutions that are integrated throughout their company, linked to other related business processes, supported by advanced technology, and delivered globally. There is a colossal need for information on the trends and strategies that dictate the success of an F&A project. This segment of the portal organizes the fast-growing industry of F&A outsourcing.

BPO in CRM and Call Center Services

Call center outsourcing is one of the fastest growing areas in BPO. Technology is shrinking the world to the point where having customer service work performed halfway thousands of miles away is not that much different from having it done in an office building across the street.

Why do firms outsource CRM and call centers? The simple answer is complexity and fragmentation. One fast growing computer manufacturer found itself supporting customers in 50 markets around the globe through a number of geographically scattered call centers, each of which performed its own discrete customer care functions. One call center, for example, primarily logged orders. If a problem arose, it was handed off to a different center for follow-up. Similarly, inbound service calls after 5 p.m. went to yet another location. The result was very little consistency in customer interaction and no good way to gather the intelligence needed to develop customer loyalty.

When growth dictated an addition to inbound customer service capabilities, the company began to consider consolidating or outsourcing its customer call centers. A focus on both immediate requirements and longer-term outcomes led to the recommendation of a fundamentally different approach - the creation of a "virtual global contact center." By tying all client centers together through common technology and consistent processes, the company with its third-party outsourcing vendor created seamless, 24x7 coverage for customers around the world. Today, all customer touch points are consolidated; customer information is centralized, and better trained and managed agents handle a wide range of customer needs.

We are witnessing a major change in the way companies outsource customer care and interaction (e.g., call center, customer relationship management, marketing services, technical support services and IT helpdesks) services. The customer care outsourcing value chain continues to evolve and is transforming the way business is being conducted.

BPO in Back-Office Transactions Processing Services

Most organizations face the tedious task of processing countless transactions, which results in the need to generate, manage and document multiple forms in an organized, accessible manner. This task, though critical, is time-consuming and forces organizations to devote resources to activities that are not necessarily their core business. Outsourcing transaction processing allows companies to either lay off employees or reassign them to tasks related to the core business.

Companies turn to transaction processing outsourcing for a variety of reasons. They include :

- The high cost of transactions
- Too much time spent on daily operations
- Few processes are considered best practice
- The high cost of upgrading applications
- Difficulty in hiring or retaining process staff
- Lack of timely or accurate reports

These "pain points" in the back office manifest themselves in a variety of drivers and inhibitors to outsourcing back-office processing services. Foremost among the drivers are the goals of focusing on the core business, improving service levels and reducing implementation costs.

BPO in Human Resources Services

Payroll processing is the oldest IT-based outsourced service. Until recently, however, the rest of the human resources (HR) function remained firmly embedded in house. In 1999, outsourcing caught up with HR in a big way as pioneers such as BP Amoco, Bank of America, British Telecom, and BAE Systems began to hand it over wholesale to external providers.

Outsourcing human resources lightens organizations' burdens by helping them screen, choose, and manage employees. What you should look for in outsourcing human resources is a company that has in-depth knowledge of country-specific human resource practices, rules, and regulations, as well as excellent communication and analytical skills.

The possible reasons for outsourcing HR include:

- The HR department wants to redefine its role by shedding administration and concentrating on human capital management and alignment with business strategy.
- CEOs and CFOs are increasingly unhappy with the HR function. They want detailed analytics, which can inform their operating strategy.
- The cost of largely paper-based, in-house systems is exorbitant.

The following reasons will give you a better understanding of what is happening in HR outsourcing.

BPO in Information Technology

In the 1960's, EDS took over the IT functions for Frito Lay. This deal became the foundation of IT outsourcing. Today, outsourcing is becoming a crucial component of the IT services portfolio. In fact, IT outsourcing is the fastest-growing segment of the technology services market. While estimates vary, we expect that IT outsourcing will grow at least 15% annually for the next five years. Its growth is creating profitable opportunities for outsourcers, but it's also causing immense dislocation among technology companies and workers.

What's driving the demand for IT outsourcing and offshoring? Mostly, lower costs. A conservative estimate for a good Java programmer in New York City is $150,000. You can get at least five high-end Java programmers for the same cost in Bangalore, India. That means, by moving the programming overseas, productivity can be improved manifold. This is a compelling argument in an environment where IT budgets are shrinking or stagnant but digitization workload is growing. The business risk is also less as the IS outsourcing to India is a proven model.

IT infrastructure management outsourcing is also another area of tremendous growth. In general, infrastructure-outsourcing providers can offer lower prices through economies of scale, as well as reduce the number of technical employees required. We estimate that companies save between 11% and 25% when they outsource IT. Companies also outsource because they can often improve their infrastructure, getting better access to new technologies, metered services, and better architectures.

IT outsourcing has been gaining momentum, primarily because of the cost reduction benefits. Lower IT costs and capital expenditure are often cited as the main motivators for outsourcing. India is having advantage of good IT service industry track record which is already an established name and fame helps BPO industry also to flourish. Indians can manage pressure well. Indians are also good at adapting to new technologies. Indians are also intelligent and hardworking. Indian firms are good at improving the productivity through business process reengineering.

The BPO industry should concern about how to retain the control over the business processes if they were outsourced. Security and confidentiality of information should also be of utmost concern. Maintaining the proprietary of information and privacy of the information are the main concerns. Improving value above the labour cost advantage is the main challenge for Indian BPO industry. A high attrition rate of the employees is the main concern. Technology is doubling at great speed. Upgradation of technology is constant endeavor. While moving up in the value chain the cost also increases proportionately. Offlate there is a pricing pressure for most of the BPO firms and their margins are shrinking. They should also go to volume business rather concentrating on margins.

28

BUSINESS PROCESS OUTSOURCING
A CRITICAL ANALYSIS

C. Naga Pavan* and **A.V.S. Ashok****

The role of Information Technology is growing tremendously in Industry and Education. It has changed the way in which the things has been done. The processes in Industry has been changed and the teaching- learning process in Education has changed. The paper presents the role of Information Technology in changing the processes of both the sectors.

When electricity was invented by Thomas Alva Edison, people said it will not be beneficial because of the high cost involved in establishing power generation stations, building high tension cables and in the event of any accident due to electricity the ultimate penalty is death. But.... Now with out electricity people cannot live.

When Internet or Information Technology came to existence, people believed it will not be beneficial to the society as well as to the individuals. But now the role of Information Technology has increased not only in Industry and Education but also in other areas. As the number of applications basing on internet one growing we can understand its impact.

* Faculty Member, ICFAI National College, Vijayawada.

** Faculty Member, ICFAI National College, Guntur.

To see Developed India with the help of Information Technology, we need to change the processes in Education, Industry and other fields simultaneously. One important element has to be changed i.e. the mindsets to make the people to accept the change in the processes and the impact of Information Technology.

Introduction

In the software industry, the strongest example outsourcing has been the banking and financial services segment. A similar story is waiting to be played out in the BPO space. BPO Progress is well documented. A recent survey by *CFO Magazine* and AMR Research found that 68.3% of companies of all sizes already outsource some business processes, and 63.6% expect to do more. A PricewaterhouseCoopers survey found an even higher number—73%—of companies that report some element of BPO outsourcing. Gartner Group has estimated that the BPO market will grow to between $235 billion and $300 billion by 2004, with the finance and accounting component to reach $37.7 billion.

If a foreign country can supply us with a commodity cheaper than we ourselves can make it, better buy it of them, with some part of the produce of our own industry, employed in a way which we have some advantage.

Adam Smith, "Wealth of Nations" (1776)

Business Process Outsourcing is an offset of the above theory, where companies' are cutting costs on less value addition tasks, and deriving more customer advantage by concentrating their efforts and resources on tasks contributing more value to customers. This trend in the developed world has opened up new avenues for the qualified human resources of the developing world both to improve individually and also move up the value chain of businesses.

Outsourcing – is this the correct word?

Outsourcing refers to a non-core activity performed by third party service providers. However, in India the Business Processes are 'outsourced' to not a third party service provider but to a captive unit of the global firm or an MNC. GE call centers best emphasis the use of captive unit as well as giving business to an MNC. In this article we refer to outsourcing as any activity of foreign origin coming to India and handled by Indian Professionals, especially in the services sector (ITES, BPO, and e-commerce services).

Present Situation

The Indian ITES-BPO industry grew by 59.1% during 2002-03 and is likely to grow by about 54% to reach US$3.6bn by the end of fiscal year 2003-04. The industry worth Rs 24 billion in 1999-2000 has grown to an industry worth Rs 71 billion. The ITES-BPO market remained a high growth segment for the Indian software and services industry during 2002-03. Despite the adverse global economic conditions, Indian players in this space logged in high growth rates. In the financial services segment, organizations are now prepared to think of outsourcing more financial functions beyond the payroll and benefits administration. Outsourcing business processes is particularly attractive for companies that need to reinvent themselves along more efficient lines. Outsourcing and building structural alliances with suppliers can help the outsource providers to bring major change through optimum resource allocation to more value added tasks. The most commonly outsourced Finance &Accounting activities—tax management, treasury, risk management—usually go to specialized accounting firms, and India should be able to take advantage of this trend happening in the United States. This changes would bring a lean financial department for the outsourcing firm and allows it to concentrate more on the better value contributors like risk management and corporate governance. In the outsourcing firm there will be a CFO with limited staff to deal with capital structure, risk management, financial statements and reporting to the board. However, there may not be a treasurer or controller and the staffs that traditionally reported to them.

However, the outsourcing in Financial & Accounting is not happening very fast because of skepticism in the market. "Follow the money," Deep Throat advised Woodward and Bernstein (Nixon's Water Gate Investigation). The risk and apprehension of revealing information that is to be kept secret is the predominant reason for not going ahead faster with the outsourcing of Financial and Accounting activities. Although most companies follow ethical financial and accounting practices, there's still a feeling that there's nothing to gain and might be something to lose if third parties had access to those most private financial records.

The apprehension that the money trail might reveal secrets to competitors' details of amounts spent on Research and Development, Product Development, Testing and Launch and also the distinctive cost advantages the outsourcing firm possess is a rational business problem. At the very least, a third party providing financial and accounting outsourcing services would have to be highly trusted. Few executives at the outsourcing firm want to depend on the discretion and integrity of a clerical workforce hired by somebody else, here the outsourced firm.

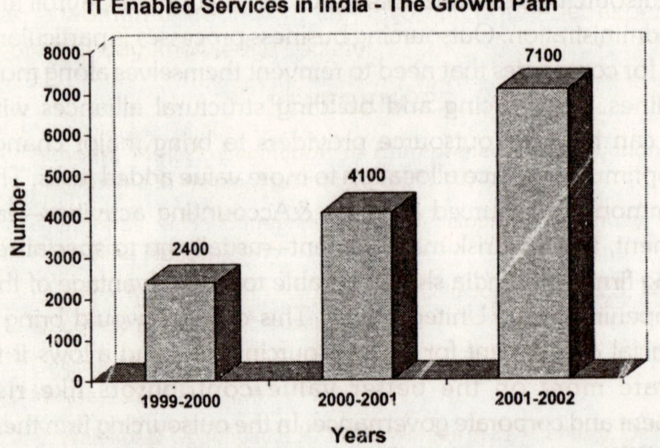

Source: NASSCOM

Overall this sector grew at over 65 percent—upping revenues from Rs. 71 billion in 2001-02 to touch Rs. 117 billion in 2002-03.

Opportunities for Growth

The factors that were mainly responsible for the growth of this sector are divided into two categories – Demand side forces and Supply side enablers. The demand side forces are the success of early movers and the efficiency they brought to outsourced activities, there by creating a brand image for Indian companies, the US market environment where the bottom line pressures faced by the American firms are one – to many to efficiently cater to them, which has necessitated cost cutting on most activities. The success in outsourcing Software development and servicing activities has also helped change the mindsets of American top executives and propel the growth of the services outsourcing to developing countries like India.

The supply side enablers that have helped India take advantage of this demand factors are:

- The reduction in the cost of data transfer (by 90%) from the other side of the globe to India.
- Increased reliability, sometimes world class of the telecom sector
- Availability of low cost talented workers.

Credible Vendor community, whose have already proven their worth in Software sector and have created a brand image for the Indian professional performing these activities.

As with the software industry which has started as a body shopping entity, the Outsourcing has also started with a routine, recurring, less qualified, manual jobs like call centers, and medical transcription, where the quality of human resource, and the work style required not a mental prowess or decision making but the ability to understand and provide service to the customers of the outsourcing firm. However the business is moving up the value chain in that more specialized functions where significantly more judgment calls are to made like in taxation, accountancy policies, and others are slowly but surely being outsource to India. A move up the value chain is happening in terms of breadth and depth of processes outsourced, from simple, standardized activities to advanced skill and some judgment required activities to extensive skill and judgment required activities.

The Indian IT and ITES growth drivers are as follows:

- Highly educated population
- Low cost because of cost savings from outsourcing and decrease in direct labor costs
- Strong IT Backbone in software mainly, but slowly improving in hardware also

- Government Incentives and support for the newly established firms in this sector.

Sectors of Growth

The Indian ITES-BPO industry continues its strong upward spiral on service lines like customer care, finance, HR, administration, billing and payments services, etc. Revenues from customer care doubled during 2002-03 registering a growth of 102%. Similar trend was witnessed in payment service, which grew by over 90% during 2002-03. Other service lines like finance, HR and administration are also expected to grow significantly over the next few years.

Challenges

Public Relations in the Customers' Country: The growth of outsourcing has created great anxiety in the primary markets. Indian IT as well as BPO industry is dependent heavily on the United States (primary market for India). The political leadership and the trade unions are dead set against the 'exporting' of jobs to other countries. This group of stakeholders for a firm involved in the business of outsourcing is very difficult to be convinced of the necessity of outsourcing as they are personally and financially affected by the action of outsourcing from businesses in their home country.

Let us just discuss the various challenges faced by the Indian industry and the associations while campaigning for the necessity of outsourcing for the home country (in this case US) economy. Outsourcing to India of activities generates greater value for the global economy. For every $ 1.00 spent by the US not outsourced to India results in a value delivery of $0.33 to Indian and $ 0.67 returns to US, and $0.45 – 0.47 in creating new value for reemploying US labor. Thus we can conclude that every $1.00 spent is creating a $1.45 – 1.47 to the global market place. This clearly shows that the benefit to the US economy is to the tune to $ 1.12. The benefit to the Indian economy is 33 cents from each dollar outsourced by the US. The benefit is accrued with 10 cents to labor, 10 cents to profits retained in India, 9 cents to Suppliers, 3 cents to central government as income tax and corporate tax, and 1 cent to the state government as sales tax – a total of 33 cents per dollar is accrued as benefit to Indian economy.

The number of job losses will also be minimum as the jobs to be outsourced to India from US is only 3.3 million where as the decline in the working population due to aging is said to at 15.6 million as per Mckinsey Global Institute in the 15 years from 2000 – 2015. The jobs outsourced to India are also a fraction of the mass layoffs. In the total mass layoffs of worker of 1.17 million trade related layoffs account for 0.27 million and outsourcing is only going to account for 0.21 million jobs (Projections).

The above facts are to be clearly presented in the public relations exercise and India should also start investing in the US economy as the Japanese did when manufacturing jobs are transferred to low cost East Asian countries where Japanese companies have major presence.

Moving up the value chain (Escaping Commoditization): The outsourcing industry has moved from being a Customer service industry where information is acquired and disseminated to the customers to a transaction processing industry where Finance and Accounting, Claims Processing and Online Collection of payments are the major activities. Both these activities are commodities in that only minimum or nil differentiation exist between firms in terms of competencies and service. The business of outsourcing has to move up the chain to perform the activities like Planning and Design, where decisions are to be made and competencies required are significantly higher. This move up the value chain will bring regular and permanent clients to Indian outsourcing companies and will also help develop the Indian manufacturing and service base.

Human Resource Challenges: Creating Real Value requires building capability, and looking beyond the immediate organizational needs. Human Capital is the key to long term success for BPO industry. The key strategic challenges in Human Capital are: Leadership, Social Image, Life Quality, and Talent Pool. Talent Pool – For creating a pool of talented service provides for BPO industry, we have to first source human resource, assess them, and recruit, and provide them with the required training in delivering service. Now a days too much emphasis is placed on assessment and recruiting of human resource, rather than on training them in delivering service. BPO industries have an average attrition rate of 30-35%. For increasing the size of the talent pool we have to undertake the following steps.

- Improve ITES/BPO image as employer
- Work with State Governments to improve English Language skills in medium to long term
- Employ more 'experienced'/part time/non-graduates

We should also reduce attrition rate through the following retention steps:

- Recruit well initially
- 'No Poaching' agreements between the competitors.
- Move from short to medium/long term option, when recruiting employees plan for the future needs and not the immediate needs.
- Improve variety of jobs undertaken by the employees to reduce boredom, and frustration with the job profile.
- Deal with timings and shift issues, affecting especially the female employees a mutually acceptable and convenient work culture would reduce the attrition of qualified human resource from the BPO industry.
- Provide good working environment/conditions – This would improve the acceptability of the work and install a sense of pride in the employees.
- Promote teamwork – in work and socially: This would reduce the frustration of competing for a flat structure of growth where only a few are given higher positions and would retain the qualified human resource more, as individuals do not like to leave a conducive social situation.
- Train and develop 'people' managers; The leader builds the team and therefore the managers with concern not only for results but also employees as individuals should be developed. The BPO industry should have a leader in the TEAM MANAGEMENT position of Managerial Grid.

The BPO industries should also accept that employee development is a key factor in growth of the business and therefore should undertake a few steps in that direction.

- Promote internally wherever possible
- Identify and develop high potential employees
- Identify and advertise career paths within businesses
- Develop skills required for the industry

Therefore we can conclude that if the Indian Business wants to be reckoned as a leader in the IT sphere and services sector, they should invest in basic infrastructure, build on the cheap, qualified labor, and should take up more challenging and competency based activities. If this is to be done, significant planning both at the company level, and association's level, as well as India Inc. should be there.

REFERENCES

1. Stuart Jefferson, *ITES/BPO HR Challenges and Strategies*, iTech 2004 – 12-13 January 2004.
2. *ITES/BPO – Opportunity to move up the value chain?* iTech 2004, McKinsey & Company Jan 13 2004
3. http://www.business-standard.com/special/bs1000/2003/bs14.htm
4. http://www.outsourcing.com/content.asp?page=02i/other/NRS-article/default.html&nonav=true
5. www.nasscom.org
6. www.outsourcing.com
7. www.mckinseyquarterly.com
8. *Why outsourcing is good for the US?* December 09, 2003 www.rediff.com
9. *BPO – A new business model*, January 13, 2004, *Progeon*, iTech 2004
10. Vikram Shah, *Made in India – The New Paradigm,* Talisma Corporation, iTECH 2004

Prof. Bala V. Balachandran, *Economic Outlook & Business Prospects shaping IT solutions investment*, iTech 2004, Strategic Leadership for Sustaining Growth.

Source: "India Offshore Outsourcing – An Investor's Perspective"

The View Group, *iTech 2004, Hyderabad.*

29

KNOWLEDGE MANAGEMENT
A STRATEGIC PERSPECTIVE

R. Suresh*

The world is moving through a phase of kaleidoscopic change caused by rapid changes in technology and it's varied applications. The Indian market scenario has gone through a massive churning, fuelled primarily two factors, liberalization of the economy and change in the market from a sellers market to a buyers market. The market place, in variance with the way it operated a decade back, has become hyper-competitive and organisations are finding it increasingly difficult to sustain their competitive advantage over a longer time period due to the elimination of information asymmetry fuelled by the phenomenal growth of Internet, value conscious customers with their ever increasing demand for change, shorter product & corporate life cycle and technological obsolescence. Organisations woke up to the reality of competing against world players and faced an urgent need for improving on all fronts in order to stay afloat, leave alone becoming profitable. They had to face the challenge of achieve more with less and in double quick time with world class quality. Towards this end, many organisations introduced many initiatives like TQM, CRM etc., but found them inadequate to sustain their competitive advantage over a longer period. In this context, continuous knowledge creation and harnessing of existing knowledge have become indispensable

* Associate Professor, Indian Institute of Financial Management and Research, Chennai.

processes to sustain competitive advantage. This paper emphasizes the need for organisations to look at knowledge management from a strategic perspective and the strategies that they could follow to achieve sustainable competitive advantage.

Preamble

"In the emerging economy, a firm's only advantage is its ability to leverage and utilize its knowledge."

Larry Prusak,
Executive Director-
The Institute for Knowledge Management

We are living in an economy of kaleidoscopic change where the only element, which is constant, is change. The industry environment is being influenced by unexpected, multiple changes reducing the period for which organizations can hold on to a competitive advantage. Every sector of industry in every corner of the globe has been affected by this change.

In the Indian context there have been two major factors, that have forced industry to look up and deliver. The first of these was the liberalization policy in 1991, which paved the way for global players to set up that shop in our country. Indian companies suddenly found themselves competing with world players in all the industrial segments. They realized that, in order to compete with the world players and come successful, they needed to improve on various fronts like quality, costs, and timely delivery and after sales service. They needed to achieve more for less and in double quick time to stay afloat, leave alone succeed and go ahead. In this context, companies felt a need for harnessing the existing knowledge and experience available in the organisation.

The other factor was the change in the market from a seller's market to a buyer's market. The buyers are more informed, thanks to the growth of Internet and consequently, information dissemination.

Organisations initiated many steps like TQM, BPR, SCM, and CRM to build and sustain their competitive advantage. These initiatives, although have resulted in firms attaining competitive advantage, are replicable and not sustainable over a longer period of time. Hence, organisations are now focusing on methods of creating new knowledge and harnessing existing knowledge to gain sustainable competitive advantage.

The importance of focus on knowledge as a source of competitive advantage is understood better when one looks at the ratio of market value to book value of a knowledge intensive firm, e-g Infosys which has got a ratio of more than 10.

This paper emphasizes the importance of harnessing and creating knowledge and the strategies that they could follow to achieve sustainable competitive advantage, especially in the current scenario of increased competition by Indian Companies.

Introduction

Strategy Concepts and Frameworks

Strategy is a method/plan adopted by a firm to balance it's external environment (opportunities and threats) and the internal capabilities (strengths and weaknesses)

Various management consultants and thinkers have defined the process of strategy in various ways. Porter's model focused on defining a firm's strategy in terms of it's product/ market positioning. Building on Porter's notion of competitive advantage, the resource based view of strategy argues that the resources and capabilities of an organisation can be a source of competitive advantage if they processes certain characteristics of being rare, durable and difficult to imitate and flexible and durable. If firms have resources with these characteristics, they can position themselves strategically on the basis of these resources and capabilities. Most of the tangible resources may not have these characteristics and hence organisations have to focus on intangible assets to be a source of competitive advantage. Many authors have stressed on the strategic importance of intangible assets for firms to achieve competitive advantage (Itami, 1987: Hall, Teece). Teece et al (1990s) in their paper on 'dynamic capabilities' emphasise on knowledge as a source of competitive advantage through the definition of the term. They define the term dynamic capabilities as follows :

"The term 'dynamic' refers to the shifting character of the environment; certain strategic responses are required when time-to-market and timing is critical, the pace of innovation is accelerating and the nature of future competition and markets is difficult to determine. The term 'capabilities' emphasizes the key role of strategic management in appropriately adapting, integrating, and re-configuring internal and external organizational skills, resources and functional competencies toward changing environment".

The emphasis, from this definition, is on adapting to the changing environment, through organizational learning and innovation, for which knowledge is the base. This knowledge based view of strategy, which emphasizes building, and sustaining competitive advantage on the basis of the knowledge resources and capabilities of a firm has gained currency due to the following reasons

- market is in a state of flux and going through a string of realignments
- resources and capabilities are easily replicable
- the unprecedented growth of information superhighway has accelerated the spread of explicit knowledge and consequently the speed of replicability
- Tacit knowledge gained through years of experience is not easily replicable.

and hence any strategy based on market and product mix or resources and capabilities may not provide the firm with a sustainable competitive advantage.

The importance of integration of knowledge available in the organisation is also stressed upon by authors like Huff, who, argue that managers look upon collective knowledge and experience in constructing mental models of strategic issues and terms this as 'strategic frames' and any strategic decision is a combination of multiple strategic frames.

Reasons for Emphasis on Knowledge Management

The need to focus on managing knowledge within the enterprise results from

- Economic and market-driven requirements created by customer demands and international competition
- Increase in customer demands for products and services that fulfill their particular needs more precisely and to a greater advantage

- Loss of knowledge to the organisation due to increased personnel turnover
- It helps organisations to be able to repeat the processes followed in past successful projects.
- Effective knowledge management practices helps organisations avoid repeating mistakes of past projects, thereby reducing the time span required for completing current projects.

The importance of knowledge is also focused on by Michael Zack, he defined a term 'strategic knowledge gap', as the gap between what the organisation needs to know and what it presently does now and Knowledge management is the process by which organisations could bridge this gap.

Value Addition through Knowledge

Many firms have evidenced substantial savings or an increase in their value by using knowledge inputs and modifying their internal processes. A case in point is Texas Instruments, which was able to save the equivalent of the investment in a new semiconductor fabrication plant, by sharing best practices between the existing plants. (O'Dell 1996).

Process of Knowledge Creation and Dissemination

There are many ways in which knowledge can be created and disseminated across organisation. Any organisation that aims to create a knowledge management system should have to follow these general knowledge management initiatives.

- Creation of knowledge teams
- Sharing of best practices
- Development of knowledge databases
- Creation of knowledge centers
- Selection and use of collaborative technologies
- Creation of Intellectual capital teams

Apart from the above, mentioned management initiatives the organisation specifically, organisations could create knowledge portal in the organizational intranet, establish communities of practice and harness the knowledge gained by persons over years of experience can adopt the processes of debriefing and mentoring among the staff organisation.

(i) Knowledge Portal

Knowledge portal is a single point reference for knowledge storage, search and dissemination within an organisation. This ideally works on the intranet and one of the major features by which tacit knowledge is captured and stored in through discussion forums from which knowledge can be mined and extracted.

(ii) Communities of Practice

The focus on knowledge as a source of competitive advantage has necessitated organisations to embark on a change in structures, which would facilitate knowledge sharing and dissemination. Some of the organizational forms created for this purpose are cross-functional teams, work groups etc. The latest organizational form created for this purpose is the Communities Of Practice (COP).

The communities of practice are groups of people informally bound together by shared expertise and passion for a joint enterprise (Wenger & Snyder).

There can be formal or informal groups within an organisation or across organisations, but it is important to focus on garnering the knowledge acquired through the discussions within this group.

COPs are more effective than teams since members of these communities organize themselves and focus on value addition and hence the commitment towards this is higher.

They help create a bank of best practices and thus help develop the critical capabilities, which are essential for organizational success and to sustain competitive advantage.

The characteristics of knowledge creation which are focused on making tacit knowledge explicit are

- To express the inexpressible through metaphor and analogy
- To disseminate knowledge converting individual knowledge to organizational knowledge

- To reduce the factors like ambiguity and redundancy in the process of knowledge creation

Creativity', Innovation and Knowledge Strategy

Creativity and innovation play a very important role in designing and driving the business strategy of any present day organisation. In the present industrial scenario, an organisation does not enjoy sustainable competitive advantage, merely by possessing resources and capabilities. They should be able to combine these resources in new and different ways or develop new capabilities to gain sustainable competitive advantage. This is possible through creative thinking and innovation.

30

KNOWLEDGE MANAGEMENT IN ACADEMIA

SEVEN Cs FRAMEWORK

Dr. Talluru Sreenivas* and **T. Sree Krishna****

An effective management of Knowledge is the key management challenge of the late twentieth and early twenty first century.

–Peter F Drucker

In the current business context across the globe, organizational knowledge is recognized as a significant source of competitive advantage. The ability to acquire, share and utilize knowledge has become a critical organizational capability as businesses attempt to cope with a rapidly changing environment. Academic Institutions which are the critical suppliers of future professionals are not immune to such environmental changes. As such many academicians have come to realize that they must adopt cultures that embrace continuous learning so that college programmes can be periodically updated to meet changing demands. Unfortunately, given the nature of academia, the implementation of many knowledge management processes is often difficult. To address such problems, this paper attempts to identify several barriers that inhibit KM in the college context and tries to present the frame work that can be used to identify the boundaries of

* Reader, Department of Management Sciences, R.V.R.& J.C.College of Engg, Guntur-19, A.P.

** Sr. Lecturer, Department of Management Sciences, R.V.R.& J.C.College of Engg, Guntur-19, A.P.

a college's knowledge base so that it can be reconciled with the body of knowledge and skills currently needed. The paper tries to offer some general concluding remarks as to the importance of Knowledge Management, its frame work for academic institutions and its role in helping these institutions remain relevant in the educational supply chain.

Introduction

In the current business context across the globe, organizational knowledge is recognized as a significant source of competitive advantage. What significantly adds value and contributes to competitive advantage in the information technology age is the ability to manage 'Knowledge' within the organization. In fact, academic settings are no exception. Hence, in this paper an attempt is made to develop a useful framework for capturing and capitalization of Knowledge in academia.

Now-a-days these academic settings are attacked by many forces such as –

- Academic Environment is changing much faster than ever before. Increasing competition, new emerging technologies, new opportunities for expansion are forcing the academic institutions to change completely. These changes are questioning the basic nature of the academics.
- There is a trend towards 'Mass Customization'. The key to adopt mass customization is to make products adapt to the users' specific preferences. Standardized designs need to be replaced with flexible and adaptive procedures.
- The world is integrating in many ways. Mobility of students, global list of academic experts, emergence of Internet etc. are forcing the universities and other academic institutions to adopt new standards, innovative and creative methods and practices. This shift is continuously changing the rules of the game.

The KM Imperative

In order to survive in this fast changing, knowledge intensive and volatile environment, Educational institutions should adopt strategies that would simultaneously address the concerns of internal efficiency and external competitiveness. A systemic and well-designed knowledge Management initiative would facilitate the assimilation of knowledge from the environment, creation of new knowledge with in the organization, sharing knowledge across the organization, and therefore, capitalization of the knowledge thus can effectively be managed. Thus, educational institutions can capitalize on the KM initiative through either embedding knowledge in their programmes and services, enhancing the efficacy of their existing processes or effective implementation of their strategies.

Knowledge Management – A Definition

Sveiby defines Knowledge as the capacity to act. This capacity to act is generated continuously by a process of knowing. Knowledge is both about issues and the context in which those issues are being dealt with. Sveiby further identifies four characteristics to knowledge – It is tacit, action oriented, supported by rules and constantly changing.

According to Bair (2001), KM is a discipline of identifying, capturing, retrieving, sharing and evaluating an enterprise's information assets.

In this context, issues central to most of the organizations are –

1. How is knowledge defined in the context of an organization?
2. How do we tap knowledge from the minds of the individuals transform the same into organizational knowledge?
3. How to disseminate knowledge within and outside the organizations?
4. How to make the best use of organizational knowledge?

Factors Affecting KM in the Academic Institutions

Effective KM is difficult to achieve in any organization. In fact, organizations are often characterized as being resistant to learning and regularly fail to learn from past experiences. Within college setting, KM is often difficult because of existing cultural and bureaucratic factors that act as barriers to the KM process. Instead of considering knowledge as an asset that increases in value when shared, many faculty members consider knowledge as proprietary and something which cannot be shared freely. Some faculty members view knowledge as a possible source of differentiation, and thus defer sharing certain aspects of their knowledge. Another barrier to knowledge sharing and creation can be attributed to a simple lack of interest among some faculty members. For a variety of reasons, some faculty members become complacent and keep away from the learning process.

The time and resource constraints also disrupt the KM process. Even when a source of knowledge has been identified and is readily available, faculty members often lack sufficient time and resources to take advantage of learning opportunities.

Knowledge Management through 7Cs Framework

A Seven Cs framework may help in identifying knowledge, organizing it into manageable units, ensuring that it is relevant and distributing it to others with in the organization. This process can be studied under the following heads – 1) Capture 2) Clarity 3) Codify 4) Collate 5) Connectivity 6) Conversion and 7) Capitalization.

1. *Capture:* This represents the identification of boundaries of a college's knowledge base and involves the evaluation of current curriculum vitae of each faculty member. It helps in establishing a preliminary list of self reported areas of knowledge and expertise. It gives brief idea of past experience, current research publications, work in progress, teaching responsibilities, service and consulting activities. Information relating to classes currently being taught and taught in the past provides a general indication of a faculty member's exposure to specific areas of knowledge.

2. *Clarity:* Once an inventory of knowledge domains has been developed for each faculty member, subsequently the data collection process begins by conducting semi-structured personal interviews with each faculty member in order to refine the list of knowledge areas. This step gives opportunity to the faculty members to elaborate on the level of expertise they possess. They can make additions and deletions to the list of general areas of knowledge. The end result of this step would be a more refined list of knowledge areas.

3. *Codify:* The third step of data collection involves using small focus groups to reduce the number of knowledge areas to a more manageable number by identifying closely related areas that can be clustered together. The master knowledge areas are identified and it becomes possible to distill several distinct areas of knowledge into a more general category. By reducing the number of discrete knowledge areas down to fewer master categories, the KM process becomes much more manageable and hence is more likely to continue as a prescriptive tool for helping colleges remain relevant. This stage helps in identifying the gaps in the knowledge base as well as areas where collaboration and synergy can be developed among faculty members.
4. *Collate:* This step involves developing a self- report survey that seeks to measure the levels of expertise that each individual faculty member has in terms of master knowledge areas. Two important tasks are accomplished with this step. The individual faculty members get an opportunity to report their skills within the context of new master areas of knowledge. Another task concerned with this step is validation of data collected in second step as well as the merging process in third step. In addition, the rationale for combining individual knowledge areas into a smaller subset of master areas is also validated in this step if they show approximately the same response pattern from faculty members. Thus this step provides a validity check.
5. *Connectivity:* This step explains need for connection to community. It involves tapping in to external sources of information in order to determine the body of knowledge and skills that students should possess in graduation. One possible source of such information comes from the other colleges and universities. By identifying college programmes that are considered forward-thinking, edge-cutting and innovative, and that correspondingly rank well in terms of recruitment and placements, many insights can be gained about what businesses are seeking from

new graduates. Another possibly more useful source of information comes from the organizations that hire college students. Whether relying on recruiter surveys, alumni surveys, seeking information from those who make the hiring decisions can be critical. However, it is important to avoid becoming too focussed on the knowledge and skills associated with any one Industry or Company.

6. *Conversion:* Once a reasonably complete picture of a college's knowledge base is developed and information concerning the knowledge and skills needed by students has been compiled, the two must be reconciled. Thus this step of KM process entails gaining insights about what areas of a college's knowledge base are relevant, what areas are obsolete, and what areas are deficient. Once such information is formalized and distributed throughout the college, faculty and administrators will be able to gain better understanding of the extent to which a college possesses specific knowledge assets, as well as gain additional insights about those knowledge assets that may be lacking. In addition, the above KM process will also help to facilitate knowledge sharing, since faculty members will now have reliable information pertaining to who is teaching, conducting research, providing service and consulting in various knowledge areas. Ultimately, decisions relating to faculty development, recruitment aspects, perks and tenure etc. should be made in conjunction with knowledge mapping process.

7. *Capitalization:* In this final stage, the academic institutions monitor the usage, assess the benefits of knowledge management in terms of the specified knowledge bases and embed knowledge into the organization's value creation activities.

Conclusion

Across the sectors, knowledge intensive organizations increasingly face similar conditions with a strong connection between the individual organization's ability to mobilize, apply and disseminate knowledge resources on one hand and their competitiveness and survival on the other. The public sector educational settings are facing rapid changes as a result of new demands for commercialization of knowledge, a need for a more efficient utilization of human resources due to cut-backs in basic funding, the introduction of new accountability measures from Government, increase in the prevalence of university-industry co-operations and increased dependence on external funding and team work. These changes are forcing Government colleges and Universities to do the work in new ways. In the private sector, the need for increased transparency and reduced complexity necessitated the institutions to use knowledge mapping extensively. The ability to acquire, share and utilize knowledge has become a critical organizational capability as these colleges and universities (both private and public) have to cope up with a rapidly changing environment. Thus, KM process helps the academic settings to remain as an important part of the educational value chain.

INDEX

C

J

K

U

V

W